Bloom's Modern Critical Views

Bloom's Modern Critical Views

Bloom's Modern Critical Views

C.S. LEWIS

Edited and with an introduction by
Harold Bloom
Sterling Professor of the Humanities
Yale University

CHELSEA HOUSE
PUBLISHERS
An imprint of Infobase Publishing

Bloom's Modern Critical Views: C.S. Lewis

Copyright © 2006 by Infobase Publishing
Introduction © 2006 by Harold Bloom

Chelsea House
An imprint of Infobase Publishing
132 West 31st Street
New York NY 10001

Library of Congress Cataloging-in-Publication Data
C.S. Lewis / Harold Bloom, editor.
    p. cm. — (Bloom's modern critical views)
  Includes bibliographical references and index.
  ISBN 0-7910-9319-0 (hardcover)
  1. Lewis, C. S. (Clive Staples), 1898-1963—Criticism and
interpretation. I. Bloom, Harold. II. Series.
  PR6023.E926Z596 2006
  823'.912—dc22   2006011658

You can find Chelsea House on the World Wide Web at http://www.chelseahouse.com

Contributing Editor: Amy Sickels
Cover design by Keith Trego
Cover photo © Hulton Archive

Printed in the United States of America.

Bang EJB 10 9 8 7 6 5 4 3 2 1

This book is printed on acid-free paper.

Contents

Editor's Note

My Introduction acknowledges C.S. Lewis's eminence as a scholar-critic of Renaissance literature, while expressing a certain resistance to his dogmatic lay theology and his allegorical fantasy-fictions.

As is inevitable, some of the essays reprinted in this volume are considerably at variance with my own stance towards Lewis, beginning with Chad Walsh's, which actually places *The Screwtape Letters* on the aesthetic level of John Bunyan's *The Pilgrim's Progress*.

Margaret Blount meditates upon Lewis's fictive animals, who culminate in *Narnia*'s Aslan, Christ the Lion, after which Margaret Patterson Hannay connects *Narnia*, literary criticism, and theology in Lewis by way of his concept of "joy" or "longing," which had a considerable role in his life.

Owen Barfield's oppositional yet close friendship with Lewis is sketched by Dabney Adams Hart, who emphasizes Barfield's deep influence upon Lewis, while Lee D. Rossi investigates divisions in Lewis's self between polemicism and fantasy and shrewdly concludes that "the more explicitly Christian his writing becomes, the less it convinces the reader."

The *Narnia* books extravagantly are judged by C.N. Manlove as capable of making us see "the Deep Magic of God," after which Joe R. Christopher praises Lewis's defenses of Christianity for their supposed wit.

In David Downing's reading, Lewis retrieves "the discarded image" of the world of Old Western Man, while the more disenchanted Kath Filmer confronts the indubitable misogyny of *Narnia* in Lewis's witches and the troubled androgyny of Glome in *Till We Have Faces*, surely the Great Apologist's most equivocal fiction, and perhaps therefore his best.

Because of the *Narnia* movie, Lewis is now best known as a story-teller for children, and is heartily praised as such by Lionel Adey, after which

Don W. King concludes this volume with a realistic account of Lewis-as-poet. I myself, who have read all of Lewis's poetry, can find in it only the truth of Oscar's Wilde's observation: "all bad poetry is sincere."

HAROLD BLOOM

Introduction

C.S. Lewis was the most dogmatic and aggressive person I have ever met. In 1954–55, I was a Fulbright scholar living at Pembroke College, Cambridge University. Lewis had just left Oxford to become Professor of Medieval and Renaissance English at Cambridge. I attended a few of his lectures, and for a while regularly talked with him at two pubs on the river. As I was twenty-four, and he fifty-six and immensely learned, I attempted to listen while saying as little as possible. But he was a Christian polemicist, and I an eccentric Gnostic Jew, devoted to William Blake. We shared a love for Shelley, upon whom I was writing a Yale doctoral dissertation, and yet we meant different things by "Shelley." Cowed as I was, the inevitable break came after a month or so, and we ceased to speak. The breaking-point was the metaphor "creation" which Lewis insisted pertained only to God. There was not a trace of creativity in Shakespeare, Dante, and Cervantes, Lewis told me. The greatest writers only rearranged building blocks provided by God. If, like Blake or Shelley, you had the illusion you were creating, what you actually created was Hell. On this, as on all things, C.S. Lewis was firm.

A profound scholar of allegory, Lewis dedicated his classic study *The Allegory of Love* (1936) to Owen Barfield, whom I met and learned from, and always revered. I remarked once to Barfield that I could not reconcile Lewis and Barfield on Shakespearean creativity. Lewis's strict view was that Shakespeare at most had reinvented Hell in *Hamlet*, *Othello*, *King Lear*, and *Macbeth*. How did Barfield receive such a judgment, since he had taught me that readers and audiences might well experience chagrin when what they considered to be *their* emotions actually turned out to be Shakespeare's thoughts? Barfield replied that dogma in Lewis might be bothersome, but much was to be learned from so great a scholar.

1

C.S. Lewis wrote more than forty books: I own and have read some two dozen of them. At seventy-five, I find it difficult to reread Lewis; he whacks me with a Christian cudgel on nearly every page. In preparation for writing this Introduction, I have just read through *A Mind's Awake*, a Lewis anthology edited by Clyde S. Kilby (1968), published five years after the polemicist's death. Kilby accurately remarks of Lewis: "He liked answers better than questions," and *A Mind Awake* certainly is a book of answers. I myself only can read, write, and teach by asking questions, which I suppose is why my contact with Professor Lewis endured just a month. Like most people I would prefer answers, but Shakespeare was not a problem-solver, and the refrain throughout *Hamlet* is "question" in its many forms.

Answer-persons attract followings: Lewis's *Mere Christianity* is a perpetual best-seller among American Evangelical Christians. His attitude towards Evolution is a touch more sophisticated than theirs, but differs from Creationism only in degree, not in kind. Indeed, Intelligent Design is a kind of parody of Lewis's general view of a Christian cosmos. I do not profess to know how many American Evangelical Christians can be considered either evangelical or Christian. C.S. Lewis, though as sedentary as myself, was a muscular Christian who is now the intellectual sage of George W. Bush's America, whose Christianity is mere enough to encompass enlightened selfishness, theocratic militarism, and semi-literacy. (President George W. Bush vaunts that he never read a book through, even as a Yale undergraduate.)

That a major Renaissance scholar, C.S. Lewis, should now be a hero to millions of Americans who scarcely can read is a merely social irony. Like Tolkien and Charles Williams, his good friends, Lewis is most famous for his fantasy-fiction, particularly *The Chronicles of Narnia*. I have just attempted to reread that tendentious evangelical taletelling, but failed. This may be because I am seventy-five, but then I can't reread Tolkien or Williams either. Lewis and Tolkien write better prose than Rowling does in her *Harry Potter* fantasies, but like Rowling they will rub down into Period Pieces, and end in the dustbins. There are of course the epic movies inspired by these works, but will they be viewable a decade hence?

I should attempt to distinguish between the scholar-critic C.S. Lewis, admirable exegete of Edmund Spenser and other Renaissance poets, and Lewis the lay theologian, who composed fictions and Christian apologies, generally fusing them together. The scholarly Lewis's masterpiece is the wonderfully brief and useful *The Discarded Image* (1971), which traces the medieval image of the universe and its survival into the Renaissance. I suppose that I cannot choose between Lewis's sermonizing fictions and fictive sermons because they all blend together for me.

Though some of Lewis's admirers wish to see him as a latter-day Dr. Samuel Johnson, that does the endlessly answering Lewis no service. Dr. Johnson was a wisdom writer, and his prudential wisdom did not depend upon dogma, though the great critic was a devout Christian. I would not even compare Lewis to G.K. Chesterton, whose best fictions far surpass the storyteller of *Narnia*, and whose Christian lay sermons are alive with wit and paradox.

The energies of C.S. Lewis were as intense as his learning was profound, and his co-religionists will maintain his public reputation for another generation or so. But he is neither an original thinker nor a canonical writer, and inflating his value will not enhance his ultimate status. It is not my lack of religious faith that renders me indifferent to Lewis's positive fervor. Kierkegaard, a great ironist, was also a religious genius. Lewis was religious, which is not in itself an achievement.

CHAD WALSH

Dreams and Letters

"A dream? Then—then—am I not really here, Sir?"

"No, Son," said he kindly, taking my hand in his. "It is not so good as that. The bitter drink of death is still before you. Ye are only dreaming. And if ye come to tell of what ye have seen, make it plain that it was but a dream. See ye make it very plain ...."

— *The Great Divorce*, p. 131.[1]

Three of Lewis's books which employ unusual literary genres are *The Pilgrim's Regress*, *The Screwtape Letters*, and *The Great Divorce*.

The first-named (subtitled: *An Allegorical Apology for Christianity, Reason and Romanticism*) will never supplant *The Pilgrim's Progress*. It lacks the simplicity and eloquent naïveté of Bunyan; it is also disappointingly empty of the wit and grace that readers of the later Lewis have come to expect. The style is heavy and wooden; the allegorical figures heavier and more wooden. And the reviewers, who bestowed a few pats on the head of the young author, complained with some justice that the book was obscure.

The *Regress* is an allegory within the framework of a dream-vision. The narrator (never named and of no importance) has a dream in which he observes the interminable adventures of the hero, John, in his flight from Puritania (a land of grim but hypocritical religion, which resembles a satirist's caricature of Ulster). John, in several dozen short chapters, pursues the never-

From *C.S. Lewis: Apostle to the Skeptics*. © 1949 by The Macmillan Company.

never vision of beauty and joy that haunts him. He tries all solutions: women, artistic movements, various schools of philosophy. Finally, with the aid of Reason, he is led to Mother Kirk, who makes him realize that his desire can be fulfilled only in Christianity, which he accepts by leaping into a deep pool and coming up through an underwater tunnel. Now a twice-born man, he retraces his steps, and sees the scenes of his earlier adventures in a radically different light. At the end, firm in the faith, he crosses the Brook (death), to the accompaniment of indifferent verse sung by the angelic Guide.

When Lewis edited the allegory for the 1943 edition[2] he added a Preface pointing out two of the principal defects:[3] a "needless obscurity, and an uncharitable temper." The temper had been directed mainly against the "counter-romantics" (such as the Neo-Scholastics and the American "Humanists") who professed to debunk the complex emotional experience which Lewis labels "Romanticism." The book is also an attack on the "subromantics" (such as the followers of Freud and D. H. Lawrence) but they are treated with more charity.

Mediocre as a work of literature, the *Regress* is invaluable for anyone tracing the development of Lewis's ideas. Practically all his later books exist within it in embryonic form. His belief in orthodox Christianity, his conviction that both "Romanticism" and Reason lead the quester to Christianity, many of his attitudes toward literary and philosophic movements—all appear in an early and incomplete form.

A much more successful use of an unconventional technique is *The Screwtape Letters*, which exploded in book form on the English literary scene in 1942 and soon bounded across the Atlantic.

The admirers of Lewis are divided into two groups: those who have read the *Letters*, and those who have read some of his other works in addition. The book has solved the gift problem for countless thousands. I know of a government office in Washington where *The Screwtape Letters* is almost invariably chosen when the girls arrange a birthday party for one of their number.

Ministers have preached from the *Letters*, and sent marked copies to parishioners in need of specific spiritual counsel. The critics, of almost every viewpoint, have loaded it with superlatives. Leonard Bacon[4] called it "this admirable, diverting, and remarkably original work," and added, "there is a spectacular and satisfactory nova in the bleak sky of satire." *The Manchester Guardian*[5] stated: "The book is sparkling yet truly reverent, in fact a perfect joy, and should become a classic."

The Screwtape Letters, then, have been adequately praised. Lewis, I suspect, is sometimes irked at the disproportionate fame of the infernal correspondence. He has confessed that writing it serially for the *Guardian* grew to be a "terrible bore," and when I talked with him he said that it was far from being his favorite.

However, I have no desire to battle the whole weight of critical and popular opinion. The *Letters* are very good indeed, in a very specialized way. They afford little scope for their author's poetic or myth-making ability, but they reveal his psychological insight and his satire at their sharpest.

The *Letters* purport to be written by His Infernal Excellency Screwtape to his young demon assistant Wormwood, who is stationed on the earth. Wormwood's mission is to undermine the faith of a recent convert to Christianity—a pallid, feckless young man, rather like a christianized Mark Studdock. Screwtape bestows a great wealth of shrewd advice on the inexperienced tempter. Wormwood, being new at the job, is inclined toward dramatic techniques, but Screwtape, with the wisdom of many victories, advises him:[6]

> It does not matter how small the sins are provided their cumulative effect is to edge the man away from the Light and out into the Nothing. Murder is no better than cards if cards can do the trick. Indeed the safest road to Hell is the gradual one—the gentle slope, soft underfoot, without sudden turnings, without milestones, without signposts....

The book seems calculated to accomplish two things. First of all, Lewis uses the wisdom of Hell to turn the tables on disparagers of Christianity. Screwtape's knowing advice in the very first letter takes for granted that modern thought, such as philosophic materialism, is based not on reason but emotion, and warns Wormwood against any action that would tempt the patient into using his own mind.

The other purpose of the *Letters* is to encourage the wavering Christian by showing him that his uncertainties are nothing unique, and in all likelihood are planted in his mind by agents of Our Father Below.

The epistolary pattern makes it possible for Lewis to take swipes at many of his pet aversions by the simple expedient of having Screwtape praise them. A hasty glance through the *Letters* will reveal that the Historical Method, flippancy (as distinguished from joy, fun, and the joke proper), "pacifism-and-Christianity," the "historical Jesus," and various fashions in feminine beauty are all targets for witty condemnation.

Quite unintentionally, it may be, Lewis accomplished in *The Screwtape Letters* what he conspicuously failed to do in *The Pilgrim's Regress*—he rivaled

Bunyan. The temptations of the patient, and his eventual victory over the team of Screwtape and Wormwood, are the twentieth-century equivalent of the salvation of Christian, as told by the good seventeenth-century tinker.

When *The Great Divorce* appeared in 1946 the dust-jacket of the American edition hopefully described it as "brilliant symbolism very like the author's famous 'Screwtape Letters.'" No blurb-writer has ever missed the mark more sadly. The two books are alike only in the acute psychological insight that both reveal.

The Great Divorce was not received with the same unmixed delight that greeted the *Letters*. It is too disturbing for easy enjoyment. The theme might well be George Macdonald's warning: "No. There is no escape. There is no Heaven with a little Hell in it." Or to quote Lewis's own words, from the Preface:[7]

> Blake wrote the Marriage of Heaven and Hell. If I have written of their Divorce, this is not because I think myself a fit antagonist for so great a genius, nor even because I feel at all sure that I know what he meant. But in some sense or other the attempt to make that marriage is perennial. The attempt is based on the belief that reality never presents us with an absolutely unavoidable "either-or", that, granted skill and patience and (above all) time enough, some way of embracing both alternatives can always be found; that mere development or adjustment or refinement will somehow turn evil into good without our being called on for a final and total rejection of anything we should like to retain. This belief I take to be a disastrous error. You cannot take all luggage with you on all journeys; on one journey even your right hand and your right eye may be among the things you have to leave behind.

Throughout the book the drastic "either-or" is being forced upon the reader. There is very little sugaring of humor and satire to kill the bitter taste, and the beauty of the fantasy somehow only deepens the solemn feeling that, as the angel says to one of the characters,[8] "This moment contains all moments."

The plot amounts to little. Like *The Pilgrim's Regress*, the story is a dream-vision, but there the resemblance ends. The dreamer is Lewis himself, who does not discover he is dreaming until near the end of the book.

In the first chapter the narrator is wandering through the endless streets of a drab, gray town, likened by some of the British reviewers to

Manchester. He boards a bus and gradually discovers that everyone there—including himself—is a transparent ghost. The entire company travel to the borders of Heaven and are given the opportunity to remain permanently. Most of them decline the offer because they cannot bear to make a clean-cut break with their favorite sins. The greater number are afflicted with some form of pride or self-centeredness, which is more precious to them than all the joys of Heaven. An artist who can think only of artistic movements and his reputation decides on the return trip, as does a woman who insists on dominating her son even after death. The only ghost with the courage to surrender his vice and stay in Heaven is a man guilty of lust—a quiet confirmation of the traditional Christian hierarchy of sins, which considers the sins of the flesh as less deadly than pride.

Each of the ghosts is met by one of the "solid people" who reasons with it and tries to prevail upon it to stay. Beyond these largely futile dialogues there is little action. The setting of the story is of great loveliness: the outlying provinces of Heaven resemble the landscapes of Perelandra.

The high point comes when Lewis encounters[9] "a very tall man, almost a giant, with a flowing beard"—George Macdonald—who, Virgil-like, explains some of the mysteries of Heaven and Hell to his disciple and commands him to inform his readers that everything he has seen is part of a dream and not to be taken literally.

One feels that *The Great Divorce* is the work of a man distinctly older than the rollicking author of *The Screwtape Letters*. The greater and more obvious seriousness is reflected in the sharper diversity of critical opinion. *The Providence Sunday Journal*[10] was bored: "Basically, 'The Great Divorce' is a sermon cast in the form of an allegory. It's a good sermon, but as allegory it's full of straw-men and cloudy symbolism." (Lewis, incidentally, insists with some vehemence that the book is a fantasy, not an allegory: none of the characters stands for anything else.) *The New Yorker*, on the other hand, said that[11] "If wit and wisdom, style and scholarship are requisites to passage through the pearly gates, Mr. Lewis will be among the angels."

John F. Dwyer, writing in *Thought*, commented that[12] you feel the joy and happiness of the Bright Spirits, you share their keen pity for the foolish, self-willed ghosts who are their own damnation," while A. C. Deane, in *The Spectator*, goes to considerable length to damn Lewis for lack of compassion:[13] "The metallic hardness of its tone, its air of disdain, untouched by sympathy, for the various weaknesses of human nature.... The 'Ghosts,' as the excursionists are called, meet 'Spirits' from heaven who argue with them deftly but in vain. The narrator seems, as it were, to place each Ghost in turn on the lecture-table, to exhibit with deliberate skill his special follies and impenitence, and then to drop him back whence he came."

This charge—lack of compassion—has been leveled against some of Lewis's other books. As though anticipating it, he has Macdonald say:[14]

> "Son, son, it must be one way or the other. Either the day must come when joy prevails and all the makers of misery are no longer able to infect it: or else for ever and ever the makers of misery can destroy in others the happiness they reject for themselves. I know it has a grand sound to say yell accept no salvation which leaves even one creature in the dark outside. But watch that sophistry or ye'll make a Dog in a Manger the tyrant of the universe."

With these words Macdonald brings Lewis—and the reader—back to the pitiless theme of the book: "no Heaven with a little Hell in it." The air-raid siren that wakes Lewis might better be the warning bell that troubled John Donne on his sick-bed: "And therefore never send to know for whom the *bell* tolls; it tolls for *thee*."

NOTES

1. From *The Great Divorce*. Copyright 1946 by The Macmillan Company and used with their permission. Published in England by Geoffrey Bles, Ltd.

2. Geoffrey Bles Ltd., London.

3. P. 5. By permission of the publishers.

4. Critique of Pure Diabolism," *The Saturday Review of Literature*, April 17, 1943.

5. February 24, 1943.

6. From *The Screwtape Letters*, pp. 64–65. Used by permission of The Macmillan Company. Published in England by Geoffrey Bles, Ltd.

7. P. v.

8. P. 101.

9. P. 60.

10. May 5, 1946.

11. March 16, 1946.

12. December 1946.

13. "A Nightmare," January 25, 1946.

14. P. 124.

MARGARET BLOUNT

Fallen and Redeemed:
Animals in the Novels of C.S. Lewis

My first stories were written and illustrated with enormous satisfaction:
they were an attempt to combine my two chief literary pleasures—
dressed animals and knights in armour.

—*Surprised by Joy*, C.S. Lewis

Invented Edens have never been equally shared between animals and
men until the decline of religious belief and man's displacement as the
centre of the universe. It is ironic that the most memorable of such places
is Narnia, a land that is under the power of Aslan, the Christian Lion. C.S.
Lewis only manages this pleasing arrangement by putting the action
outside the earth and into a parallel world (*The Lion, the Witch and the
Wardrobe*) or on Mars, where animal and human sharing is even more
marked, in *Out of the Silent Planet*. Mars, or Malacandra, reduces the
humans to animal status; Narnia raises the animals to human heights by
turning them into Talking Beasts.

The animal strain is present in all the *Narnia* books, and in the science-
fiction trilogy. It shows itself in two ways: the homely (the dressed mice in
Snug Town) and the heroic (the knights in armour) combine not only in C.S.
Lewis's unpublished juvenilia, the stories of Animal-Land or Boxen, but in
his children's stories, culminating in Aslan himself and the courtly mouse
Reepicheep.

From *Animal Land: The Creatures of Children's Fiction.* © 1974 Margaret Ingle-Finch.

Mouse Town is not everyone's idea of heaven, but it is significant that an imagination whose first promptings of beauty (we are told) came from the illustrations to *Squirrel Nutkin* should indulge in 'dressed animals' and perhaps, wanting to write grownup novels or histories that were not allowed to get interesting on the first page but only on the second, should change this into the country of Boxen, the name given to the invented place 'Animal-Land' that adjoined India. It was the way that this imagination wanted to go; it is no coincidence that among the children's stories he most quotes from and must have most enjoyed, *The Wind in the Willows* is prominent.

The animals in Boxen are there because they have to be, but as animals they are rather an arbitrary assortment—a bull, an owl, horse, sheep or cat, ruled over by a frog (Lord John Big). It seems to have been as natural for C.S. Lewis to write about animals as it was to write religious allegory. The *Narnia* books and the science-fiction trilogy combine the two and it is interesting to see how in both series, ideal worlds are shown to be populated first by animals, later by humans, who tend to bring evil, conflict and doubt. In every case the animals exist as themselves, never as counterfeit men, always 'good' and uncorrupted. From Boxen—which, in its way, must have been rather like *Reynard the Fox*—we have moved to worlds containing rational, talking creatures in animal form, equal to men but quite different from them.

But in the first two novels of his science-fiction trilogy—*Out of the Silent Planet* (1938) and *Perelandra* (1943)—Lewis describes worlds of astonishing beauty with virtually no human populations at all, but very definite animal ones, with fur, feathers and scales. Earth is made to appear dull by comparison, its inhabitants dark, flattened and bulging to a Martian eye. In much science fiction other planets are alien and terrifying; to describe them otherwise is as untraditional as writing successful children's stories full of explicit religious allegory (of which there is far more in Narnia than in the work of George Macdonald).

Ransom's arrival on Mars in *Out of the Silent Planet* is marked by terror. He is a reluctant, kidnapped traveller and when he overhears that he is to be given to creatures called Sorns, he immediately thinks of horrors—perhaps of the two things that most frightened the author as a child—insects and ghosts.

'Wait till he sees a Sorn,' say the villains Weston and Devine; and Sorns are bird-ghosts of giant height, disturbingly almost human. Ransom's one thought on seeing one is to escape. He runs through, and hides in, the beautifully coloured and strangely elongated country, until he meets more living things, a herd of tall, pale, furry giraffe-kangaroos who are eating the tops of trees. Reassured with the idea that the planet has animals on it as well as ghosts, he is still unprepared for his first meeting with yet another inhabitant: a gleaming black creature six or seven feet high, 'something like a penguin, something like an otter, something like a seal, something like a giant stoat'. He is rooted to the ground with fear, until, in one of the great passages of this book and the key to the *Narnia* stories, the creature opens its mouth and begins to make noises. Ransom—a scholar and a philologist—at once realises, in spite of his terror, that it is talking. That animals could be rational had not occurred to him, and as it did, it overturned the world: animal and human had no more meaning.

This, one feels, is how C.S. Lewis wanted things to be, for he had created a world in which it was so. Hross and man confront each other with a kind of balletic advance and retreat, each afraid, yet each attracted—it was 'foolish, frightening, ecstatic and unbearable all in one moment'. Later, when they have learned each other's names, Ransom and Hyoi sit on a river bank eating a kind of Martian vegetable, Ransom is struck with fear because the creature is not a man, but is seven feet high, covered in hair and whiskered like a cat. But it is when he can make the change and consider it as an animal that he can love it 'as though Paradise had never been lost and earliest dreams were true', for it has the charm of speech and reason. Here is the romantic Eden before the fall, glimpsed in John's Island in *The Pilgrim's Regress*, 1933, where man and animal are not only equal, but friends. In more mundane fashion, it is the old story of the child who longed for his dog, or his Teddy bear to speak, and as a man, made up stories in which they did. It is Animal-Land and Paradise combined. All the science-fiction stories and the whole of the *Narnia* cycle are played on this note. In *Out of the Silent Planet* there is Eden, in *Perelandra* the reader witnesses the story of the fall, in *That Hideous Strength*, the fall has already happened. But in all three there is the reminder that the fall of man brought the fall, or fate, or exploitation of animals with it.

Out of the Silent Planet has other interesting ideas concerning Mars—or Malacandra, in Martian language—as an idealised Animal-Land. Ransom comes to realise that this is a planet with no countries, only three different races. Manlike, he tries to rationalise their society (late Stone Age?) and to wonder which of the three species—the Hrossa, the ghostly birdlike Sorns, or the reptilian Pfifltriggi—is the dominant one. He finds out that they are equal but different in nature, one poetic, one philosophical and one physically creative, and that the same God that made them made men too. He hears of an earlier race which has died out, for none are intended to live for ever.

In one sense in this book there are man-bird, man-seal and man-toad, yet in another the men in the story are made to feel small, insignificant, ugly and at the end, for all their space ships, foolish.

At the very end comes animal vengeance which C.S. Lewis uses and re-uses to remind us that since the fall animal creation has been consistently killed, enslaved and abused. In this novel it is comic vengeance taken on one of the men, the wicked scientist Weston who is here the villain, later to become the arch villain of Perelandra. He is removed to have his head bathed in cold water, 'to cool him off'.

This is a joke to the Hrossa and Pfifltriggi but to Weston, whose plans would have prostituted and exploited both animals' and humans, it is a real revenge. From first to last he has never realised the Malacandrian's nobility, but takes them to be animals or creatures of a low order: he can never regard the non-human as equal.

> We dipped his head in the cold water seven times (says a hross). The seventh time something fell off it. We had thought it was the top of his head but now we saw it was a covering made of the skin of some creature ... then we dipped it seven times more. The creature talked a lot between the dips and mart between the second seven, but we could not understand it.

The ignominy was cruelty to Weston, who was expecting torture and a martyr's death. A very similar incident happens in the *Narnia* story at the end of *The Magician's Nephew* where the Wicked Uncle, another Weston figure (but even worse because he is a magician as well as a scientist), is dealt with by the Narnian Talking Beasts of whom he is naturally terrified and whose language he does not understand. The Beasts' intention is kind but the result is nightmare, quite unbearable if it was not comic. They think he is a tree and try to plant him, the wrong way up.

The animals' revenge in *That Hideous Strength* is nightmare come true, brought about, significantly, by confusion of language and man's reduction to the level of the animals he has been exploiting. Once again the animals are not guilty—they are doing nothing except obeying instinct.

In both the Edens of Mars and Venus the evil comes from without in the shape of a man, and animal characters, rational or otherwise, are shown to be guiltless and uncorrupted. They do not even understand evil; it is so rare among them that it has to be explained in terms of something of almost legendary rarity, strange and unfortunate.

The classical and northern elements which always combined in Lewis's work—making the inhabitants of Narnia a combination of Chiron and Squirrel Nutkin—reappear in Perelandra, the Venus of the trilogy, a planet as warm and fluid as Malacandra was hard and cold. Ransom speculates among other things on whether situations and creatures regarded as legendary on one planet become real on another: an idea which appealed greatly to Lewis and which he used in Narnia and in the science-fiction short story 'Forms of Things Unknown'. On Malacandra Ransom is shown comparing the Sorn Augray with the Cyclops of Ulysses, and throughout the *Narnia* books there are an astonishing and not always happily mixed number of creatures from different legends—the ones that appealed to the author most—inhabiting a created world that is obviously England only better.

In *Perelandra* the legend is that of the temptation of Eve, which Ransom is allowed to witness in the hope that he will be able to prevent it. But the tempter is not an animal, not even the most unpopular one of all, whose only apologist has been Rudyard Kipling; it is the wicked Weston again, the power-mad humanist, a type Lewis regarded as the worst in existence and who is later taken over by the forces of evil becoming, like them, unkillable and all but invincible.

The animals in this novel do not speak and are all in a state of nature in an Eden which, allowing for differences of climate and ecology, is rather like that of the Bible. Eve is shown at the summit of creation, 'The Lady' whom the animals know and love and obey. The devil in the form of Weston tries to bring about her downfall by argument and persuasion, leading up to the great temptation—the invitation to walk on the fixed land, the forbidden place. The interesting idea is advanced that God put it there in order to be able to say No; it would have been equally interesting if C.S. Lewis had suggested that Adam was the one vulnerable to temptation (but in the last novel of the trilogy a man is tempted, by the offer of power: Eve in Perelandra is tempted through latent feminine vanity).

The Perelandrian animals are beautiful, mythical and heraldic: a tame, winged dragon, flying frogs, rideable dolphins and a creature called the Singing Beast which suggests an okapi but which is described as being like a dog with the legs of a camel, the neck and head of a horse, but vast in size. It is a cuckoo beast, suckled and reared by a mother of another kind. Lewis shows it existing with such strange, hidden, sad joy, beauty and shyness that words other than his own reduce it to a cartoon anomaly.[1]

The animals in *That Hideous Strength* are earthly ones, non-rational, but important enough to be heroes or victims, in the former sense pets (of a kind), in the latter, inhabitants of a zoo. C.S. Lewis's insect fear, exorcised by a harmless monster in *Perelandra*, also suggested 'either machines that have come to life, or life degenerating into mechanism', and dominance of the female and the collective. *That Hideous Strength* shows just such a process beginning to take hold when the mysterious Ministry, the National Institute of Coordinated Experiments with its ambiguous initials, takes root and gains power by infiltration and persuasion as a prelude to inevitable force. One of its principal officers is the sadistic lesbian Miss Hardcastle.

A subsidiary interest of this devilish symposium is animal experiment and a large zoo is kept for this purpose. The opposing side, who live in a place called The Manor, St Anne's, an almost enchanted country house, have animals as pets including a vast bear called Mr Bultitude who has escaped from a circus and whose delight it is to sit in the bathroom on cold days. It is Eden again; all the pets seem to have arrived by their own free will and to lead lives of equality with the humans, unencumbered by leads, fences or locked doors, in harmony with man and each other. The opposition torture their animals in cages.

The 'good' humans are an odd collection of the simple and the intelligent. Perhaps one is justified in peopling Eden, or even Heaven, with the characters one has most loved and admired (in *The Great Divorce* George Macdonald is Heaven's interpreter and guide) and Hell with those for whom one feels the most horror—scientists, experimenters, those whom sheer logic has rendered inhuman, the power-mad manipulators, the merely vain. In a scene of orgiastic horror during after-dinner speeches at a banquet, the humans lose the power of language and with it their ascendancy, and the beasts from the laboratories attack and destroy them. The 'good' bear Mr Bultitude annihilates the evil 'head' of the Institute by eating it, prompted by simple hunger. The animals are neither good nor bad; they are themselves, simple and amoral, creatures with whom the planet is unequally shared, neither agents of witchcraft nor of heaven. Though at the end a few of them appear to speak in the manner of Balaam's Ass, they are not rationally intelligent; but in the war between good and evil they have a large part to play. At the end, when the occupants of the Manor are revealed to each other in beauty that has always, in mundane life, been hidden, the mating of the animals in the garden is part of the joy of revealed love.

It would appear to have been as difficult for C.S. Lewis to avoid religious allegory, as it was to avoid the prominent role that animals, usually intelligent and often humanised, play in it. It is, of course quite in order to write heroic romance dealing with the struggle between good and evil without any religious theme. *The Hobbit* is such a book. When *The Lord of the Kings* first appeared one critic found its lack of religious feeling remarkable enough for comment—as remarkable as its lack of women. But aim at the distant hills and you find yourself going in at the front door, as Alice did. Whatever kind of story Lewis thought he was going to write, religious allegory appeared. This is illustrated yet again in the recorded conversation between Lewis, Kingsley Amis and Brian Aldiss (*Unreal Estates: Of Other Worlds*, 1966) when Lewis remarks, 'The starting point of my second novel, *Perelandra*, was my mental picture of the floating islands. The whole of the rest of my labours in a sense consisted of building up a world in which floating islands could exist. And then, of course, the story about an averted fall developed.' To which Aldiss replied, 'I am surprised you put it this way round. I would have thought that you constructed *Perelandra* for the didactic purpose,' which shows how wrong one can be.

In a sense, Narnia is Malacandra and Perelandra over again; in another, it is Mouse Town and Knights-in-armour; but it is a long, long way from Animal-Land.

In the beginning of *The Lion, the Witch and the Wardrobe*, Lucy, exploring, enjoying the feel of the fur coats, discovers with a beautiful tactile pun that they are turning into pine and spruce and the mothballs into snow. Lewis uses the device of the Parallel World, a favourite in Fantasy literature. It is a world not reached by space ships but by magic (Lewis quickly abandoned the space ship as a device for travel). Lewis Carroll does this too, and so does E. Nesbit who has exactly the same opening of a cupboard or wardrobe door in a story called 'The Aunt and Amabel'; it is used by contemporary writers such as Alan Garner. C.S. Lewis makes Narnia an ideal world in which the oreads and enchanters mingle with dwarves and talking mice. Few writers have given a magic place such definition, such solid geography and such a gallery of characters. From the mind of a writer so stocked with images of the classical and 'northern' kind, so coloured by Christianity, the first elements of the story appear; the faun, the ice-queen and the golden lion. The result is a wonderful and at times uneasy mixture of ingredients, like a rich but indigestible Christmas cake. Critics of Narnia have tumbled out the words *rich* and *strange*, thought for a bit, and then come up with *strange* and *rich* again, as if almost at a loss; indeed, it has some affinities with Prospero's island. This ideal land has, for the sake of adventure and dramatic conflict, to have evil in it, and it is presented as an unredeemed country, waiting for Aslan's death and resurrection.

As the books progress, one can see the creative imagination at work. At first, the classic strain—the fauns, dryads, centaurs and others—is far stronger. It blends with the Northern European element, the witches, giants, dwarves and earthmen, and the inevitable Talking Beasts, ruled over by Christ the Lion, Aslan, son of the Emperor over the sea. Perhaps the uneasiness that adults feel is not shared by children, who do not notice that the child Edmund is made to play the part of Judas, being led astray by such ordinary means as sherbet and Turkish Delight (evil confections from *The*

Arabian Nights that Lewis disliked as a child); or that Susan and Lucy are like the two Marys at the tomb on the morning of Easter Day.

The Talking Beasts come, in the end, to dominate the whole narrative, resulting in the wonderful animal characters of Reepicheep, Bree and Puddleglum. Aslan is shown creating and dissolving the world, and at the very end it is animal nature that brings about its destruction. The cycle has returned to its beginning, in Animal-Land, and Mouse Town. The animals have become human enough to have heroes and villains, tragedy and triumph, but C.S. Lewis never quite returns to his original. There is never any confusion as to *which* order his creatures belong to: they are always themselves.

But in the first book, this element is muted, the classical and religious elements are strong. It is interesting to note that in all the *Narnia* stories the classical characters are invariably 'goodies'. There is never an evil dryad, faun or centaur; creatures like hydras, gorgons, chimeras or harpies have not found their way into Narnia. But when one comes to the 'Northern' animals, Lewis seems more at home and characters are more flexible. The White Queen is a snow queen rather than a Circe, some dwarves are good and some corrupt, there are good and bad giants (but no clever ones) and even a pleasantly childlike and enthusiastic lion. The really bad characters are all from the Northern kind—wolves, fungi, ogres, ghosts and werewolves. Northern and classical do not emulsify with smoothness. Perhaps it is inevitable that they find themselves in opposing armies.

The only non-human characters to be given any depth in this first story—which is full of ideas, images, descriptions and incident without much character interest apart from the reform and repentance of Edmund the traitor—are the beavers, and Mr Tumnus the faun. They are all essentially homely, and the faun, a highly intelligent person, is Northernised. He lives in a cave and serves tea. The cave has a carpet, chairs, table and dresser, and bookshelves with such titles as *The Life and Letters of Silenus, Men, Monks and Gamekeepers: a study in popular legend*. If a faun could be found living in an English wood, his home would certainly be like this. The beavers are even more literally Northernised: they live in a log cabin with snowshoes, rocking chair, stove, sewing machine and fishing tackle. They are completely humanised (apart from Mr Beaver's fishing by paw). Mrs Beaver, when at last they leave the lodge in haste, wants to bring her sewing machine. 'I can't abide the thought of that witch fiddling with it and breaking it,' she says. On the journey the beavers walk on two legs and hand round spirits in a flask. There is even the odd adjective 'wrinkled' applied to one of Mrs Beaver's paws, indicating age and slight animal-person confusion.[2]

The later animals that join in the battle with Peter to help win him his kingdom are all of the fairy-tale, heraldic or mythical kind: bears, leopards, stags, lions, horses, nothing either odd or ordinary and nothing comic, no elephants, giraffes, cats or monkeys (these appear in later books). It is clear that the animal strain is not the strongest, or even among the strongest strains, of this story which is concerned with human sin and redemption in an invented world. The animals are always present, they talk and fight and everything ends with a mixture of thrones and sand-between-the-toes, the four children living happily ever after into a courtly middle age before they find their way out through the wardrobe into the world again. Everything is harmony—animal, myth, classical and northern are all united as is suggested by the little party in the wood that is the sign of the end of the witch's rule: squirrels, fox, dwarves and fauns all having Christmas dinner together. Father Christmas and Silenus should surely have joined them.

In the second and less successful book *Prince Caspian*, the animal element is stronger—as with each succeeding instalment. The Prince's lost kingdom consists almost entirely of Talking Beasts who are exiled or in hiding, and who later make up the rebel army with a number or dryads, fauns, dwarves, centaurs (why is it that Northern myth does not supply any heroic or delightful animal-human creatures?). Here we see the Narnian creatures beginning to form themselves into a workable population. The 'small' animals are larger than life and the 'large' ones smaller; and as in Malacandra, the racial mixture is slightly comic.

The book is most notable for the introduction of C.S. Lewis's best animal character, significantly, a mouse. But Reepicheep is not part of Snug Town, a place that the faun Mr Tumnus belongs to, but of the Knights-in-Armour and Courtly Mice mentioned in *Surprised by Joy*. He is described as 'gay and martial', makes grand gestures and talks like a mixture of Sir Thomas Malory and an old-fashioned general: he wears a rapier and twirls his long whiskers as if they were moustaches

> 'There are twelve of us, Sire,' he said with a dashing and graceful bow, 'and I place all the resources of my people unreservedly at your Majesty's disposal.' Caspian tried hard (and successfully) not to laugh.

The joke, even though Reepicheep is described as over a foot high, is his smallness—always the joke with Mouse characters in stories displaying them as bustling housewives in doll's houses, or triumphing over impossible odds (*The Rescuers*). Reepicheep starts off as part of this tradition, the joke being made even more pointed by the largeness of his heart, the size of his courage and self-esteem and Caspian's and Peter's tact and politeness in dealing with him.

At the end of the book, Reepicheep actually answers Aslan back—a thing that no other animal, creature or human dares to do, in any of the *Narnia* stories. Aslan is rather like a schoolmaster with an outsize but invisible cane. He tells the Mouse that he should think a little less of honour and glory, and the Mouse reminds him that 'a very small size has been bestowed on us Mice' and that they cannot help guarding their dignity above all. It is a courageous and prompt answer and Aslan is won by it.

This is a very long way from the tiny Aesop creatures who, mouse-sized and dumb, gnawed away the ropes that bound Aslan in *The Lion, the Witch and the Wardrobe.* The third and best of the *Narnia* books, *The Voyage of the Dawn Treader*, has Reepicheep the mouse as its central, tragic hero; and this, in a fairy tale involving humans, is unique. At last, animal creation has taken human status and intelligence; we are back with the Hrossa and Sorns again. The status of the Mouse is the same as that of the courtly members of the crew (he is a Knight of the Order of the Lion) and the story concerns, among other things, his quest for the end of the world culminating in his strange and poetic death which has true heroic sadness. But there is a difference between Reepicheep and the humans—he is not quite a human in disguise. He is in some ways better and braver (in the adventure of The Dark Island and the Magician) and more level headed (with the Sea Serpent). He gains and loses by being a mouse and not a man, and the differences are explicit. He does not feel the shudders of horror that the others feel in the Dark Island; he has no dreams and cannot understand human fear of nightmare; he feels no exhaustion in the tropics and can stay awake to guard the water supply (or else is able to subdue the flesh more easily than the humans).

It is odd, perhaps, that *The Voyage of the Dawn Treader*, the most satisfying of the *Narnia* books, is the one with the least of Aslan in it and the fewest Talking Beasts. Religious allegory is unobtrusive and there is a strong Arthurian odour. Part of the interest, especially at the beginning, is the improvement and redemption of Eustace, the ordinary boy. We first see Reepicheep through his eyes.

> Something very curious indeed had come out of the cabin in the poop and was slowly approaching them ... it was a Mouse on its hind legs and stood about two feet high. A thin band of gold passed round its head under one ear and over the other and in this was stuck a long crimson feather. (As the Mouse's fur was very

dark, almost black, the effect was bold and striking.) Its left paw rested on the hilt of a sword very nearly as long at its tail. Its balance, as it paced gravely along the swaying deck, was perfect, its manners courtly.

This personage is unstrokeable, uncuddleable. Indeed Reepicheep and Talking Beasts in general inspire a certain amount of awe; the only people who do not feel it and do not like the situation are the strangers or evil humans or those who have got into Narnia by some sort of mistake, such as the Telmarines, who, when given the chance to stay in Narnia, decline.

'Live here, with a lot of blooming performing animals! No fear,' they said. 'And ghosts too,' some added with a shudder. 'That's what those Dryads really are' ... 'I don't trust 'em,' they said. 'Not that awful Lion and all.'

This is Uncle Andrew's reaction in *The Magician's Nephew*; it is also that of Professor Weston in *Out of the Silent Planet*. 'Ugh, take it away,' says Eustace when, brought unwillingly and by mistake into Narnia, he sees Reepicheep. 'I hate mice. And I never could bear performing animals. They're silly and vulgar and—sentimental.' One feels a certain sympathy for him, though this is far from the author's intention. Reepicheep immediately has cause for single combat with Eustace; and one can hardly blame Eustace for disliking this adventure into which he has been pulled. It promises to be uncomfortable, messy, dangerous, and starts by making him seasick and is going to be full or characters and situations he has never met and would not have chosen (this is blamed on the wrong school—a potent Progressive source of corruption, responsible for the treachery of Edmund—and the wrong books, or rather, lack of the right ones). Eustace does the only things he knows; complains and threatens, tries to contact the British consul, tries to maintain his identity by talking about liners and aeroplanes, and in the end keeps an aggrieved diary. In short, he behaves in typical Professor Weston fashion. The first half of the book has considerable pace and fascination through the conflict between Eustace and his surroundings.

Of course Eustace cannot win; Heaven is larger than the world. He must learn to like Heaven, or Eden, with its Equality for Animals, or go away. There is an exactly similar situation in *The Great Divorce* where the visitors from Hell neither recognise not like Heaven. The scene is set for the Animal Revenge, which here is two-pronged. Eustace tries to humiliate Reepicheep—it was meant as a joke, he says afterwards, but the Mouse has no sense of humour and again offers single combat. 'I'm a pacifist,' says Eustace, but the Mouse has never heard of them and Eustace is beaten with the flat of his sword. As he has never experienced corporal punishment at the Progressive school, the sensation is new. His subsequent dragon adventure—being changed not only into an animal but into the ugliest, most feared and hated creature in the world, with a boy's consciousness but carnivorous and cannibalistic instincts, to say nothing of a painful iron band immovably stuck on his foreleg—is a punishment almost too terrible to contemplate; far beyond anything meted out to Weston or Uncle Andrew. But as this is a children's story Eustace emerges at last, a sadder and a wiser boy. He has been made to fit into Narnia, like a bulgy Lost Boy into his tree (Peter did something to him and it was all right).

The Mouse throughout behaves with gallantry and courage so great as to be almost foolhardy, but never comic; always as immune from human envy, fear and greed as if he were lacking in some faculty. The end of the book becomes more and more like the quest for the Grail as they reach Ramandu's Isle with its holy relic, and the Utter East, where prophecy has told the Mouse that he will meet his heart's desire. And so dies Reepicheep, launching himself over the world's edge in his tiny coracle, heroic, courteous, tiny, humourless and unforgettable, nonhuman, lesser and greater and completely other.

The only other characters to compare with Reepicheep in stature are Puddleglum the Marsh Wiggle and Bree the horse. Puddleglum, in 'The Silver Chair', is hardly animal; he is a humanised Pfifltrigg, animal in his webbed feet and fingers with serious saurian views of life. It is made quite clear that Wiggles are a separate species in the Narnian world. Puddleglum is something between Mark Tapley and a frog. His arms and legs are very long—long enough to frighten the Giant Queen; Pauline Baynes' illustration shows Puddleglum on the floor before the Giant's feet in a half-collapsed position, rather as if a small human grasshopper or locust was poised for a spring, its knees higher than its ears. Puddleglum's hair is green-grey and flat like reeds, and he smokes strange, heavy tobacco that trickles out of his pipe like foggy water.

He—always 'he' and not 'It' as Reepicheep is described—appears to hope for disaster and to thrive on it, to court it by mentioning the worst before it can possibly happen. In reality he is well prepared, sensible and the best companion Eustace and Jill could have chosen for their adventure (or have had chosen for them by Aslan, who, though absent, influences the happenings in this story, Will-of-God fashion). Puddleglum is slow, sure, steady and has the reptilian virtues of being cold blooded and reliable. One would imagine that in winter he might hibernate, but on the contrary, he leads the children through storms and snows to the wild lands of the North, his only weakness being drink, his greatest strength his clear-sighted, unemotional pessimism—always ready to doubt a honeyed voice or a deceitfully fair face. He is not taken in by the Lady, the wicked queen who is an enchantress and a shape-changer. (Beware! Aslan has warned elsewhere against half-and-halfers. It appears that the author only admits the fixed and finished off categories into the animal Eden; there is no evolution and certainly no blurring. It is all like Genesis.)

Puddleglum remembers Aslan's rules when the children have forgotten them, is unexpectedly brave and—another animal virtue similar to that of the heroic Mouse—toughly immune when the witch tries to drug and hypnotise the party into forgetfulness and make them believe that the counterfeit, underground world is the real one. Puddleglum has a heroic last stand in which he uses his cold webbed feet to stamp out the Lady's fire, and asserts his belief in the sun and his determination to spend his life, however short, in looking for it.

As a character he is vivid and unique and earns the children's love and gratitude. As a species he is lacking, as he is the only one of his kind we are allowed to see; Wiggles are said to be solitary. He is the most manlike of Narnian creatures, perhaps only a canny, careful East Anglian after all.

If Reepicheep is the most memorable mouse ever created, Bree is one of the most interesting horses. 'The Horse and his Boy' has the amusing situation of animal creation being not merely equal or different from human but, in its own rather snobbish opinion, better. Aslan, after all, created the animals in his image, and humans were an afterthought, a transplant, as is shown in 'The Magician's Nephew'. 'The Horse and his Boy' takes place outside Narnia and had the most purely human excitements about it—battle, treachery and fugitives—but in many ways it is the least characteristic of the *Narnia* books and bears about the same relation to the others as *A Tale of Two Cities* to the rest of Dickens. It concerns the adventures of a Narnian Talking Horse (trained by mistake as a warhorse of Calormen), a Boy who is from Archenland and does not know it, and their struggles to find their way home.

Calormen, the Eastern land on the borders of Archenland and Narnia, is neutral, but inclined to burst into enmity and conquest. Its inhabitants are practical, money-minded, devious and reflect the sad fact that the author as a child could not stand *The Arabian Nights*; his allegiance appears to have gone as far south as Greece and no further (the strongly Eastern flavour of Christianity has been absorbed into Europe for so long that it has almost lost its original tang).

The adventures are exciting and dangerous and of the two main rational characters the Horse is much the stronger. It is older than the Boy Shasta, wiser, better educated, capable of leading him out of danger and saving both from slavery. Some of the strange amusement of the story comes from the un-Narnian situation of the Horse's having to be ridden if the two are to get anywhere, partly for speed and partly for disguise. (One does not suppose that Narnians rode Talking Horses, except by invitation, as Jill and Eustace were invited to ride Centaurs in 'The Silver Chair'; a ride with learned conversation as an awe-inspiring accompaniment.)

The Horse teaches the Boy to ride; later they are joined by a Girl and a Mare, similarly running away. They make a perfect quartet, and the situation is an appealing one. But 'The Horse and his Boy' is the least magic, the least poetic of the *Narnia* books, and Aslan has a sterner, redemptive effect on all four main characters except perhaps for Hwin the Mare, who is, unusually for C.S. Lewis, a female of great charm and courage. (The human heroine, Aravis, is described as rather a tomboy: 'interested in bows and arrows and horses and dogs and swimming'.)

The names of the horses have interest. It is always difficult to name a humanised animal according to the sound it makes. Only Swift has ever attempted this with the horse, with a result that is as unspellable as it is unpronounceable. The easier way is to name the animal by what it does, or what it looks like: Goldenshoes, Trufflehunter. Occasionally comes a really inspired name like Mrs Tiggiwinkle or a beautiful foreign one such as Shere Khan. Bree and Hwin are pronounceable, accurate ideas of what a horse sounds like, having clear sexual indications. Lewis's names have not the inspiration of some of those in the *King* saga, such as Meriadoc Brandybuck or Belladonna Took, but he is writing with careful simplicity while Tolkien is writing as the historian of a distant—if imaginary—period which children may enjoy but which is not presented for their entertainment. Thus the capital of Calormen, Tashbaan, is a noise of cymbal and gong, while the names Gondor, Lothlorien have a flavour of another language—as the author intended.

Bree's greatest weakness is his personal pride. Part of the comedy of his character is that a dignified creature or person, when he loses his dignity, can be very funny indeed. Bree persists in talking to Hwin, rather than her girl rider. He worries about whether he looks funny when rolling and wonders if rolling 'isn't done' in Narnia—he is a very socially conscious horse. He is patronising to Shasta and thinks humans are 'funny little creatures' and quarrelsome. He objects to having to disguise himself as a working, dumb horse and is awkward and difficult about it. He loses his pride at last by becoming too intellectual. He is caught out trying to explain rather pompously to Aravis and Hwin why Aslan is not a real lion (or why religion is just a myth). One feels that it would be a bit unfair to humanists if God should come and tap them on the shoulder; one of the facts of life in the last few centuries is that God does not seem to have had much of a hand in it. But in Narnia things are different, and when Bree finds that Aslan is true, he feels almost as unpleasant as Edmund and Eustace did. By the end of the book he has not quite recovered and is still worried about rolling, a subject on which Hwin is quite at her ease.

In comparison with Bree, the horse Fledge in 'The Magician's Nephew' is a simple creature. He starts life as Strawberry the cabhorse and is the only animal of note in this, the sixth book of the series, which concerns the founding of Narnia and creation, by Aslan, of all the animals.

'The Magician's Nephew' is the most obvious blending of parts. It has a great number of possible sources which have been used and transformed and made new; there is the Bastable world of Digory and Polly, the similarly E. Nesbit magic rings which transport when touched, the Rider Haggard city of Charn with its Hall of Effigies, the Arthurian Deplorable Word, the Siege Perilous warning on the magic bell and the Dolorous Stroke effect when it is rung in anger by Digory. There is the morbid Victorian Theme of Digory's dying mother, who is cured with a magic apple which, in this story, is as if one of Iduna's could have been grafted on to the tree in the garden of the Hesperides.

The greatest theme is the creation of Narnia by Aslan out of Nothing. It grows gradually from stars to mountains and rivers, grass and trees and last of all the animals, its natural and uncorrupted inhabitants, who rise out of the earth as if they were made from it. The group of human onlookers are intruders, by a magic mistake.

From the animals, Aslan chooses certain pairs to touch and breathe on. They become Talking Beasts, and Narnia is founded at last with creatures whose first act is to do the most human thing of all—'they began making various queer noises which ... no one has ever heard in our world'—and animal laughter is heard, perhaps for the first time ever. The animals observe the people present but do not recognise them, thinking they are vegetables (a legitimate mistake; Narnian Talking Beasts are never dressed, and Aslan has already created walking trees).

Strawberry the cabhorse, who has been given speech with the others and later becomes Fledge the hippogriff, is no ordinary horse. The cabman has already mentioned that his sire was a cavalry charger (the old warhorse, Captain, of *Black Beauty?*). But he is grateful to the cabman who has treated him kindly. Even with wings and a changed status—he has thrown off his earthly slavery and become free—he is both proud and humble, recognising that the cabman who put him in harness had no choice, being just as much a slave as he. Of course the cabman and his wife are the same and have simple, animal souls. Aslan at once transforms them into the King and Queen of Narnia, the Adam and Eve from whom all humans spring.

The story explains and in part contradicts the others; the author is filling the gaps and providing causes for effects which were there because they were there, like the tree of knowledge.[3]

The animals' revenge on Uncle Andrew, already mentioned, is a milder version of what happens in two earlier science-fiction novels. The scientist Weston is punished, not through malice, but because the Malacandrian creatures are trying, in a fairly simple way, to do what they think best. Neither man nor creature really understands what the other is trying to do or say. The animals in the banquet scene in *That Hideous Strength* are not rational. The humans have brought about their own downfall. There is an interesting parallel in 'The Terror', a short story by Arthur Machen, in which domestic and farm animals begin to murder humans in revenge for the human exploitation which they cannot escape. But Machen did not suggest that the animals were conscious killers, only that man's murderous instincts had turned against himself.

It is quite natural that the newly created Talking Beasts, who have mistaken the children for cabbages, mistake Uncle Andrew for a kind of tree. When they discover he is Animal, they make a cage and try to feed him; it is the scientist-magician's logical fate—in a land where animals are his equals—the tables are turned at the Zoo. The joke is that the animals are no more sensible than humans usually are, and shower Uncle Andrew with their favourite food, much as Tigger was given everything except Extract of Malt. Uncle Andrew has everything except the brandy he wants. He is terrified of Aslan, and hears only roars, squeaks and growls as the Beasts try to speak to him.

In the final *Narnian* story, 'The Last Battle', the fall of Narnia is brought about by animal means and not human. The only delinquent Talking Beasts occur here—the Ape, Shift, and the Cat.

Shift, who is lazy, artful, ambitious and greedy, starts by exploiting the gentle donkey Puzzle and goes on to exploit all the other Talking Beasts by working on their simple, loyal credulity. In a way, he is a Beast descending into Humanity, for this is what humans do. Shift even ends by dressing like a human. The Ape's aim is to sell Narnia to Calormen. Only the Cat sees through the Ape's trickery and connives at it, and is punished in the inevitable way by losing its faculty of speech, becoming witless and wild. Cats are often heroic or treacherous in folklore or fairy tale, seldom neutral. This cat is very cool and logical. It is the dogs which are preferred, as in Maeterlinck, they are all heart and rather mindless affection. They join eagerly in Prince Tirian's last stand and are among the first to enter heaven. It seems that the good characters are to be defeated, and the harshly neutral dwarves (ambiguous characters, sometimes out of Snug Town, sometimes very much not so) and the wicked *Arabian Nights* people out of Calormen, are going to win; but Aslan defeats them by putting an end to Narnia, Calormen and all.

It is difficult to be neutral about Aslan, as character or animal or symbol. He is always *there*, the instrument of the author's ideas, and it seems at times as if he is the author, who is rather enjoying himself. Aslan is the eternal Big Brother, the irrefutable and ultimate authority, the person who not only upholds the rules but also seems to have made them. To disobey is unthinkable and always brings disaster, sometimes swiftly as happens to Aravis when she is attacked and scored by ten claws in retribution for ten strokes given to a serving maid she has tricked. Sometimes the retribution is horribly and inevitably slow: the sad death scene of Caspian at the end of 'The Silver Chair' springs partly from the unpleasant tempers and disobedience of Jill Pole and Eustace Scrubb at the beginning. Indeed the book is notable for the set of instructions or commandments given by Aslan which must always be followed even when not understood.

Aslan cannot ever be ignored. The rather worldly and un-Narnian Susan, present in the first two stories, is banished from the rest. Aslan cannot be laughed at. Edmund has a feeble try in *The Lion, the Witch and the Wardrobe* and soon feels sorry for it. It is impossible to look Aslan in the eyes and tell a lie or make an excuse: even his name has a shaking, unpleasant effect on wrongdoers, as it cheers the good characters and fills them with hope. His very presence in the Earth world (back view only) is enough to unmake a whole Progressive school. The religious tones are explicit: if Talking Beasts disobey, they lose their speech. A 'lapsed bear' is mentioned. It has to be hunted, fought and killed; the fate of the wicked cat is similar.

Aslan made Narnia, and when all the nasty people of Eastern fairy tale break into it and start to ruin its Classical-Northernness, he unmakes it again in scenes of apocalyptic, sunset grandeur. Casting God into a story in the form of a lion is bold and unique; the *Pilgrim's Progress* does not do as much. Aslan is an heraldic lion, bright, fearsome and wonderful, but his lion nature is appearance only—he never kills or eats. His mane is a 'tossing sea of gold'. His best appearances concern themselves only with beauty and joy. He comes frequently into the early books like an Old Testament Jehovah and less in the later ones. The most memorable occasions are those of the two girls' ride on his back in *The Lion, the Witch and the Wardrobe* and at the end of 'Prince Caspian' where he joins Bacchus, the Maenads, animals and trees in a glorious game that overcomes everything—even old age, tyranny and death. 'And so at last, with leaping and dancing and singing with music and laughter and roaring and barking and neighing, they all came to the place where Miraz's army stood flinging down their swords and holding up their hands.' When the Talking Beasts meet him they greet him as the King of the Beasts, and not with words. He seems to speak to their innocent goodness. 'They surged round the Lion with purrs and grunts and squeaks and whinneys of delight, fawning on him with their tails, rubbing against him, touching him reverently with their noses.'

It is the schoolmasterly, godlike Aslan which adults often dislike. C.S. Lewis tells in an essay (not the short piece 'It All Began with a Picture' which appeared in the *Radio Times* and was peppered with capital Hs for the personal pronoun, but 'Sometimes Fairy Tales may say best what's to be said') how he hoped to 'steal past those watchful dragons', i.e. the Sunday School inhibitions which many children may feel when thinking of religion. It is possible that children do not feel such inhibitions at all, but with many adults the watchful dragons are still there, very much awake.

At best, Aslan is the King of Beasts in an animal land where humans are put very much in their place. 'This elegant little biped' runs the giant's cookery book 'has long been valued as a delicacy. It forms a traditional part of the Autumn Feast and is served between the fish and the joint.' Humans are, therefore, just another kind of Talking Beast, with a mandate to rule under Aslan. And the only secret of happiness lies in the lumbering phrase Peaceful Co-existence, with the giants paying tribute, the Calormenes confined to Calormen keeping their nasty god Tash to themselves, and none of the Narnians eating each other (eating dumb beasts is permitted).

But the presence of Aslan does give the *Narnia* books another dimension—not of magic, but of miracle. As legends concern the presence of Gods in human affairs, and the Old Testament the dealings of one God with one race, so C.S. Lewis has written of a world where God constantly takes a hand in person. It makes for strange retributions and rewards, miraculous happenings, healing and punishment, prophecies and destinies that do not occur in *The Lord of the Rings*—the only other comparable work, where God is never present and never even mentioned. It can even lead to pantomime situations such as that of the boastful horse whose audience would have shouted 'Look behind you' had they not been rooted to the spot in awe.

The real test is that, in spite of a few awkward particles, the mixture works. The *Narnia* stories have magical invention, great beauty, enormous and compelling epic drama. Together they form a unique literary classic that will surely remain, like the Lord Octesian's ring, hanging 'as long as that world lasted', on an odd, unreachable pinnacle.

NOTES

1. It seems to be extremely difficult to make up a convincing new animal. The best most science-fiction writers and others do is to add up pieces of old ones, as in the game of head, body and legs. The animals of heraldry, legend and the Bestiaries are formed in this fashion, so that in theory one could draw quite an accurate picture of the Questing Beast from the list of parts given. Usually in science fiction a new animal is a new monster put together from the parts of insects, plants, fish, etc. that most terrify and repel, i.e. John Wyndham's Triffids when analysed, come apart as Venus Fly Trap pineapple rattlesnakes. But one of this author's most telling pieces of black humour occurs in *The Chrysalids* when, after atomic pollution animal and human deviants are hunted down with fanatical religious fervour, one of the characters meets and recoils from a creature 'as obvious a deviant as ever I saw'. It is, equally obviously to the reader, a hyena, one of the few creatures that looks, in reality, as if it had been put together from spare parts like Frankenstein's monster.

2. This same adjective is used in *The Wind and the Willows* when Toad, disguised as a washerwoman, has been soaping the clothes on the barge for a long time and to no purpose (an unconvincing episode; clothes-washing is not difficult). He begins to get worried because his 'paws' are becoming wrinkled, not with age, but with water-soaking; odd, in a Toad, but it isn't a Toad—it's the irresponsible, car-stealing, jail-breaking man.

3. It is interesting to speculate on sources again; i.e. on its first day of creation the fertile soil of Narnia grew a lamp post from a piece of iron, gold and silver trees from loose change and a toffee tree from a sweet. It all sounds rather like the fertile valley at the end of David Lindsay's 'Voyage to Arcturus', much admired by Lewis, where any seed or branch or leaf that dropped sprouted and grew visibly.

MARGARET PATTERSON HANNAY

The Inconsolable Secret: Biography

C.S. Lewis wrote children's fairy tales, adult fantasy, literary criticism, Christian apologetics, and poetry, making him fit, as Chad Walsh observes, rather "oddly in our accustomed literary categories."[1] At first glance there may not seem to be much connection between Narnia and literary criticism or theology, but there is a unifying theme—*Sehnsucht*. *Sehnsucht* is Lewis's own term, one which he variously translates as "joy" or as "longing." When he introduces the concept in "The Weight of Glory," he confesses to a certain shyness: "I am trying to rip open the inconsolable secret in each one of you.... The secret we cannot hide and cannot tell, though we desire to do both." We cannot hide the secret because "our experience is constantly suggesting it"; we cannot tell it "because it is a desire for something that has never actually appeared in our experience." We are likely to name it "Beauty" and act as if the name took care of it. But the beautiful things that evoke this feeling are only images of what we desire, "only the scent of a flower we have not found, the echo of a tune we have not heard, news from a country we have never yet visited."

Similar to the German and Scandinavian motif of the Blue Flower of Longing, *Sehnsucht* is partially explainable as a melancholic longing, a joyous glimpse of paradise immediately followed by the realization that it is unattainable; the joy and the longing are inseparable. Both mystical and romantic, *Sehnsucht*, much more specific than either of those terms, is an insatiable longing for something that can never be grasped: "Most people, if they had really learned to look into their own hearts, would know that they do want, and want acutely, something that cannot be had in this world. There are all sorts of things in this world that offer to give it to you, but they never quite keep their promise." We may think when we fall in love, or plan a trip to an exotic place, or begin a new field of work that our longings will be satisfied, but somehow they never are. "There was something we grasped at, in that first moment of longing, which just fades away in the reality."

This search for the inexpressible was the basis of Lewis's life. His autobiography, *Surprised by Joy*, records that his first experience of *Sehnsucht* was a memory of a toy garden his brother had brought into the nursery. "It is difficult to find words strong enough for the sensation which came over me; Milton's 'enormous bliss' of Eden ... comes somewhere near it. It was a sensation, of course, of desire; but desire for what? Not, certainly, for a biscuit-tin filled with moss, nor even ... for my own past.... Before I knew what I desired, the desire itself was gone, and the whole glimpse withdrawn, the world turned commonplace again, or only stirred by a longing for the longing that had just ceased. It had taken only a moment of time; and in a certain sense everything else that had ever happened to me was insignificant in comparison." This longing, poignant and joyous, continued to haunt him, evoked by things as diverse as the concept of autumn in the *Squirrel Nutkin* story, the Norse myths, or the beauty of nature.

When he was a young man, an atheist, he equated that longing with an escape from God in his first book, *Spirits in Bondage*:

> Ah, sweet, if a man could cheat him! If you could
> flee away
> Into some other country beyond the rosy West,
> To hide in deep forests and be for ever at rest
> From the rankling hate of God and the outworn
> world's decay!

Some fourteen years later, after he had become a Christian, he wrote an allegorical autobiography, *The Pilgrim's Regress*. John, the hero, flees Puritania with its forbidding mountains, searching for an island he saw in a revelation of Joy. When, after many adventures, he finally reaches the island, he discovers it is the mountains of Puritania seen with the eyes of faith; so Lewis discovered that *Sehnsucht* was his longing for God. Once he found God, the "old stab, the old bittersweet" still came to him as often as ever, but it was no longer important. "It was valuable only as a pointer" to God. He believed that this longing was in itself an indication of supernatural reality: "If I find in myself a desire which no experience in this world can satisfy, the most probable explanation is that I was made for another world." Each of his imaginative works and most of his apologetics evoke this sense of longing, then hint that this "inconsolable wound with which man is born" will one day be utterly healed.

This inconsolable and yet joyous longing was more important to Lewis than the data of his own life. When he wrote his autobiography, he observed, "I am telling a story of two lives. They had nothing to do with each other." His search for *Sehnsucht*, then, may be imagined as a deep underground river, flowing beneath the surface of his daily life.

Born in Belfast in 1898, Clive Staples Lewis's childhood was typical for the nineteenth-century Irish professional classes. His nurse, Lizzie Endicott, used to tell him the folk tales of Ireland; his mother started tutoring him in French and Latin before he was seven; after he was ten, he was sent to boarding school in England, crossing the Irish sea between Belfast and Liverpool some six times a year. His love for County Down never waned, although he did not live in Ireland as an adult. Writing to a friend in 1958, he quoted Milton's words—"isles which like to rich and various gems inlay the unadorned bosom of the deep"—to describe "the first bit of Ireland, set in the dark sea ... like jewelry." Although he was raised as an Ulster Protestant, a nominal Christian, it is difficult to tell just how much those early lessons influenced his later journey from atheism to the Church of England.

As was the usual case with Irish boys sent across to England for their education, he soon found himself an Englishman who went "home" to Ireland only on holidays; his accent was formed by Oxford, leaving only the faintest hint of an Irish brogue. His writings, too, sound like those of an Englishman, except for an occasional description of scenery, a jocular allusion to the little people, or his difficulty in forgiving Edmund Spenser for his part in the oppression of the Irish in the sixteenth century.

Lewis called himself "a product of long corridors, empty sunlit rooms, upstairs, indoor silences, attics explored in solitude ... the noise of wind under the tiles ... endless books." His father built a house in the suburbs of Belfast, named it Little Lea, and filled every corner with books. Warren Lewis, C.S. Lewis's older brother, remembers that the new house, "perhaps the worst designed house I ever saw, was for that very reason a child's delight. On the top floor, cupboard-like doors opened into huge, dark, wasted spaces under the roof, tunnel-like passages through which children could crawl, connecting space with space."[2]

The wet Irish weather meant that the boys spent most of their childhood indoors together, exploring the house and creating their own imaginary world. Before Lewis was six, he had begun to invent Animal-Land, a country populated by "dressed animals," with its own geography, history, and politics. Jack, as Clive decided he must be called, worked on the medieval history of Animal-Land; Warren developed its modern phases, its trains and its steamships. The two eras of Animal-Land, and Warren's imaginary India, were then connected in illustrated chronicles spanning four hundred years; the whole area was eventually known as Boxen. The stories of Boxen were kept up on holidays after the boys were sent to school, although the tales written in Jack's early teens are more like novels about individual characters such as Lord John Big (a frog) than straight chronicles. Focused on what Jack thought adults were interested in, politics, they completely lack the romance and imagination of his later writings.

He was driven to write by "extreme manual clumsiness," Lewis recalls. Jack and Warren both had only one joint in their thumbs, making them totally unteachable with "a tool or a bat or a gun, a sleeve link or a corkscrew." Unable to construct their play world out of cardboard or wood, they wrote about it instead.[3]

Their writings were undoubtedly encouraged by their mother, Flora Hamilton, a writer and a brilliant mathematician, who had received her degree in Mathematics and Logic from Queen's College in Belfast in 1885. Her son Jack unfortunately did not inherit her mathematical ability. He failed Responsions in Mathematics—an entrance examination roughly equivalent to our Scholastic Aptitude Test—and was fully accepted at Oxford only when that requirement was waived for veterans; no matter how hard he tried, the sums always came out wrong. But he did inherit his mother's love for literature and her interest in language.

Flora was a loving, cheerful person, who called her husband "My dear old bear," and teased him out of his habitual pessimism. After ten years of marriage she still wrote him passionate letters when he was away on business trips: in a month "we will be back in our own comfy bed together again."[4] Albert Lewis was a successful lawyer, who had courted Flora for seven years before she finally accepted him; they were married in 1894. While Flora lived, the family was apparently quite happy, but in 1908 she died of cancer, depriving the boys of both mother and father. Albert Lewis was inconsolable, driving away his sons just when they all needed each other the most. He promptly sent them off to boarding school in England, choosing the worst possible place. Wynyard in Hertfordshire once had a fine scholastic reputation, but the headmaster, the Reverend Robert Capron ("Oldie"), had become mentally unstable and increasingly cruel; he was certified insane and the school closed in 1910, but the Lewis boys had already been there for two years. Significantly, this chapter in Lewis's autobiography is titled "Concentration Camp." The lasting damage this experience did to the young Jack may be indicated by a letter he wrote in July 1963, shortly before his death: "Do you know, only a few weeks ago I realised suddenly that I at last had forgiven the cruel schoolmaster who so darkened my childhood. I'd been trying to do it for years."

Never able to overcome his grief, Albert Lewis became increasingly eccentric. Despite his considerable financial success, he frequently told his young sons that they would all end up in the county poor house; naturally, they believed him. He began to insist that the house windows never be opened, regardless of the temperature, to force his sons to eat an enormous hot dinner at noon in the summer heat, and to lecture them in long Latinate words they could not understand. While they were young, he was a figure of terror; as they grew older, he became almost comic to them.

But little time was spent at home. The boys were sent to schools in Malvern, England, a place where Warren was apparently quite happy, but Jack was miserable. Clumsy at games in a hierarchical society based largely on one's skill on the playing fields, he became a target of ridicule. Like so many English writers of his generation, he later recalled his school days as the most unhappy period of his life. Although Warren later got Jack to admit that it was not as bad as he pictured it in his autobiography, the hierarchy also involved a good deal of homosexuality, with the younger boys heavily pressured to please the more powerful. "The deadly thing was that school life was a life almost wholly dominated by the social struggle; to get on, to arrive, or, having reached the top, to remain there, was the absorbing preoccupation." During this period Lewis denied his Christian faith, wore flashy clothes, and experimented with sex, admitting "I began to labour very hard to make myself into a fop, a cad, and a snob." He also excelled in scholarship, for the library was the one place of safety at Malvern.

Finally he was able to persuade his father to remove him from school. This time Albert Lewis made a brilliant decision; he placed Jack with his own teacher, W. T. Kirkpatrick, to be tutored for the Oxford entrance examinations. In *Surprised by Joy* Lewis recounts how this tutor met him at the train, demolishing all his pleasantries in a few sentences. Jack said that the countryside was a bit "wilder" than he had expected. "'Stop' shouted Kirk with a suddenness that made me jump. 'What do you mean by wildness and what grounds had you for not expecting it?'" After Lewis had tried several answers (still "making conversation"), and each answer was torn to shreds, he at last realized that Kirk really wanted to know. It was quickly established that Lewis had no clear idea of "wildness," and that it was a particularly inept word. "Do you not see then that your remark was meaningless.... Do you not see, then, that you had no right to have any opinion whatever on the subject?"

This was the first three and a half minutes of his acquaintance with the "Great Knock." Kirkpatrick could not comprehend that a human being would ever say anything except in an attempt to discover truth: "the most casual remark was taken as a summons to disputation." Such rough treatment would have terrified most adolescents, but Lewis quickly learned to meet Kirk on his own ground. He had never been good at small talk; now he developed the habit of "talking for victory." He was completely happy in the isolated house, learning to think in Greek, to increase his fluency in Latin and French, and to read in Italian and in German. His days were spent in reading, in discussion, and in walks through the countryside; this became his ideal of the "settled, calm, Epicurean life."

Kirkpatrick did his job well. Lewis won a classical scholarship at Oxford and was elected to University College. After election to a college, the student must pass the university-wide examination, Responsions. Knowing he would have difficulty with the mathematics, Lewis went to Oxford in April of 1917 to prepare for that exam, but he was recruited into the army before the end of the term. After military training at Oxford, he was sent to the front lines in France, arriving at the trenches on his nineteenth birthday as a second lieutenant in the Somerset Light Infantry. (A second lieutenant in the trenches had a life expectancy of about six weeks.) Just before leaving England, Lewis wired his father to come see him, but Albert Lewis misunderstood the telegram and did not come.

In his autobiography, Lewis entitled the chapter dealing with the war "Guns and Good Company." The army "was, of course, detestable. But the word 'of course' drew the sting." The army differed from school in that no one liked it, pretended to like it, or said one ought to be happy. "Straight tribulation is easier to bear than tribulation which advertises itself as pleasure." He laughed off the capture of sixty prisoners: "That is, I discovered to my great relief that the crowd of field-grey figures who suddenly appeared from nowhere, all had their hands up."

His letters home from France were deliberately cheerful and primarily concerned his reading. For example, on January 19, 1918 he wrote to his father: "You will be anxious to hear my first impressions of trench life. This is a very quiet part of the line and the dugouts are much more comfortable than one imagines at home.... I am now at 'The Mill on the Floss' ... do you know of any life of George Eliot published in a cheap edition? If you can find one, I should like to read it."[5] This was not affectation; one simply did not write home about "the horribly smashed men still moving like half-crushed beetles, the sitting or standing corpses," the rats gnawing bodies. And his concern with his reading was quite genuine. As he wrote to his boyhood friend Arthur Greeves, "I do hope I shall not forget all I know, and come back from the war a great empty-headed military prig!"[6]

Three months later he was wounded at the Battle of Arras by a misplaced English shell and sent across to England as a stretcher case. By the end of May he was established in Endsleigh Palace Hospital, London, and begged his father to come see him: "I know I have often been far from what I should be in my relation to you, and have undervalued [your] affection and generosity.... But, please God, I shall do better in the future. Come and see me, I am homesick, that is the long and the short of it."[7] Inexplicably, his father chose to ignore this plea and the others that followed. By September Lewis was writing, "It is four months now since I returned from France, and my friends laughingly suggest that 'my father in Ireland' is a mythical creation."[8]

But someone did come, Mrs. Moore, the mother of Lewis's roommate Paddy, who had been killed in France. His father's desertion goes far toward explaining an arrangement which seemed incomprehensible to his closest friends; he and Mrs. Moore adopted each other, living as mother and son. Unfortunately, she was the opposite of the brilliant and loving Flora Lewis—irascible, petty, illogical, domineering. According to Warren Lewis, "What had actually happened was that Jack had set up a joint establishment with Mrs. Moore, an arrangement which bound him to her service for the next thirty years and ended only with her death in January 1951. How the arrangement came into being no one will ever know, for it was perhaps the only subject which Jack never mentioned to me; more than never mentioned, for on the only occasion when I hinted at my curiosity he silenced me with an abruptness which was sufficient warning never to re-open the topic."[9] The arrangement was kept secret from Albert Lewis, causing an added strain in that relationship. So alienated did Lewis feel, he called himself "I, the orphan" long before his father's death. But whatever their differences may have been, his father did support him at Oxford—not realizing that he was also supporting Mrs. Moore and her young daughter Maureen, for the three already had set up housekeeping as a family.

In 1915 Kirkpatrick had written to Albert Lewis that his son "was born with the literary temperament and we have to face that fact with all that it implies. This is not a case of early precocity showing itself in rapid assimilation of knowledge and followed by subsequent indifference or torpor.... It is the maturity and originality of his literary judgements which is so unusual and surprising," adding later, "He is the most brilliant translator of Greek plays I have ever met." Kirkpatrick warned that, "while admirably adapted for excellence and probably for distinction in literary matters, he is adapted for nothing else. You may make up your mind on that."[10]

Fortunately, Lewis was indeed well adapted to Oxford life. His first book, poems entitled *Spirits in Bondage*, was published in 1919, as he was studying for Honor Mods (Greek and Latin literature); he took a First in 1920. In 1922 he took a First in Greats (classics and philosophy). Since there were few academic jobs available for returning veterans, his father generously continued to support him while he "added another string to [his] bow," taking a First in English the following year and winning the Chancellor's Prize for an English essay. He told his father that the "atmosphere of the English School ... is very different from that of Greats. Women, Indians, and Americans predominate and ... one feels a certain amateurishness in the talk and the look of the people."[11]

The academic distinction was considerable; the closest American equivalent would be graduating *summa cum laude* with a triple major in classics, philosophy, and English literature. But, in the widespread unemployment that followed the war, his job search continued to be discouraging, particularly since he was still secretly supporting Mrs. Moore and her daughter on his father's allowance. He earned small sums by correcting examination papers and tutoring a few students. Then in the fall of 1924 he was asked to replace his own philosophy tutor, E. F. Carritt, while Carritt went to America for a year. Finally, in May of 1925, he was elected to a fellowship in English language and literature at Magdalen College, Oxford, a position he retained until 1954. For over thirty years he held the same rooms at Oxford, rooms with a magnificent view of the deer park on one side and of Magdalen tower on the other.

It took more than ten years for Lewis to establish himself at Oxford, but in 1936 he published *The Allegory of Love*, a work of medieval scholarship that won the Israel Gollancz Award for Literature. (Writing it as a young tutor with a heavy teaching load, he had completed about one chapter a year.) His belief in the objectivity of poetry was debated at length with the scholar E. M. W. Tillyard; their controversy was published under the title *The Personal Heresy* in 1939. In the same year a collection of essays entitled *Rehabilitations* was published, dealing with the British educational system and with English literature. That title would fit most of his scholarly work, including his rehabilitation of Milton in 1942, *A Preface to Paradise Lost*.

Lewis was chosen to write *English Literature in the Sixteenth Century Excluding Drama*, volume III of the Oxford History of English Literature series, and produced a work that is readable, stimulating, and highly controversial. Although he was always fascinated with the history of words, *Studies in Words*, in 1960, was Lewis's first formal treatment of philology. *An Experiment in Criticism*, in 1961, was a new approach to criticism, focusing on the reader. *The Discarded Image*, completed shortly before his death, provides a "map" to medieval and Renaissance thought for the student. At the time of his death, Lewis was revising his lecture notes on Spenser for publication; that task was completed by Alistair Fowler in *Spenser's Images of Life*.

In the midst of this scholarship, his professional writing, Lewis wrote as a hobby some eleven theological works, seven children's stories, three interplanetary novels, three books of poetry, and a hauntingly beautiful retelling of the Cupid and Psyche myth in novel form. In addition, there are twelve volumes of collected essays and addresses on literature, philosophy, theology, and ethics; so far three volumes of letters, two anthologies, and two books of short stories have been published posthumously. These do not include, of course, all of Lewis's articles, reviews, and letters, which run into the hundreds. Not surprisingly, in light of this achievement, Lewis was a very bookish man, fulfilling Kirkpatrick's prophecy. His days were spent reading, writing, and talking about reading and writing. One brash reporter for *Time* magazine asked Lewis if his life were not monotonous. "I like monotony," he replied.[12] He delighted in cross-country walks with close friends, in strolls around the lovely Addison's Walk near his rooms at Magdalen, in swims in the pond at his home The Kilns, and in various literary societies.

Literary societies had always been a major part of his life at Oxford, beginning with the Martlets, the literary and debating society of University College. Lewis was elected to membership in 1919 and remained active, first as undergraduate and then as a don, until 1940. From the minutes preserved in the Bodleian Library, we receive a portrait of the young man fighting for the old ways in the face of modernism: "The President [Lewis] commenced his paper on narrative poetry. He took up, from the first, a fighting attitude. In an age of lyrical activity he was come to defend the epic against the prejudice of contemporaries.... The real objection of the moderns was based on the fact that they would not make the effort to read a long poem. That effort ... was necessary to the true appreciation of the epic: for art demands co-operation between the artist and his audience."[13]

Another literary club he belonged to for several years was the *Kolbitars*, a group who worked their way through the Old Icelandic sagas in the original language. Lewis discovered that J. R. R. Tolkien, founder of the group, shared his love for northern mythology and for fantasy. That discovery was the beginning of a long friendship, and the indirect cause of a more famous gathering, the Inklings, a group that met in Lewis's rooms at Magdalen on Thursday evenings and before lunch on Tuesdays at the Eagle and Child pub. Tolkien read most of *The Hobbit* and sections of *The Lord of the Rings* to that group. Charles Williams, an editor at Oxford University Press, joined the Inklings when the press was moved to Oxford from London during World War II; he read to the group from his supernatural novels and from his Arthurian poetry.

A third important member of the group was Owen Barfield, a solicitor and a philologist who developed provocative theories about the origin of language. Tolkien recorded the events of one meeting: "O.B. [Owen Barfield] is the only man who can tackle C.S.L. making him define everything, and interrupting his most dogmatic pronouncements with subtle *distinguo*'s. The result was a most amusing and highly contentious evening, on which had an outsider dropped he would have thought it a meeting of fell enemies hurling deadly insults before drawing their guns."[14] Warren Lewis became a regular member, as did Nevill Coghill, Colin Hardie, Hugo Dyson, and others of the Oxford community, most of them Christians. Lewis said later, "What I owe to them all is incalculable.... Is any pleasure on earth as great as a circle of Christian friends by a good fire?"

Christian friends, indeed, for the one jolting event in Lewis's early residence at Oxford was his reluctant conversion. His autobiography is primarily the story of how he passed from atheism to Christianity. In the chapter entitled "Checkmate," Lewis declares, "Amiable agnostics will talk cheerfully about 'man's search for God.' To me, as I then was, they might as well have talked about the mouse's search for the cat ... That which I greatly feared had at last come upon me. In the Trinity Term of 1929 I gave in, and admitted that God was God, and knelt and prayed: perhaps, that night, the most dejected and reluctant convert in all England. I did not then see what is now the most shining and obvious thing; the Divine humility which will accept a convert even on such terms."

Within a few years of his conversion, he began his long series of radio talks and publications about Christianity. The book which first made him famous in America was *The Screwtape Letters*, an ingenious presentation of Christian doctrines and ethics "upside down," from the devil's point of view. Although it is still widely read, it is a book that the Oxford community found embarrassing, both for its flagrant Christianity and for its popular success, particularly when a *Time* magazine cover (September 8, 1947) featured a picture of Lewis with a cartoon devil. Lewis's wry British humor had not been understood by the American reporter, who quoted a radio talk in which Lewis had said: "I know someone will ask me, Do you really mean ... to reintroduce our old friend the devil-hoofs and horns and all? ... I am not particular about the hoofs and horns. But in other respects my answer is 'Yes, I do.'" He was, of course, expressing a belief in the reality of evil, which had nothing to do with devils in red tights, but he became associated in the public mind with those very cartoon figures, prompting him to tell a group of undergraduates in 1944 that he would speak to them on the world, not on the flesh, which they already understood, or on the devil: "The association between him and me in the public mind has already gone quite as deep as I wish: in some quarters it has already reached the level of confusion, if not of identification."

Oxford never forgave him for violating the code of detached irony, for crusading instead of keeping his conversion private. His theological writings caused virtual social ostracism at Oxford, a heavy burden for him. He cared not at all for the thousands who idolized him in America, but felt deeply the disapproval of his peers. Regardless of whether or not one agrees with his theology, one must admire the steadiness of vision that kept him true to his convictions at what was, for him, enormous cost. He was also prepared to pay for that faith with substantial amounts of time spent in uncongenial tasks and with most of his income. Though he valued freedom from interference above all else, Lewis maintained an extensive correspondence with hundreds of people who wrote for spiritual or literary advice; one lengthy correspondence with a particularly difficult woman has been published posthumously under the title *Letters to an American Lady*. He grew to "dread the postman's knock," but continued to spend several hours a day writing letters, letters he did not know would be preserved as part of his literary achievement. He also had an extensive list of private charities. For example, when two young girls were evacuated to The Kilns during the war, he encouraged their career choices, later paying tuition for one to go to Oxford and the other to train as a nurse. His friend Owen Barfield, the solicitor, helped him set up a charitable foundation so that he would not fulfill his father's prophesy by ending up in the county poorhouse after giving away all his income. He also put up with the incessant demands of Mrs. Moore, breaking off his writing in midsentence to help her with housecleaning or making marmalade. "He is as good as an extra maid in the house," Mrs. Moore claimed.[15] Warren Lewis said that he never saw his brother able to work more than half an hour without being called by Mrs. Moore. He would roar, "Coming," lay down his pen, rush to help her, and then return to his work, all with inexplicable patience.

During the war years he was asked to explain Christian doctrine in a series of radio talks for the British Broadcasting Corporation and to speak to various groups of the Armed Forces. A more congenial area of service was the Socratic Club, a group that grew out of a meeting at the Somerville Junior Commons Rooms when Stella Aldwinckle decided that Oxford needed "an open forum for the discussion of the intellectual difficulties connected with religion in general and with Christianity in particular.... Mr. C.S. Lewis [was] the obvious President."[16] He accepted the position, serving as president from 1941 until he left for Cambridge in 1954. The usual pattern at the Socratic Club was for a Christian to be answered by an atheist, or vice versa. Lewis admitted, in his preface to the first *Socratic Digest*, that "Those who founded it do not for one moment pretend to be neutral. It was the Christians who constructed the arena and issued the challenge," but, he added, "the committee has scoured *Who's Who* to find intelligent atheists who had leisure or zeal to come and propagate their creed."

Regardless of the formal program, Lewis was generally present to defend the faith with erudition and witty repartee. One night a Relativist ended his presentation with the ringing conclusion: "The world does not exist, England does not exist, Oxford does not exist, and I am confident that I do not exist!" Lewis rose, asking, "How am I to talk to a man who's not *there?*"[17]

A less flattering picture is painted by John Wain, a poet and novelist who was one of Lewis's students, in his autobiography *Sprightly Running*:

> The more simple-minded undergraduates, particularly the birds of passage who did not stay at Oxford long enough to pick up any (real or simulated) sophistication, generally turned out to hear Lewis at the 'Socratic Club' and gave him much the same docile reception as his BBC and Service audiences.... The Socratic Club was the ideal framework for this kind of teaching: ostensibly a club without any doctrinal bias, committed only to following any argument wherever it might lead, it was in practice a kind of prize-ring in which various champions appeared to try conclusions with Lewis.

However, Wain concludes that Lewis "week after week put on a knockdown and drag-out performance that really was impressive. Our time has produced no better debater."[18]

Lewis was "talking for victory," as he had learned from his tutor Kirkpatrick. He carried that same method over into his teaching, with very uneven results. John Wain thrived on the weekly session by "turning myself, for this hour at least, into a miniature Lewis." He couldn't copy the burly physique, of course, "But I could become a quick-fire debater, I could supply a torrent of illustration and metaphor, I could talk fast and know all the answers—if only I tried hard enough. I tried."[19] The poet John Betjeman reacted differently, escaping all the tutorial sessions he could, refusing to do his Anglo-Saxon; Lewis retaliated by acting formal and fierce, giving stern admonitions to work harder, admonitions which were disregarded. Betjeman later wrote, in the preface to a forty-five-page book of poems, *Continual Dew*, that he was "indebted to Mr. C.S. Lewis for the fact on page 256."[20]

Whether they loved or despised Lewis, his students and colleagues agree that his memory was phenomenal. One of many legends about it was set down by John Leyerle, now Professor of English at the School of Graduate Studies, University of Toronto. At dinner Lewis had grumbled that he was concluding many of his paragraphs with iambic pentameter:

> Selig said, "If you *will* end your paragraphs in iambic pentameter, why do you grumble about it, Sir?"
>
> Lewis replied, "As usual, Selig, you missed the point. The difficulty is that I remember everything I've ever read and bits pop up uninvited."
>
> "Surely not everything you've ever read, Mr. Lewis?"
>
> "Yes, everything, Selig, even the most boring texts."

Selig put him to the test of Lydgate's "Siege of Thebes," a sufficiently obscure work. When prompted by a few lines, he began to recite the poem, stopping only when Selig was convinced.[21] Others recall that given one line of *Paradise Lost*, he could usually recite the next line, or that he could recite a passage from memory if given its location in his library, minus title or author. Such a phenomenal memory was an enormous advantage for a scholar; however, it did lead him into the habit of quoting from memory in his writings, making occasional slips in the wording. He once admitted that he would make a poor editor. "I'm not accurate."[22]

Lewis lived most of his life not in the modern world, but in the world of his reading and of his imagination. Even his personal life seems to have been filtered through books. He recalls that walking through the countryside of Surrey "gave one the same sort of pleasure that there is in the labyrinthine complexity of Malory or *The Faerie Queene*." In a letter to his brother he speaks of the battle in an Italian epic: "I had the feeling that if one knew anything about sword-technique one would be able to follow them in detail.

Talking of that, if we had money to spare on whims, I should like to have a fencing-master when you come home.... It would ... make many passages in literature, which at present are mere words, start into light."[23] His first reaction to war was similar. On first hearing the whine of a bullet he wrote "This is War. This is what Homer wrote about." And even his idea of love was, for most of his life, a bookish one. Writing in his sixties, he admitted, "Years ago when I wrote about medieval love-poetry and described its strange, half make-believe, 'religion of love,' [in *The Allegory of Love*] I was blind enough to treat this as an almost purely literary phenomenon. I know better now."

He knew better because he had experienced erotic love. By the early 1950s Lewis was a confirmed bachelor, suspected of despising his women pupils, certain that the female intelligence was somehow inferior to that of the male. He was famous for his popular theological works, especially in America, and carried on extensive correspondence with many who sought his advice. One of these was Joy Davidman Gresham, a Jewish Communist who had become a Christian, partly as a result of reading Lewis's books. When she wrote that she was coming to Oxford, he invited her to visit him and set up a lunch party in her honor; he was unfailingly courteous to his many visitors from America. A longer visit followed in 1953, after Joy's divorce from William Gresham; she brought her two young sons for a four-day visit at The Kilns with Jack and Warren Lewis, an exhausting ordeal for the two middle-aged bachelors. (Lewis dedicated *The Horse and His Boy*, his next Narnia story, to the boys.)

In 1955 Joy rented a house near The Kilns; early the next year, the Home Office refused to renew her permit to stay in England. To keep her from being deported, Lewis married her as "a pure matter of friendship and expediency" in a civil ceremony on April 23, 1956. Because he did not believe they were married in the eyes of God or the church, they continued to live separately. Then doctors discovered that Joy had bone cancer, and Lewis discovered that he loved her: "No one can mark the exact moment at which friendship becomes love," he later said. They decided to be married in a Christian ceremony. When a priest performed the marriage at her hospital bed on March 21, 1957, they both knew her case was terminal.[24]

Then Joy had a miraculous remission, giving them three years of married life. Lewis delighted in her quick mind, showing her off to the Inklings, including her as their intellectual equal. He told a friend: "I never expected to have, in my sixties, the happiness that passed me by in my twenties."[25] Later he wrote: "For those few years H. [Joy] and I feasted on love; every mode of it—solemn and merry, romantic and realistic, sometimes as dramatic as a thunderstorm, sometimes as comfortable and unemphatic as putting on your soft slippers. No cranny of heart or body remained unsatisfied." But the cancer returned, and Joy died on July 13, 1960. The shattering effect of her death was recorded by Lewis in a book published anonymously, *A Grief Observed*. He became dangerously ill himself that year and never totally regained his health.

During this period of private joy and anguish, his professional life had gone on. He had served in the same position at Oxford for thirty years, having been passed over for a professorship on several occasions; one colleague admitted to voting against him as the author of *Screwtape*.[26] So when Magdalene College at Cambridge unanimously offered him the newly established chair of Medieval and Renaissance Literature in 1954, he accepted on the condition that he keep his home at The Kilns, commuting to Cambridge for lectures. He fitted into his new world comfortably, delighted in the "new boy's" task of pouring the port for the residents with seniority, and found the community congenial. "Many of my colleagues are Christians, more than was the case in my old College." The college itself "is smaller, softer, more gracious than my old."[27] He observed that, since colleges provide more money and less work as one advances through the ranks, he had more leisure to devote to his writing, and to walks around Cambridge. Soon he fell into the old pattern of life he had had at Kirkpatrick's, a day spent writing and reading, with a break for an afternoon walk and for tea.

At his Cambridge inauguration, Lewis gave a provocative address, "*De Descriptione Temporum*." He began by quoting Professor Seznec with approval: "As the Middle Ages and the Renaissance come to be better known, the traditional antithesis between them grows less marked." He then asserted that the great divide comes not between the medieval and Renaissance periods, but some time between Jane Austen and ourselves, offering the following evidence: in politics, rulers have been replaced by leaders; in art, ambiguity has replaced the ideal of teaching by delight; in religion, Christianity has been replaced by materialism; in popular mythology, machines have restructured our perception of the world, creating a belief that what is newer is inevitably better. Having established the great divide, he then made the startling assertion that "I myself belong far more to that Old Western order than to yours.... I read as a native texts that you must read as foreigners." This is not mere arrogance, he hastened to add, for "who can be proud of speaking fluently his mother tongue?" He was convinced that "in order to read Old Western Literature aright you must suspend most of the responses and unlearn most of the habits you have acquired in reading modern literature." Because he had never acquired these habits, he believed that his reactions to the old texts should be useful as a specimen of a forgotten way of thought. He closed with the warning: "Speaking not only for myself but for all other Old Western men whom you may meet, I would say, use your specimens while you can. There are not going to be many more dinosaurs."

His appropriation of the label sent scholars rushing for their pens to tell the world that they too were "Old Western Men" or, alternatively, that Lewis was the victim of a serious delusion. One critic said that Lewis had completely lost his objectivity, that he was a paleontologist who thought he was a fossil. Graham Hough analyzed the controversy that swirled about the address, making the dismaying observation that

> Hardly anyone ... had time to listen to Professor Lewis's argument, which was about the Renaissance and whether it really marked a crisis in our civilization; they were too busy lining up for or against his essay on miracles. The fact that he obviously approved of a culture based on supernatural presuppositions aroused such intense partisanship, or intense disgust, that the really important matter that lay behind his lecture, and behind the whole discussion, went quite unnoticed.[28]

Lewis did have some claim to be a dinosaur. Earlier, he had written to a friend: "I usually love anachronisms and boasted to be one myself."[29] He was in complete sympathy with the Flat Earth Society, an organization which pretended to believe in the theory of a flat, not spherical earth. He told the Society for the Prevention of Progress, another eccentric British club, that he was in full agreement with their aims. Much of this was dry British humor, but it was not all a jest. He did love the old ways, feeling out of place in the speed and noise of the twentieth century. And he is surely right that the generations raised on the classics are disappearing; few children now learn to think in Latin or Greek.

His final years were pleasantly divided between Cambridge and Oxford. He was often ill and had ceased to "see pictures," his way of composing imaginative works, but he continued to write theology and literary criticism. In fact, he was working on a completely new approach to Spenser's *The Faerie Queene*, when a heart attack complicated his prostate trouble and kidney disease. He died on November 22, 1963, the same day that Aldous Huxley died and that President Kennedy was assassinated.

NOTES

1. Chad Walsh, *The Literary Legacy of C.S. Lewis* (New York: Harcourt, Brace, Jovanovich, 1979), p. 251.

2. Quoted in Roger Lancelyn Green and Walter Hooper, *C.S. Lewis: A Biography* (New York: Harcourt Brace Jovanovich, 1974), p. 20. Green was Lewis's student and then his close friend for many years; in 1953 Lewis suggested that Green write his biography after his death. Hooper, an American Anglican priest who visited Lewis sometime during 1963, the last year of Lewis's life, is "Editorial Trustee of the Estate of C.S. Lewis" and editor of most of the volumes of Lewis's work published posthumously.

3. Samples of the Boxen stories are available in C.S. Kilby and Douglas Gilbert, *C.S. Lewis: Images of His World* (Grand Rapids, Michigan: William B. Eerdmans Publishing Company, 1973), pp. 98–105.

4. "The Lewis Papers," unpublished materials compiled by Warren Lewis (The Marion E. Wade Collection, Wheaton College, Wheaton, Illinois).

5. *Letters of C.S. Lewis*, ed. W. H. Lewis (London: Geoffrey Bles Ltd., 1966), p. 41.

6. *They Stand Together: The Letters of C.S. Lewis to Arthur Greeves* (1914–1963), ed. Walter Hooper (New York: Macmillan, 1972), p. 192. Lewis certainly was not alone in his concern for literature in the trenches. Robert Graves, Siegfried Sassoon, Wilfred Owen, David Jones, and others wrote poems between battles; like Lewis, Robert Graves saw his first book of poems through press from a hospital bed in England, after he was sent home with wounds. Graves gives a much fuller account of life in the trenches than does Lewis. See *Goodbye to All That* (Garden City, New York: Doubleday and Company, 1957; revised version of 1929 edition). Graves's misery in the English public school system was also parallel to Lewis's, as was John Wain's and many other English writers'; the sports hierarchy punished those who were literary rather than athletic.

7. Lewis, *Letters*, p. 43.

8. Lewis, *Letters*, p. 44.

9. Green and Hooper, p. 66.

10. Humphrey Carpenter, *The Inklings: C.S. Lewis, J. R. R. Tolkien, Charles Williams, and their friends* (Boston: Houghton Mifflin Company, 1979), p. 8.

11. Lewis, *Letters*, p. 81.

12. "Don V. Devil," *Time* (8 September 1947), p. 65.

13. Minutes of The Martlets Society, meeting #211, 3 November 1920, III, p. 108 (The Bodleian Library, Oxford). Substantial quotations from these minutes are given in Walter Hooper, "To the Martlets," in Carolyn Keefe, *C.S. Lewis: Speaker and Teacher* (Grand Rapids, Michigan: Zondervan, 1971), pp. 37–61.

14. Carpenter, p. 177.

15. Green and Hooper, p. 228.

16. Ibid. I p. 214.

17. Ibid., p. 217 (italics his).

18. John Wain, *Sprightly Running: Part of an Autobiography* (London: Macmillan and Co., 1963), p. 140.

19. Wain, p. 138.

20. Carpenter, pp. 20–21.

21. John Leyerle, "No Glory Please, I'm Cringing," *The Canadian C.S. Lewis Journal* (March 1979), p. 12.

22. Carpenter, p. 156.

23. Unpublished letter to Warren Lewis, 8 April 1932 (Wade).

24. Carpenter, p. 240.

25. W. H. Lewis, "Memoir of C.S. Lewis," in *Letters, p. 23.*

26. Carpenter, p. 229.

27. Carpenter, p. 231.

28. Graham Hough, "Old Western Man," *Twentieth Century* 157 (1955), pp. 102–110.

29. Unpublished letter to Ruth Pitter, 29 December 1951 (Bodleian).

DABNEY ADAMS HART

The Power of Language

> ... we should become aware of what we are doing when we speak, of the ancient, fragile, and (well used) immensely potent instruments that words are.　　　　　　　　　　　　　—STUDIES IN WORDS

Lewis's concept of myth, which was fundamental to everything he wrote, is a significant factor in his increasing popularity. A generation disillusioned with technology and progress is returning to the roots of our culture, to natural foods, folk arts, and fantasy. Whether Lewis and Tolkien have stimulated the renewed interest in myth or merely contributed to it is debatable. Lewis's own interest, which began with a boyhood love of Norse mythology, was given a new direction by the thinking of a university friend, Owen Barfield. Any facet of myth, in the sense of story, or of *Idea*, involves assumptions about the origins of human thought and language that Lewis attributed to the influence of Barfield.

Barfield and Lewis, both of whom were awarded Oxford scholarships in December 1916, became friends when Lewis returned to the university in January 1919 after war service. In *Surprised By Joy*, Lewis described Barfield as the type of friend who

> ... disagrees with you about everything. He is not so much the *alter-ego* as the anti-self. Of course he shares your interests;

From *Through the Open Door: A New Look at C.S. Lewis.* © 1984 by The University of Alabama Press.

49

otherwise he would not become your friend at all. But he has approached them all at a different angle. He has read all the right books but has got the wrong thing out of every one. It is as if he spoke your language but mispronounced it. How can he be so nearly right and yet, invariably, just not right? ... Actually (though it never seems so at the time) you modify one another's thought; out of this perpetual dogfight a community of mind and a deep affection emerge. But I think he changed me a good deal more than I him. Much of the thought which he afterward put into *Poetic Diction* had already become mine before that important little book appeared.[1]

The stimulating conflict is illustrated by the first reference to Barfield in the published extracts from Lewis's journal:

... we walked to Wadham gardens and sat under the trees. We began with "Christian dreams"; I condemned them—the love dream made a man incapable of real love, the hero dream made him a coward. He took the opposite view, and a stubborn argument followed.[2]

Their compatibility was expressed in Barfield's dedication of *Poetic Diction* to Clive Hamilton (Lewis's pseudonym for his early poetry) with the epigraph "Opposition is true friendship," from Blake's *Marriage of Heaven and Hell*. The records of this friendship in seventeen published letters from Lewis to Barfield show that the relationship continued to be close, mutually stimulating, controversial, often teasing. In one, Lewis referred to the six heavily satirized villains of *That Hideous Strength*: "Did I ever mention that Weston, Devine, Frost, Wither, Curry, and Miss Hardcastle were all portraits of you? (If I didn't, that may have been because it isn't true. By gum, though, wait until I write another story.)"[3] In fact his next story, *The Lion, the Witch and the Wardrobe*, was dedicated by her godfather to Barfield's daughter Lucy, whose name was used for its major character. The figure of the Professor, far from being a satire of Barfield, could be identified as Lewis himself expressing his friend's influence. He assures the two older children that little Lucy's tale about being in Narnia for hours, when she had been away from them less than a minute, is "... likely to be true.... If there really is a door in this house that leads to some other world ... I should not be at all surprised to find that that other world had a separate time of its own."[4]

Lewis affirmed the importance of Barfield's ideas in the dedication of his first major critical study, *The Allegory of Love*: "To Owen Barfield, wisest and best of my unofficial teachers." More specifically, in the preface he said: "... the friend to whom I have dedicated the book has taught me not to patronize the past, and has trained me to see the present as itself a 'period.' I desire for myself no higher function than to be one of the instruments whereby his theory and practice in such matters may become more widely effective."[5] This attitude toward the past and the present is based on a theory of the development of language that Barfield delineated in two books written during the early years of his friendship with Lewis, *History in English Words* and *Poetic Diction*.[6] According to Barfield, poetic diction is closest to the original concrete meaning of language. He argued that development has been from the figurative toward the abstract. For example, the theory that *pneuma* or *spiritus*, originally meaning "breath" or "wind," was employed as a metaphor to mean "the principle of life within man or animal" assumes an advanced degree of abstraction; it is more logical to assume that "breath," "wind," and "principle of life" are later distinctions and subtleties discovered by the intellect in the original single concept of *spiritus*.[7] The original concrete figurative language seems metaphorical now because the process of abstraction has obliterated the original unity of meaning, which Barfield considered inherent rather than invented:

> It is these "footsteps of nature" whose noise we hear alike in primitive language and in the finest metaphors of poets. Men do not *invent* these mysterious relations between separate external objects, and between objects and feelings or ideas, which it is the function of poetry to reveal.... The language of primitive men reports them as direct perceptual experience. The speaker has observed a unity, and is not therefore himself conscious of *relation*. But we, in the development of consciousness, have lost the power to see this one as one.... it is the language of poets, in so far as they create true metaphors, which must *restore* this unity conceptually, after it has been lost from perception.[8]

This is the basis of the development of poetic diction: language that achieves as much as possible of unified and concrete meaning. As meaning becomes fossilized in the evolution of human thought, the poetic imagination must revive the language by deliberately creating through metaphor the unity that the primitive imagination perceived.

The metaphoric basis of language is a dominant theme in Lewis's first space-fiction novel, *Out of the Silent Planet*. The idea that our planet—

controlled by evil—is silent, unable to communicate, is emphasized by the role of a philologist, Ransom, as spokesman, advocate, or intercessor for the human race. The Malacandrian way of life is revealed through Ransom's gradual comprehension of their language. He learns that each of the three species has its own language but all study that of the *hrossa* because, being the most poetic, it expresses ideas most powerfully. Since neither Weston, the scientist, nor Devine, the entrepreneur, has learned more than a pidgin variety of Malacandrian, Ransom must interpret when Weston makes his speech of self justification before the highest authority, Oyarsa. Ransom has difficulty in translating Weston's abstractions into the concrete Malacandrian terms. The scientist not only speaks a parody of technical jargon, but also is out of touch with the physical realities of the creation he claims to understand. For Weston's introductory "'To you I may seem a vulgar robber, but I bear on my shoulders the destiny of the human race,'" Ransom finds his own version rather unsatisfactory: "Among us, Oyarsa, there is a kind of *hnau* who will take other *hnaus'* food and things, when they are not looking. He says he is not an ordinary one of that kind. He says what he does now will make very different things happen to those of our people who are not yet born."[9] This contrast is reminiscent of Gulliver's attempts to explain European customs in other languages. Just as the Houyhnhnms have no word for "lie" and can express the concept only with "to say the thing that is not," so the Malacandrians, having no abstraction meaning "evil," use the figurative word "bent" as the opposite of "good." But the difference between these examples is as important as the similarity: Swift was merely calling attention to the contrast between Houyhnhnm and human values, while Lewis was also making a point about language itself. The literal meaning of "bent" makes its metaphorical sense much more precise and powerful than the vague term "evil."

The importance of language per se is further developed in the story of Ransom's second extraterrestrial journey. He speculates that he is being sent to Perelandra because he already knows the language, which he calls Old Solar, "originally a common speech for all rational creatures inhabiting the planets of our system, ... lost on our own world, when our whole tragedy took place."[10] The philologist hero is much more than a convenience. In contrast to the materialist aim of Weston, Ransom's professional pursuit is the fundamental meaning of language. Although he and the green lady of Perelandra can communicate in speech, they are often bewildered as they use words in different ways. Their attempts to understand each other dramatize the tension between abstract and concrete, between metaphor and reality. When Ransom speaks of a long time, the lady learns a new concept: "'You think times have lengths. A night is always a night whatever you do in it, as from this tree to that is always so many paces whether you take them quickly or slowly. I suppose that is true in a way. But the waves do not always come at equal distances.'"[11] She realizes that the relationship between time and length in one world may not apply equally in another. Ransom himself comes to this realization while struggling against the conviction that he must fight Weston's body in order to prevent evil from corrupting the first mother of Perelandra. When the Voice reminds him that his name is "Ransom," the surname derived from "Ranolf's son" becomes more than a pun or play on words: "All in a moment of time he perceived that what was, to human philologists, a merely accidental resemblance of two sounds, was in truth no accident. The whole distinction between things accidental and things designed, like the distinction between fact and myth, was purely terrestrial."[12] In this context, the philologist represents the first Adam's naming the creatures as well as the second Adam's redeeming man. The power of language is no more accidental than the creation itself.

The same theme is prominent in the third and last Ransom novel, *That Hideous Strength*. The title comes from a description by Sir David Lindsay (one of the Scottish medieval poets praised by Lewis) of the Tower of Babel:

The Shadow of that hyddeous strength
Sax myle and more it is of length.

This epigraph stresses the identification of human corruption with corruption of language. The novel (set on our own planet, in an English university town) concerns the conflict between a small Christian community under the leadership of Ransom and a politically powerful institute of applied science dedicated to the control and manipulation of society. Both sides want to make contact with Merlin, whose anticipated return brings about the crisis of the plot. Ransom has the advantage as a Latin and Celtic scholar also familiar with Old Solar, which he expects Merlin to understand or at least recognize as a language of power. He has taught Dr. Dimble, the middle-aged professor of English, to speak in the Great Tongue:

And Dimble ... raised his head, and great syllables of words that sounded like castles came out of his mouth.... The voice did not sound like Dimble's own: it was as if the words spoke themselves through him from some strong place at a distance—or as if they were not words at all but present operations of God, the planets, and the Pendragon. For this was the language spoken before the

Fall and beyond the Moon, and the meanings were not given to the syllables by chance, or skill, or long tradition, but truly inherent in them as the shape of the great Sun is inherent in the little waterdrop. This was Language herself, as she first sprang at Maledil's bidding out of the molten quicksilver of the star called Mercury on Earth, But Viritrilbia in Deep Heaven.[13]

Such language is the antithesis of that used by the directors of the National Institute for Coordinated Experiments (N.I.C.E.). When a young sociologist asks what job he is being recruited for, the Director replies: "'Everyone in the Institute feels that his own work is not so much a departmental contribution to an end already defined as a moment or grade in the progressive self-definition of an organic whole.'"[14] Since Wither always speaks in this jargon, he is slower than the psychologist Frost to recognize the signs of disaster during an N.I.C.E. banquet:

He had never expected the speech to have any meaning as a whole and for a long time the familiar catchwords rolled on in a manner which did not disturb the expectation of his ear. He thought that ... even a very small false step would deprive both the speaker and the audience of even the power to pretend that he was saying anything in particular. But as long as that border was not crossed, he rather admired the speech.... He looked down the room again. They were attending too much, always a bad sign. Then came the sentence, "The surrogates exemplanted in a continual of porous variations."[15]

This speech is the beginning of Merlin's defeat of the N.I.C.E. The organization has made the fatal mistake of disregarding the importance of language in communicating with him:

"This throws a quite unexpected burden on our resources," said Wither to Frost.... "I must confess I had not anticipated any serious difficulty about language."

"We must get a Celtic scholar," said Frost. "We are regrettably weak on the philological side."[16]

Their need to advertise for a Celtic scholar to speak to the tramp whom they have mistaken for Merlin gives the real Merlin easy access to their headquarters. In effect the turning point of the plot hinges on the power of language.

In Lewis's final novel, *Till We Have Faces*, the importance of language is stressed not in the plot but in the complex mode of its first-person narration. Queen Orual of Glome explains that her story is written in Greek, which she learned from her slave tutor, since she hopes that it may be found by a traveler and taken to Greece, where there is freedom of speech even about the gods. But she points out also that all names of people and places are in the language of Glome. This opposition, first intimated in terms of language, between the culture of Greece and that of Glome is one of the many thematic contrasts throughout the novel. The fact that Orual and her youngest sister, Istra, call each other by Greek names—Maia and Psyche—is a linguistic equivalent of the dominant duality: the distinction between appearance and reality. (The identification of *Maia* with the Buddhist *Maya*, which is corroborated by her use of the veil, emphasizes this theme.[17]) Orual's purpose in writing her story is to make this distinction as she charges the gods with deceiving men. At the end she realizes the difficulty of her undertaking:

> Lightly men talk of saying what they mean. Often when he was teaching me to write in Greek the Fox would say, "Child, to say the very thing you really mean, the whole of it, nothing more or less or other than what you really mean; that's the whole art and joy of words." A glib saying. When the time comes to you at which you will be forced at last to utter the speech which has lain at the centre of your soul for years, which you have, all that time, idiot-like, been saying over and over, you'll not talk about joy of words. I saw well why the gods do not speak to us openly, nor let us answer. Till that word can be dug out of us, why should they hear the babble that we think we mean? How can they meet us face to face till we have faces?[18]

The right words, according to Lewis, are more likely to be those of the poet than those of the philosopher, because poetic language is closest to original meaning.

Lewis demonstrated "the art and joy of words" throughout his children's series. On the most obvious level, although English children can understand and speak the language of Narnia, it is not taken for granted that Narnian animals can do so. They receive this power at the creation, lose it when enchanted by the White Witch, and regain it after the sacrifice of Aslan. The enslaved animals of Calormen cannot speak, and the bad giants speak meaningless words of twenty syllables each, a detail reminiscent of

Dante's Nimrod as well as the N.I.C.E. Another example of the negation of language's purpose and power is the speech of the Duffers, whose trite and meaningless catchwords and phrases parody the jargon of mass communication:

> "That's right, that's right," said the Chief Voice. "You don't see us. And why not? Because we're invisible."
> "Keep it up, Chief, keep it up," said the Other Voices. "You're talking like a book. They couldn't ask for a better answer than that."[19]

For Lewis such linguistic parodies indicated not just a failure to communicate any real meaning but a fundamental flaw at the depths of the imagination.

Another way in which the mythic significance of language is stressed is in the connotative names of the characters. This familiar convention is given a deeper dimension by Aslan's reaction when Mr. Beaver objects to the White Witch's calling herself Queen of Narnia. "'Peace, Beaver,' said Aslan. 'All names will soon be restored to their proper owners.'"[20] The four children have names that suit them: Peter the leader, Edmund the follower, Susan the practical sister, and Lucy the imaginative one. The two who must be converted, Eustace Scrubb and Jill Pole, call each other by their drab surnames. The good kings of Narnia have euphonious names like Caspian, Rilian, and Tirian, while the worst is Miraz, whose chief advisers are Glozelle and Sopespian. The good Dwarfs have rough, sturdy names like Trumpkin and Trufflehunter, while the enemy Calormenes are Arsheesh and Lasaraleen. Some of the animals' names are onomatopoetic, like Reepicheep the mouse and Hwin the mare; and some names are descriptive, like Queen Prunaprismia or Puddleglum, the pessimistic Marshwiggle. In general, the names of both people and places are as original and evocative as Cair Paravel (the castle of the Narnian kings).

The power of language is suggested also by the use of refrains. In *The Lion, the Witch and the Wardrobe*, Mr. Beaver first whispers a secret: "'They say Aslan is on the move—perhaps has already landed.'"[21] Repetition of "Aslan is on the move" thrills the reader as it does the children even before they know who Aslan is. In *The Horse and His Boy*, the escape from Calormen is encouraged by the repeated signal, "Narnia and the North." Even more haunting is the call of the friends of Aslan, "Further up and further in." At the end of *The Last Battle* this rallying cry marks stages in the crescendo of action and imagery. Such refrains function almost as spells; but when Lucy reads the Magician's book containing real spells, the author says: "Nothing will induce me to tell you what they were."[22] Some language is too powerful.

This emphasis on the power of language, traceable as a leitmotif throughout Lewis's imaginative writing, operates also in his critical and scholarly works. One of his most consistent aims was to distinguish between the meanings that words have accrued over the centuries and to strip them back to the native grain of their meaning for the original audience. In *The Allegory of Love*, Lewis's primary purpose of "reconstructing that long-lost state of mind for which the allegorical love poem was a natural mode of expression"[23] required careful attention to the metaphoric power of words. He noted, for instance, the "coming and going between the natural and the allegorical senses of his 'love' that makes Usk [a fifteenth-century poet] so profoundly interesting to the historian of sentiment."[24] In Latin literature, Lewis found the names of picturable deities such as Venus used instead of abstractions like "love," in passages ranging from lyric poetry to the prose of Caesar. He concluded that

> ... a distinction which is fundamental for us—the distinction, namely, between an abstract universal and a living spirit—was only vaguely and intermittently present to the Roman mind. Nor need we despair of recovering, for a moment, this point of view, if we remember the strange border-line position which a notion such as "Nature" occupies to-day in the mind of an imaginative and unphilosophical person who has read many books of popularized science. It is something more than a personification and less than a myth, and ready to be either or both as the stress of argument demands.[25]

These two words—"love" and "Nature"—are important examples of changes from concrete meaning to widely differentiated abstraction. Lewis analyzes both of them in two books published in 1960, twenty-five years after *The Allegory of Love*.

In *The Four Loves*, the main focus is on the psychological, moral, and spiritual implications of different types of love: Affection, Friendship, Eros, and Charity, each related in complex degrees to what Lewis called "Gift-love" and "Need-love." But throughout the book, he called attention to the metaphoric power of the words. "Affection" in Greek was *storge*, especially the relationship of parents to offspring. Lewis identified parental love as "the original form of the thing as well as the central meaning of the word. The image we must start with is that of a mother nursing a baby, a bitch or a cat with a basketful of puppies or kittens."[26] In another context he explained a key word by ending rather than starting with an image. In making the transition from the natural loves to love for God, Lewis affirmed: "It remains certainly true that all natural loves can be inordinate. *Inordinate* does not mean 'insufficiently cautious.' Nor does it mean 'too big.' It is not a quantitative term. It is probably impossible to love any human being simply 'too much'... the question whether we are loving God or the earthly Beloved 'more' is not, so far as concerns our Christian duty, a question about the comparative intensity of two feelings. The real question is, which (when the alternative comes) do you serve, or choose, or put first?"[27] *Inordinate* is thus shown to mean "out of order," a precise figurative concept rather than an abstraction.

In *Studies In Words*, a book based on Cambridge lectures about changes in meaning that make the understanding of older literature difficult, Lewis began with "Nature," as related to the Greek *phusis*, Latin *natura*, and English *kind*. He traced fifteen different senses of the word, beginning with "sort," "type," or "essential characteristic": "nature shares a common base with *nasci* (to be born); with the noun *natus* (birth); with *natio* (not only a race or nation but the name of the birth-goddess).... there is obviously some idea of a thing's natura as its original or 'innate' character."[28] With increasing abstraction, meanings proliferate. For instance, the "innate character" of something may be contrasted with man's manipulation of it. In this sense,

> a yew-tree is *natural* before the topiarist has carved it.... This distinction between the uninterfered with and the interfered with will not probably recommend itself to the *philosopher*. It may be held to enshrine a very primitive, an almost magical or animistic, conception of causality.... What keeps the contrast alive, however, is the daily experience of men as practical, not speculative, beings. The antithesis between unreclaimed land and the cleared, drained, fenced, ploughed, sown, and weeded field—between the unbroken and the broken horse—between the fish as caught and the fish opened, cleaned, and fried—is forced upon us every day.... If ants had a language they would, no doubt, call their anthill an artifact and describe the brick wall in its neighbourhood as a *natural* object. *Nature* in fact would be for them all that was not "ant-made."[29]

Philosophers might also object to the sense of "Nature" identified particularly with eighteenth- and nineteenth-century poetry, but Lewis justified this common use on the grounds that its contrast with the man-made urban environment is something most people genuinely feel. "People know pretty well what they mean by it and sometimes use it to communicate what would not easily be 'communicable' in other ways."[30] But the abstraction can be ridiculous if it is used with no sensitivity to its original meaning, as in Lewis's example of "a railway poster which advertised Kent as 'Nature's home.'"[31]

All the words Lewis traced in this study are related in some way to man's perceptions of his own "nature," collectively or individually: *sad, wit, free, sense, simple, conscious, conscience.* The histories of such words are most likely to illustrate subtle and complex changes from original simple meaning, in which the material and immaterial senses were indistinguishable, to increasingly self-conscious abstractions. Lewis's main purpose was to call modern students' attention to the changes, to show them *how* to read literature of different periods. He included a chapter, "At the Fringe of Language," to elucidate a principle about the use of words: he pointed out that the vocabulary of praise, abuse, and expression of emotion in general is being diminished by the fading of metaphoric meaning. Words formerly "stimulated emotion because they also stimulated something else: imagination."[32] "Sickening," "villain," and "bitch" no longer evoke images.[33] Many modern writers, according to Lewis, lack his beloved Spenser's "profound sympathy with ... the fundamental tendencies of the human imagination as such."[34]

Because language is based on the most fundamental processes of the human consciousness, the history of the language has important implications for history as a whole. It was this aspect of Owen Barfield's theory that Lewis wanted to promote. Their mutual friend Tolkien expressed this conviction when he related the origin of fairy tales to the origin of language in the perception of concrete meaning. The key to the significance of the fairy story is in the double meaning of *spell* as story and as incantation.[35] It is interesting to note that the word *gospel,* the "good spell," incorporates both these meanings; by implication, the present-day translation "good news" reflects a change in the human imagination. (The complete *Oxford English Dictionary* gives a fascinating analysis of the history of *gospel.*) We have retained the meaning of *story* only, since we are now more readily persuaded by news than by spells. However, the word *spell* reveals, in what Barfield might call a fossilized form, the fundamental power of language: the idea that to pronounce the right name is to exercise power—to say the letters in the right order is to cast a spell.

Barfield's theory of the history of language as a movement from concrete metaphor to abstraction illustrates that history is not necessarily evolutionary in the sense of continual improvement. He considered the "progressive" view of history responsible for misunderstanding the past: this assumption has resulted in too much emphasis on those features of the past that have survived and too little emphasis on features perhaps more important that have been lost. Lewis, following Barfield, attempted to understand past literature on its own terms rather than to repudiate what seemed "dated" and to praise the "up-to-date." It can be equally difficult, in other ways, to see the literature of one's own period in the right perspective. Lewis noted, for instance, that the contemporary student's inability to scan poetry, which he had observed as a teacher, was parallel to the contemporary poet's use of free verse; but he speculated that there might be no direct relationship: "More probably the ignorance, and the deliberate abandonment, of accentual meters are correlative phenomena, and both the result of some revolution in our whole sense of rhythm—a revolution of great importance reaching deep down into the unconscious and even perhaps into the blood."[36] He made no attempt to identify this revolution more precisely; it serves as an illustration of our ignorance of the pattern of history. Lewis believed that there is a pattern, which can be apprehended imaginatively through myth—Arthurian, Malacandrian, Narnian, or some other. Art can imply but logic cannot prove what stage of the pattern has been reached in actual history. He considered the least dangerous philosophy of history to be "simple Providentialism": "It is a method which saves minor historians from writing a great deal of nonsense and compels them to get on with the story."[37]

In his fascination with the mythic power of language, in his stimulating analyses of changes in meaning from the metaphoric to the abstract, Lewis was continually propagating Barfield's theories, as he had intended to do. By showing that the history of language involves losses as well as gains, he suggested that the same is true for the history of our literature and our culture as a whole. The only way to understand any of these patterns is to realize that they are, fundamentally, mythic. In a letter to Barfield in 1939, Lewis predicted the increased interest in this approach during the succeeding forty years:

> You could hardly expect the man in the T.L.S. to know the esoteric doctrine of myths.
>
> By the bye, we now need a new word for the "science of the nature of myths," since "mythology" has been appropriated for the myths themselves. Would "mythonomy" do? I am quite serious. If your views are not a complete error, this subject will

become more important; and it's worth while trying to get a good word before they invent a beastly one. "Mytho-logic" (noun) wouldn't be bad, but people would read it as an adjective. I have also thought of "mythopoetics" (cf. "metaphysics"), but that leads to "a mythopoecian," which is frightful; whereas "a mythonomer" (better still "The Mythonomer Royal") is nice. Or shall we just invent a new word—like "gas." (Nay sir, I meant nothing.)[38]

The blend of gravity and humor in the letter is typical. He took the subject seriously, but he never took himself too seriously. Had the post of Mythonomer Royal been established, he would have recommended Tolkien or Barfield for it rather than himself. Lewis was right about the increasing importance of the subject. Now Barfield, as a trustee of Lewis's estate, continues the interdependent relationship that began more than half a century ago. Barfield was a catalyst for a chain reaction in Lewis's approach to literature.

NOTES

1. C.S. Lewis, *Surprised By Joy: The Shape of My Early Life* (New York: Harcourt, Brace and Company, 1955), pp. 199–200.

2. Lewis, *Letters*, p. 76.

3. Ibid., p. 217.

4. C.S. Lewis, *The Lion, the Witch and the Wardrobe* (London: Geoffrey Bles, 1950), p. 50.

5. Lewis, *The Allegory of Love*, p. viii.

6. Owen Barfield, *History in English Words* (London: Faber and Gwyer, 1926) and *Poetic Diction* (London: Faber and Gwyer, 1928).

7. Barfield, *Poetic Diction*, pp. 80–81.

8. Ibid., pp. 86–87.

9. C.S. Lewis, *Out of the Silent Planet* (London: The Bodley Head, 1938), pp. 152–53.

10. C.S. Lewis, *Perelandra* (London: The Bodley Head, 1943), p. 26.

11. Ibid., p. 67.

12. Ibid., p. 168.

13. C.S. Lewis, *That Hideous Strength* (London: The Bodley Head, 1945), pp. 280–81.

14. Ibid., p. 62.

15. Ibid., pp. 426–27.

16. Ibid., p. 338.

17. See the discussion of *Maya* in Owen Barfield, *Romanticism Comes of Age* (Middletown, Conn.: Wesleyan University Press, rpt. 1966), pp. 29–33.

18. C.S. Lewis, *Till We Have Faces: A Myth Retold* (New York: Harcourt, Brace and Company, 1956), p. 294.

19. C.S. Lewis, *The Voyage of the Dawn Treader* (London: Geoffrey Bles, 1952), p. 127.

20. Lewis, *The Lion, the Witch and the Wardrobe*, p. 129.

21. Ibid., p. 67.

22. Lewis, *The Voyage of the Dawn Treader*, pp. 142–43.

23. Lewis, *The Allegory of Love*, p. 1.

24. Ibid., p. 227.

25. Ibid., p. 49.

26. C.S. Lewis, *The Four Loves* (New York: Harcourt, Brace and Company, 1960), p. 53.

27. Ibid., pp. 170–71.

28. C.S. Lewis, *Studies in Words* (Cambridge: Cambridge University Press, 1960), p. 25.

29. Ibid., pp. 45–46.

30. Ibid., p. 74.

31. Ibid.

32. Ibid., p. 224.

33. Ibid., pp. 223–25.

34. Lewis, *The Allegory of Love*, pp. 312–13.

35. J. R. R. Tolkien, "On Fairy-Stories," in *Essays Presented to Charles Williams* (London: Oxford University Press, 1947), pp. 50–51.

36. C.S. Lewis, "Donne and Love Poetry in the Seventeenth Century," in *Seventeenth Century Studies Presented to Sir Herbert Grierson* (Oxford: Clarendon Press, 1938), pp. 72–73.

37. Lewis, *Sixteenth Century*, p. 148.

38. Lewis, *Letters*, p. 163.

LEE D. ROSSI

"Logic" and "Romance": The Divided Self of C.S. Lewis

In an essay on "C.S. Lewis: The Man and the Mystery," Chad Walsh, an Episcopalian priest and author of *C.S. Lewis: Apostle to the Skeptics*, notes that "the mystery of C.S. Lewis is that there seems to be no mystery. None, at least, if one views the man through his books."[1] Clyde Kilby, a personal friend of Lewis and the author of *The Christian World of C.S. Lewis*, remarks similarly but in a more personal vein, "My impression is that few people ever faced the delusive nature of selfishness more thoroughly than Lewis.... What his detractors do not understand—or maybe what they understand only too well—is that Lewis had come out on the other side of a door most of us never manage to enter."[2] Likewise, another friend, Austin Farrer, observes that Lewis's apologetic writings "express a solid confidence." He calls Lewis "a bonny fighter" and observes that, "From temper ... he loved an argument."[3] What most impresses these writers—and they are representative of the majority opinion—is Lewis's stability of character and purpose. He is one of the very few authors of the twentieth century to whom individuals in spiritual turmoil turn again and again for consolation and guidance. There is hardly a memoir in the volume, *These Found the Way; Thirteen Converts to Protestant Christianity*, in which Lewis is not mentioned as one of the authors responsible for bringing the individual to Christianity. He figures, for instance, in the conversion narratives of such

From *The Politics of Fantasy: C.S. Lewis and J.R.R. Tolkien*. © 1984 by Lee D. Rossi.

different individuals as Chad Walsh, an American Southerner who, in reacting to the narrowness of his upbringing, became an atheist; Hyatt Howe Waggoner, a university professor noted for his writings on American literature; and William Lindsay Gresham, a writer and a Communist veteran of the Spanish Civil War. Most striking of all is the narrative written by Gresham's wife, Joy Davidman. A poet and an editor of the Communist periodical, *The New Masses*, she tells how she had reached a crucial moment in her life, her faith in the Communist Party shattered, her marriage dissolving, her husband an alcoholic. She was without any belief to guide her life. At the very worst moment, she says that she experienced the presence of God. In solemn testimony to Lewis's helpfulness, she says that after that experience she started reading Lewis and "learned from him, slowly, how I had gone wrong. Without his works, I wonder if I and many others might not still be infants 'crying in the night.'"[4] She recounts that later she and her husband were reconciled and that, after an intensive study of Christian writers (Lewis, in particular), they both converted to Christianity.[5]

For many readers and critics, then, Lewis has an enviable sureness about the nature of the universe and his place in it. He is a spiritual father for those who like Joy Davidman are "infants crying in the night." Yet, for many other readers, Lewis's almost pugnacious certitude betrays a lack of appreciation for the complexities of the spiritual life. His friend and Oxford colleague, Nevill Coghill, observes that "Underneath all, I sense in his style an indefeasible core of Protestant certainties ... but the strength that [he] derive[s] from this hard core deprived him of certain kinds of sympathy and perception."[6]

Chad Walsh, elaborating on this point, declares that Lewis paid a price for his conviction "that in the Christian faith there is available the essential things one needs to know in order to be a proper part of the totality." He observes that just as his religious thinking is somewhat shrill and moralistic, so too his literary judgments are a little too clear-cut and simplistic. These habits of mind infect his creative work as well. Whereas Lewis is capable of creating characters who are "vivid and believable," they evince the same mysterious quality that one finds in Lewis himself. Says Walsh, "After he presents them to a certain depth, the curtain descends, and the reader is not sure whether anything exists behind."[7] For Walsh, the basic limitation of Lewis's thought is its lack of spiritual depth, and he relates this to Lewis's complete lack of interest in his own psychology. But ultimately he finds "Lewis's total absorption in the world outside himself" refreshing and healthy in an age full of "Ego-searching and Id-probing."

Still other readers find the key to Lewis's personality in the depths that Lewis leaves unexplored. In the introduction to *Light on C.S. Lewis*, a volume of memoirs and essays, Lewis's very close friend, Owen Barfield, observes that there was a peculiar enigmatic quality to Lewis's literary personality. Incapable of writing in the idiom of his own time, Lewis was nevertheless capable of breathing life into the motifs of the literary past. And yet there was something curiously forced, not insincere but unnatural, about this bravura performance.[8] The problem for Barfield lies in deciding what is depth and what surface, what is real and what is the product of the will. He feels that there is more to Lewis than the forceful and pugnacious apologist for Christianity. In fact, as time went on he came to feel more and more strongly that there were actually two Lewises. One was the shy and friendly student he had known at Oxford after the war, an uncertain young man hovering between rationalism and romanticism. The other developed after Lewis's conversion to Christianity. This new Lewis had put all his force of will and skill as a dialectician to work on behalf of Christianity. "There was both a friend and the memory of a friend; sometimes they were close together and nearly coalesced; sometimes they seemed very far apart."[9]

As Barfield indicates, there seems to have been a basic duality in Lewis's personality. As a corollary, we might see some basic distinction between Lewis's apologetic and religious discourse, the work of the "new" Lewis, and his works of fantasy, the work of the "old" Lewis. This view contradicts the usual judgment about the place of Lewis's fantasy in his total career. Following Lewis's account in his autobiography, most of the critics see in his conversion a resolution of the tension, which Lewis had felt as a young man, between romanticism and rationalism. As Walsh says, "The two strands that run through C.S. Lewis's books are 'logic' and 'romance,' to give them the names he chose. Jointly they led him back to Christianity."[10] Moreover, most writers on Lewis hold that Lewis's fantasy is merely another mode of a basically apologetic activity. Richard Cunningham presents the usual view when he remarks, "In the case of C.S. Lewis, his apologetic method is inseparable from its literary vehicle; the Logos (something said) is intimately bound up with Poiema (something made)."[11] Others, notably Walsh and Kilby, spend a great deal of time elucidating the Christian content of Lewis's fantasies.

Yet the evidence, both literary and biographical, strongly suggests some kind of duality in his work. Lewis's fiction, for example, oscillates between two poles—the satire predominant in *The Screwtape Letters* and *That Hideous Strength* and the "marvellous" landscapes and characters of *Out of the Silent Planet*, *Perelandra*, and the Narnia books. Of the two, satire is obviously the genre most closely related to the ends of Christian apologetics. It assumes, as the critical focus, the morality and world view of Christianity. The imaginary landscape presupposes no such underpinning. It can be enjoyed for its own sake. Perhaps this is why the Christian writers who have dealt with Lewis's work have been so anxious to point out the moral of his so-called mythic fantasies. The kind of wonder and joy which they evoke and which originally attracted Lewis to "marvellous literature" are as far removed from the prescriptions of Christianity as they are from the realities of everyday life.

Secondly, the tone of Lewis's fiction involves the same kind of polarities. His satires are serious, sober-minded affairs; their humor, if any, mordant. The Lewis of the fairy tales, on the other hand, is unquestionably ebullient. He expresses real joy in the company of his Narnian characters and in their surroundings. Yet this joy is not a result of their conformance to Christian morality but rather of the freedom and magic of the imaginary world.

Finally, the uses of language oscillate between two poles. We might call them the rational and the romantic, or the didactic and the playful. Here is an example from his imaginary voyage to Mars, *Out of the Silent Planet*; a Martian creature is trying to explain to the hero Ransom the nature of "eldils" (angels):

> Body is movement. If it is atone speed, you smell something; if at another, you hear a sound; if at another you see a sight; if at another, you neither see nor hear nor smell, nor know the body in any way. But mark this, Small One, that the two ends meet. If movement is faster, then that which moves is more nearly in two places at once. But if the movement were faster still—it is difficult, for you do not know many words—you see that if you made it faster and faster, in the end the moving thing would be in all places at once, Small One. Well, then, that is the thing at the top of all bodies—so fast that it is at rest, so truly body that it has ceased being body at all. But we will not talk of that. Start from where we are, Small One. The swiftest thing that touches our senses is light. We do not truly see light, we only see slower things lit by it, so that for us light is on the edge—the last thing we know before things become too swift for us. But the body of an *eldil* is a movement swift as light; you may say its body is made of light, but not of that which is light for the *eldil*. His "light" is a swifter movement which for us is nothing at all; and what we call light is for him a thing like water, a visible thing, a thing he

can touch and bathe in—even a dark thing when not illumined by the swifter. And what we call firm things—flesh and earth—seem to him thinner, and harder to see, than our light, and more like clouds, and nearly nothing. To us the *eldil* is a thin, half-real body that can go through walls and rocks: to himself he goes through them because he is solid and firm and they are like cloud. And what is true light to him and fills the heaven, so that he will plunge into the rays of the sun to refresh himself from it, is to us the black nothing in the sky at night. (*OSP*, 94–95)

Clearly we have here two kinds of discourse. One is a definition, the other a hypothesis, a metaphor; one is abstract and the other concrete. The first is discursive and proceeds by a logical progression. The argument starts at one kind of speed which is available to our senses and progresses until the speed outstrips our senses. Ultimately, the only recourse of the argument is speculation, the only language paradox. But notice that with the repeated "Small One" Lewis is trying to give his speaker an authority which his argument doesn't have of itself. Obviously this kind of discourse is unsatisfactory, if not from a doctrinal point of view at least from a literary one. The Martian has to start again "from where we are." The vocabulary becomes more concrete, the syntax less authoritative. And the Martian is able to satisfy Ransom's curiosity. It is a moment of imaginative clarity, in which a possible other world is suggested in all its ramifications. We see side by side in this example what we see in various mixtures in Lewis's other fiction: a kind of language which emphasizes logic (as in his polemical works) and a language which is more playful and concrete.

Those who have written about Lewis have not been wrong in appraising the virtues of his writing.[12] There is general agreement that he is at his best when creating imaginary worlds full of wonder and whimsy. But they have not noticed that these virtues are not a direct result of his commitment as a Christian. Instead his fantasy expresses an impulse much older than his Christianity, the romanticism which, as John Lawlor points out, can never find a permanent home in the clearly structured logical world of medieval Christianity. Lawlor, a student of Lewis during the thirties, observes that Lewis's "emergent romanticism challenges religion as the revelation of final reality.... The myth ... flies at the touch of a colder religion."[13]

At the bottom of this romanticism we find a pattern basic to Lewis's temperament, the escape into an imaginary world. The other touchstones of Lewis's imagination, the love of inanimate nature and the consolation of a small circle of friends, are variations on this basic theme of escape. Moreover, we may turn the critical cliche around and say that it is not so much that Lewis's fantasy is an aspect of his Christian commitment, as that his Christianity is an aspect of his commitment to fantasy. Both are evidence of his profound desire for a reality alternative to modern bourgeois society. And, as we shall see, this desire is grounded in Lewis's experience as a child and a young man.

C.S. Lewis was born in Belfast, in Protestant Ireland, in 1898. He was the son of a well-to-do solicitor. His father belonged to the first generation of professionals in a family of Welsh farmers. His mother was the daughter of a naval chaplain, and the descendant of clergymen, lawyers, and sailors. He tells us that his father was an extremely emotional man with a strong love of rhetoric; he was by far the dominant figure in the family. His mother was a much less powerful presence, but Lewis remembers her for her cheerfulness and quiet affection. Both parents were bookish people, and instilled their love for literature in both their sons.

The two most important things about this early period of Lewis's life was his inability to get along with his father, and the death of his mother before he was ten. His father was an aggressive and domineering person who took little cognizance of the people around him. At times this was not without its comical aspects. "Tell him that a boy called Churchwood had caught a fieldmouse and kept it as a pet, and a year, or ten years later, he would ask you. 'Did you ever hear what became of poor Chickweed who was so afraid of the rats?' For his own version, once adopted, was indelible, and attempts to correct it only produced an incredulous, 'Hm! Well, that's not the story you *used* to tell'" (*SbJ*, 13–14). In general, however, his inability to really listen to other people completely frustrated all attempts at communication. Of his mother's death Lewis says that "all settled happiness, all that was tranquil and reliable, disappeared from my life. There was to be much fun, many pleasures, many stabs of Joy; but no more of the old security. It was sea and islands now; the great continent had sunk like Atlantis" (*SbJ*, 21). The last sentence, especially, is extraordinarily intense and reflects the extent to which his mother's presence guaranteed his own emotional stability. Moreover, the effect of his wife's death was to make Lewis's father harsher and more demanding of his sons at a time when they most needed sympathy and guidance. "Under the pressure of anxiety his temper became incalculable; he spoke wildly and acted unjustly. Thus by a peculiar cruelty of fate, during those months the unfortunate man, had he but known it, was really losing his sons as well as his wife" (*SbJ*, 19). Nor did the gap between father and sons ever really close. In 1916 Lewis was preparing for a scholarship examination at Oxford. But faced with the imminent necessity of going into the army, he was losing interest in preparing for the exam. "I once tried," writes Lewis, "to explain this to my father; it was one of the attempts I often made ... to break through the artificiality of our intercourse and admit him to my real life. It was a total failure" (*SbJ*, 183). The elder Lewis could only respond with platitudes and homilies.

As a result of this thoroughly unsatisfactory relationship, Lewis and his brother were thrown completely on their own resources. The extent to which this alienation from his father provoked feelings of sadness and disappointment is evident in Lewis's remark that he and his brother "drew daily closer together ... two frightened urchins huddled for warmth in a bleak world" (*SbJ*, 19).

This tendency to view the world in terms of a small group huddled together against a threatening reality was reinforced by Lewis's disastrous experience at his first school. His brother was already there, and Lewis was sent at age ten. The master—called Oldie by his victims—was cruel and the work pure drudgery. This experience of a cruel and tedious schoolmaster repeated the pattern set at home, and Lewis responded by banding together with his classmates in opposition to the master, much as he had drawn closer to his brother at home. Lewis suggests that these two experiences had an indelible, formative effect on his personality. He writes, "To this day the vision of the world which comes most naturally to me is one in which 'we two' or 'we few' (and in a sense 'we happy few') stand together against something stronger and larger" (*SbJ*, 32). Moreover, his experience with his father's horrible temper was repeated when Oldie, at the death of his own wife, became even more cruel and violent. "You will remember that I had already learned to fear and hate emotion," Lewis tells us. "Here was fresh reason to do so" (*SbJ*, 33).

But these experiences, crucial as they were, only served to confirm a reticence that seems certainly the result of a leisurely if isolated bourgeois way of life. From his earliest moments, Lewis's most intense experiences seem to have been primarily imaginative. The "New House" in the suburbs of Belfast, which his family moved into in the summer of 1905, is an extremely important factor in Lewis's development. "I am a product of long corridors, empty sunlit rooms, upstairs indoor silences, attics explored in solitude, distant noises of gurgling cisterns and pipes, and the noise of wind under tiles" (*SbJ*, 10). This sense of isolation was further increased by the departure of his older brother to school. We can see that eventually this solitude became a matter of choice and of habit rather than a matter of necessity. It was at this time, when Lewis first learned to read and write, that he began drawing and composing stories. "I soon staked out a claim to one of the attics and made it 'my study.' Pictures, of my own making or cut from the brightly colored Christmas numbers of magazines, were nailed on the walls. There I kept my pen and inkpot and writing books and paintbox; and there: Than to enjoy delight with liberty? What more felicity can fall to creature" (*SbJ*, 12–13). This recourse to art and literature (and not to more ordinary boyhood pursuits) was necessitated by a physical defect both sons inherited from their father. Each had only one joint in the thumb and were consequently disqualified from every kind of activity involving manual skill. Lewis remembers compulsory games at school as being some of the most dreadful times in his life. But Lewis seems always to have been a person who could make a virtue of necessity, and devoted great energy to the creation and elaboration of his private world, even to making a map and a history separate from the stories. "At this time—at the age of six, seven, and eight— I was living almost entirely in my imagination; or at least the imaginative experience of those years now seems to me more important than anything else" (*SbJ*, 15).

This imaginary world was called Boxen, and it was very different from Lewis's adult stories. (For a complete description of this work, see Walter Hooper's introduction to the volume *Of Other Worlds*.) Matters of ethics and personal choice which were to become so important to his adult fictions are completely nonexistent in the copious domains of Boxen. Moreover, they are noticeably lacking in the "marvellous" aspects of his later work. "My invented world was full (for me) of interest, bustle, humor, and character; but there was no poetry, even no romance, in it. It was almost astonishingly prosaic" (*SbJ*, 15). The absorbing interest of these early stories is politics. The most important character is Lord John Big of Bigham, a frog of powerful personality and Prime Minister of Boxen. We follow his career through two volumes of *Boxen: or Scenes from Boxonian City Life* and three volumes of *The Life of Lord John Big of Bigham*. The other characters are equally concerned with making a place for themselves among Boxen's rulers. Walter Hooper, Lewis's secretary, tells us that "The characters in *Scenes from Boxonian City Life* all relish a place in the 'Clique' though none of them, not even the author, appears to have any clear idea what a 'clique' is. Which is not surprising for, as Lewis wanted his characters to be 'grown-up', he naturally interested them in 'grown-up' affairs. And politics, his brother says, was a topic he almost always heard his elders discussing" (*OOW*, vii). Certainly we can detect in this singular effort an imaginative attempt to close what even at that early date before the death of his mother must have seemed an immense gap between himself and his father. Lewis recognizes quite clearly in his autobiography that Lord Big resembles his father. More than just an exercise in emulation, it was also an attempt to portray and satirize the family situation. Lord Big, for example, is described as "immense in size, resonant of voice, chivalrous (he was the hero of innumerable duels), stormy, eloquent, and impulsive" (*SbJ*, 80). Lord Big's charges, the two young kings, however, are not yet suitable replacements for their regent. They are much more concerned with their own private pleasures than with any serious political end. Throughout this piece, then, we notice Lewis's very strong ambivalence, not only toward his father but also toward himself.

These early stories also provide interest as they become material for parody for the adult writer. His later rejection of all striving for social success could not go further. Concern with politics comes to seem, especially in a figure such as Orual in the novel *Till We Have Faces*, a sign of spiritual desiccation. The desire to become one of the "clique" is the basic motivation of Mark Studdock in *That Hideous Strength*, yet he finds that desire leading him into greater and greater evils.

Lewis notes, as we have seen, that his first imaginary world was "astonishingly prosaic." But his childhood was also filled with an imaginative experience of a completely different character, full of "romance" and "poetry." This experience of the romantic, which he calls in his autobiography "Joy," is perhaps the most important experience of his life. It is the touchstone by which he measures the value of every other experience. It is the basis for his love of inanimate nature and his lifelong interest in fantastic literature. Moreover, it is the basis of the wonder-filled landscapes of his adult fiction. Most simply put, it is the experience of longing or desire (Lewis uses the German word *Sehnsucht*) for that which would somehow fill up the void at the core of his family and emotional life.

When he began to read, this fundamental imaginative reflex became part of his literary experience. Everything from Beatrix Potter to Norse mythology was able to awake in him this intense desire. In fact, Lewis recounts that except for a short period during his early adolescence, this experience formed a permanent and (until his conversion) important aspect of his life.

After his disastrous experience with Oldie, Lewis attended a number of other schools. In 1910, after an unhappy term at Campbell College, he was taken ill and had to be removed from the school. Between the ages of thirteen and fifteen, he attended a small boarding school he calls Chartres. He was happy there, making friends and showing promise for the first time as a student. But there also he lost his religion. At fifteen Lewis won a scholarship to Wyvern College, a school which his brother had already attended. We have already noted the difference between Lewis's half-envying picture of the scramble in Boxen and his strongly disapproving parody of it in *That Hideous Strength*. What this shift signifies is a hardening of attitude toward his father and what his father represents. What it signifies is his retreat and ultimate disgust with the English middle class. What had been ambivalent in his attitude toward his father becomes outright hostility when confronted with the English public school.

Lewis tells us that as a result of his experience with the public school at Wyvern, he became "a Prig, a Highbrow," a member of the alienated intelligentsia spawned by, but directly opposed to, the English middle class. The change was not particularly dramatic or rapid. At first Lewis was simply a typical British schoolboy with a taste for reading. But he quickly discovered that this taste separated him from most of the rest of the school and especially from the school's social elite, a group called "the Bloods," whose only interests were sports and social life. He detested the thought of playing toady to an upperclassman. Moreover, he was very clumsy in sports. Consequently, the only routes of advancement for a lad of not very distinguished origins were closed to him. His intellectual interests were shared by only a few others. But their taste for such things, he discovered, was actually "good" taste, the best taste. Lewis later felt, however, that this consciousness of one's own intellectual superiority was already very dangerous; it "involves a kind of Fall. The moment good taste knows itself, some of its goodness is lost" (*SbJ*, 104). From that point on, the temptation to scorn the more conventional members of the school was ever present, and Lewis succumbed. To some extent this was a necessary result of the system itself. As Lewis says, it is "interesting," I think he means ironic, "that the public-school system had thus produced the very thing which it was advertised to prevent or cure. For you must understand (if you have not been dipped in that tradition yourself) that the whole thing was devised to knock the nonsense out of the smaller boys and 'put them in their place'" (*SbJ*, 104–5). Yet for Lewis, his reaction to the situation was itself a great moral evil.

Yet if Priggery was a moral disaster, it did involve an uncommon emotional clarity concerning the character of the social life at Wyvern. For Lewis the social life of the school was dominated by the struggle to achieve prominence. All other values and virtues, friendship, morality, fairness, were abandoned in the race to be popular. At Wyvern, Lewis, already something of a loner, found plenty of reasons for remaining one.

Eventually Lewis quit Wyvern and was sent to a tutor, W.T. Kirkpatrick of Bookham, to prepare for Oxford. Lewis was very happy living with Kirkpatrick and his wife. Here he was able to indulge his two passions, literature and long walks in the country. Kirkpatrick himself was very important to Lewis. From him Lewis learned the dialectical skills which were so important to his career as a Christian apologist. "If ever a man came near to being a purely logical entity, that man was Kirk. Born a little later, he would have been a logical Positivist. The idea that human beings should exercise their vocal organs for any purpose except that of communicating or discovering truth was to him preposterous. The most casual remark was taken as a summons to disputation" (*SbJ*, 135–36). It was very difficult, at first, for Lewis to defend what he calls his "vague romantic notions," but eventually he was able to contest with his master on something like an equal footing. In fact, Lewis was so impressed by Kirkpatrick that he afterwards adopted his style of discourse for his own. John Lawlor, a student of Lewis's during the 1930s, remarks this fact, and adds that it left Lewis in the lamentable condition of being unable to engage in more mundane forms of conversation. "I could as readily as anyone deplore the influence of 'the Great Knock' [Kirkpatrick]: his meeting with Lewis was perhaps one of the least fortunate in intellectual history. The shy boy from Belfast, making his naive comments on the Surrey countryside, became the one who had no small talk; who talked habitually, as Johnson did, for victory."[14]

Lewis remarks in his autobiography that all the while he was getting on in these various schools and meeting new friends, he kept having recurring experiences of joy." But so different was the everyday life of schoolwork and boyish camaraderie from this other experience, that it seemed to him that he was living two lives. "The two lives do not seem to influence each other at all. Where there are hungry wastes, starving for Joy, in the one, the other may be full of cheerful bustle and success; or again, where the outer life is miserable, the other may be brimming over with ecstasy" (*SbJ*, 78). What's important about this is that already in his adolescence the life of "joy," of ecstatic experience, came to seem radically distinct from the everyday life. This kind of dualism finds its way again and again into his fantasy as he creates new worlds which pose a radical alternative, an escape from mundane existence.

After one semester at Oxford in 1917, Lewis was drafted. As we have already noted, the important thing about the war for Lewis was not its harsh realities but the friends he made and the books he read. Of one occasion when he came down with "trench fever" and had to be taken to the hospital, he says, "Perhaps I ought to have mentioned before that I had had a weak chest ever since childhood and had very early learned to make a minor illness one of the pleasures of life, even in peacetime. Now, as an alternative to the trenches, a bed and a book were 'very heaven'" (*SbJ*, 189). During this time he first read Chesterton, and as he says, "I did not know what I was letting myself in for" (*SbJ*, 191). Already his atheism was beginning to crumble. This process was accelerated by the influence of another soldier, an Oxford scholar like himself, named Johnson, who was a skilled dialectician, full of "youth and whim and poetry" but above all "a man of conscience." Lewis was very attracted to his unselfconscious display of moral goodness. Lewis's own judgment about the experiences in the war is that they led him for the first time consciously on the road to theism and Christianity. But if he was learning to sing a different tune, it was played in the key of his childhood. The pattern which developed in those early years, of finding a private and personal alternative in the face of a threatening reality, is repeated again here. The reference to his childhood in his description of his wartime illness points up this connection very nicely.

After the war he returned to Oxford, and after three years there took the examination in "Greats." Although taking a "First" in the exam, he was unable to find a position teaching and decided to stay a fourth year at Oxford to study English literature. He was able to do this, however, only because of the generous financial aid of his father, who was determined that his son should find a position teaching. By then, it had become clear to both father and son that Lewis was unsuited for any profession but the academy. As Kirkpatrick had told his father, "You may make a writer or a scholar of him, but you'll not make anything else. You may make up your mind to *that*" (*SbJ*, 183). In 1925 he was elected Fellow of Magdalen College, where he remained until taking a chair at Cambridge in 1956.

In his autobiography, Lewis recounts that the path which led him back to Christianity was mainly intellectual. During these early years at Oxford, his practice of the logical virtues implanted by Kirkpatrick, strengthened by his contact with such individuals as Johnson and Owen Barfield, led him from the atheism and "popular realism" he had learned at Bookham to philosophical idealism to theism, and finally to Christianity (*SbJ*, 205). Yet more than just pure reason was involved. The crucial fact which led him to reject "popular realism" was that it caused him to doubt his experience of "joy." The new psychology had taught him that it was merely a subjective phenomenon, valuable perhaps, but certainly not real. After rejecting realism, Lewis embraced first idealism, then theism, and finally Christianity. With idealism, theism, and Christianity, he could believe that *Sehnsucht* was putting him in touch with the really real. We must not, of course, minimize the differences between these last three stages; we should especially note that Lewis was moving toward something more solid, more "normal," less "highbrow" by which to identify himself. But the fact remains that for Lewis, the authenticity of this fundamental experience could only be guaranteed by referring it to some reality outside of himself (*SbJ*, 217–21).

During this time he published his first two volumes, both of which are marked by his long interest in "romantic" literature and which clarify to some extent the issues which led him back to Christianity. The first book, a volume of poetry with the Neo-Platonic title *Spirits in Bondage*, was published in 1919. Already his conception of literature as escape was apparent in this work. The poems abound in what he called 'thoughtful wishing' (not wishful thinking), and his purpose is clearly expressed in the opening lyric:

> In my coracle of verses I will sing of lands unknown,
> Flying from the scarlet city where a Lord that knows no pity
> Mocks the broken people praying round his iron throne,
> —Sing about the Hidden Country fresh and full of quiet green,
> Sailing over seas uncharted to a port that none has seen. (*Poems*, v)

Already in this early lyric we find a distinct anticipation not only of the hidden green country of Narnia but also of the plot of one of the Narnia stories, *The Voyage of the Dawn Treader*.

In 1926, as a Fellow of Magdalen College, Lewis published *Dymer*, a long narrative poem in rime royal. It tells of a hero born in "The Perfect City":

> There you'd have thought the gods were smothered down
> Forever, and the keys were turned on fate.
> No hour was left unchartered in that town,
> And love was in a schedule and the State
> Chose for eugenic reasons who should mate
> With whom, and when. Each idle song and dance
> Was fixed by law and nothing left to chance.[15]

For a while, Dymer endures this brave new world. Finally, however, he strikes his teacher (killing him instantly), and joyfully escapes to the forest. So far this is very like the project of escape in *Spirits in Bondage*. But complications arise for Dymer which signify in Lewis a new stage of awareness about the consequences of his literary stance of revolt. Dymer's escape touches off a rebellion in which the tyrannical authorities are overthrown. But what replaces it, a continuous round of murder, arson, and pillage, is even worse. Moreover, Dymer's union with "a girl of the forest" (who is later in the poem disclosed to be a projection of his own lust) results in a monstrous offspring which wreaks great harm on men. Finally, he resolves to do battle with it and is killed. He is reborn, however, as—

> A wing'd and sworded shape, through whom the air
> Poured as through glass: and its foam-tumbled hair
> Lay white about the shoulders and the whole
> Pure body brimmed with life, as a full bowl.[16]

In this later poem we see Lewis troubled by his responsibility to society. The twin dangers of his romantic alienation from society are narcissism and anarchism, and the only way to guard the project of escape and at the same time render it morally acceptable is to anchor it in an extramundane principle of goodness. It is precisely these emotional issues which were involved in the intellectual process that led him to Christianity.

We can perhaps make this anxiety about the narcissistic tendencies of "joy" and "romanticism" more concrete by referring once more to Lewis's autobiography. Lewis recounts that he came to recognize God's claims on him slowly and with great reluctance. He insists that the greatest moral struggle he had was in overcoming the habit of privacy and introspection. Lewis's notion of a "perfect day," limned in great detail in his autobiography, is singularly solipsistic. It is a carefully orchestrated chronology of meals and work. Recreation, such as a solitary walk after lunch, is regarded as necessary, but intercourse with others is viewed as an annoying distraction (*SbJ*, 141–43). Lewis declares that "it is a life almost entirely selfish." Lewis felt that this tendency was leading him toward the unbridled and self-centered cultivation of sensibility and subjectivity à la Symonds. His enthusiasms for "Northernness," for Norse mythology and Wagnerian music, is one of many eruptions of that "joy" which for Lewis is the most fundamental experience of his life. Yet the "joy" did not last but for a moment and his attempts to recapture it are indicative of his subjectivist tendencies. "To 'get it again' became my constant endeavor; while reading every poem, hearing every piece of music, going for every walk, I stood anxious sentinel at my own mind to watch whether the blessed moment was beginning and to endeavor to retain it if it did" (*SbJ*, 169). Lewis says that he came to realize later that he had erred in seeking the emotion itself rather than the object, or rather, the person who had caused it. "From the fading of the Northernness I ought to have drawn the conclusion that the Object, the Desirable, was further away, more external, less subjective, than even such a comparatively public and external thing as a system of mythology—had, in fact, only shone through that system" (*SbJ*, 168).

In Christianity, then, Lewis finally achieved an intellectual position which would save him from narcissism but would not jeopardize his experience of "joy." But the fact is that neither would it satisfy that experience. Christianity, especially the Anglican Christianity in which Lewis was raised, tends to be very suspicious of ecstatic emotional experiences like those of Lewis. The patient performance of one's duty is much more important than an elusive contact with some preternatural reality. In fact, from Lewis's viewpoint as a practising Christian, "joy" came to seem merely a means to an end. He says toward the end of his autobiography, "I now know that the experience, considered as a state of my own mind, had never had the kind of importance I once gave it. It was valuable only as a pointer to something other and outer" (*SbJ*, 238). Lewis states that he continued to have such experiences, but that his work as a teacher and a Christian writer were much more important to him.

Christianity, however, is a term which stands for many things. Besides a hard-nosed, aggressive critique of human nature and human society, we also find a longing for the Other World. This aspect of Christianity promises freedom from all economic and social evils, as well as that glowing realm of the impossible which so attracted Lewis. Thus, besides satisfying his need to find a place for himself in society, Christianity could also satisfy his hunger for "Otherness."

In the years after his conversion, we can see a reappearance of the split between logic and romanticism which had troubled him as a young atheist at Oxford. John Lawlor makes a very perceptive comment about Lewis's continuing interest in medieval *fyne amour* and rebellious romanticism: "Each was in some measure an opponent of, and each became in some degree a successful usurper on, the fullness of religious experience."[17]

On the one hand, we have his apologetic and philosophical writings, heavy with the influence of Kirkpatrick: *The Problem of Pain* (1940); *The Abolition of Man* (1943); *Miracles* (1947); and *Mere Christianity*, a series of talks on theology broadcast on the BBC. Included in this list should be his didactic fictions: *The Pilgrim's Regress* (1933), a barely disguised account of his own intellectual wanderings modeled on Bunyan's *Pilgrim's Progress*; his first popular success, *The Screwtape Letters* (1942), originally published weekly in the *Manchester Guardian*, and *The Great Divorce*, a short half-satiric, half-autobiographical work. We should also mention along with this aspect of his work the numerous talks on theology he gave during World

War II at various R.A.F. bases. In all these works there is an amazing consistency of tone and project, a pugnacious defense of Christian orthodoxy.

As John Lawlor has said, Lewis's interest in medieval allegory and romance at times displaces Christianity at the center of his interests. Now this is undoubtedly true, but we should also realize that Lewis's scholarly interest in medieval literature and civilization feeds directly into his defense of Christianity. Beginning with *The Allegory of Love* (1936), an examination of the rise of medieval love poetry, and including his volume in the Oxford History of English Literature *English Literature in the Sixteenth Century, excluding Drama* (1944), as well as *The Discarded Image* (1964), an examination of the content and sources of the medieval world view, he has been one of this century's leading interpreters of the strengths and beauties of medieval Christian culture. It is only when he gets interested in what he calls the "mythic" qualities of medieval literature (what he might also call its "romantic" qualities) and in "worlds of fine fabling," and when he begins to say things like "the old gods had to die before they could wake again in the beauty of acknowledged myth," that Lawlor's comment makes sense.[18]

What is startling about Lewis's career as a writer is that despite his enormous success as a scholar and a Christian apologist, he continued to be intensely interested in fantastic and romantic literature. The fundamental aim of his critical writings, in such volumes as *Rehabilitations* (1939), *An Experiment in Criticism* (1961), and *Of Other Worlds* (1964), has been to establish the value of genres which come outside the realistic canons of modern literary criticism. He praises writers like George MacDonald, William Morris, H.G. Wells, David Lindsay, and E. Nesbit, and their work in such genres as the fairy romance, science fiction, and children's stories for putting readers in touch with a realm of literary experience not available to realistic fiction. As Lewis says apropos of MacDonald's myth-making abilities: "In poetry the words are the body and the 'theme' or 'content' is the soul. But in myth the imagined events are the body and something inexpressible is the soul" (*GM*, 16).

It is precisely this "something inexpressible" which Lewis at his best is able to capture. In his two science-fiction novels, *Out of the Silent Planet* and *Perelandra*, in his children's stories *The Chronicles of Narnia*, and in his retelling of the Cupid and Psyche myth, *Till We Have Faces*, he gives his readers the magic and the mystery of great myth. Moreover, we get some of the man's amiability, a trait too often absent from his earnest but shrill apologetic and satiric writings.

Before going on to examine the fiction itself, we should mention a few of the more personal details of his later life. After his conversion Lewis still remained a loner. He entered into the life of the church community only with great reluctance. In a revealing comment, he compares going to church with going to the zoo. He much prefers, he says, to pray alone or to meet with one or two other people to discuss spiritual matters (*SbJ*, 233–34).

Though Lewis later lost some of his distaste for church-going, he never approached it with the zest he felt for masculine conversation and companionship of a group of Christian intellectual friends called the Inklings. In the introduction to *The Letters of C.S. Lewis*, his older brother, Warren Lewis, describes the character of the group's meetings and Lewis's enthusiasm for them. After tea had been drunk and pipes readied, one of the group would read a new manuscript. The group would then either praise or criticize the work. Criticism could be fierce, and Warren Lewis admitted to feeling a great deal of fear when he read the first chapter of his first book to the group. When on occasion there was nothing to read, there would just be good conversation. "On these occasions the fun would be riotous, with Jack [C.S. Lewis] at the top of his form and enjoying every minute" (*L*, 13–14).

We notice that, even to the inclusion of his brother, this circle replicates the pattern begun at home and continued at Oldie's. Only this time the threatening reality is not an individual but the secular atmosphere of society at large. In a letter of 18 February 1940, at a time when the Inklings' meetings were most frequent, Lewis writes his brother that, "The world as it is is becoming, and has partly now become, simply *too much* for people of the old square-rigged type like you and me. I don't understand its politics or its economics or any damn thing about it."

Moreover, we should note that Lewis did not marry until he was 58. In fact, except for Mrs. Moore, the mother of an Oxford friend killed in the First World War, and his women students, whom he tended to regard with a good deal of arrogance, Lewis had very little to do with women at all. As a result his notions about women's psychology and about their place in society tended to be extremely narrow and conventional, and his fictions suffer for it. His polemics on the role of women are among the least attractive aspects of his work. During most of the years of his tenure at Oxford he lived with his brother and with Mrs. Moore, whom he called "my mother." It was not an easy life; especially at first, money was a problem. Moreover, Mrs. Moore was always difficult to get along with. She died in 1952, and a couple of years later Lewis took Joy Davidman as his secretary. In 1956 they were married. It was a new and in many ways liberating experience for the aging don, though I find it strange that Lewis waited to marry her until she was on her death-bed, dying of cancer. Lewis, whose mother died of cancer, seems to have had a mother-complex, and any woman who got close to him was in danger of becoming his mother. But Joy experienced an almost miraculous remission and lived for another three years. As a result, Lewis gained a new and unexpected happiness. Lewis once told his close friend Nevill Coghill, "I never expected to have, in my sixties, the happiness that passed me by in my twenties" (L, 23). Moreover, he also gained a new depth of understanding about human love and human relations. *A Grief Observed*, written after the death of his wife, shows Lewis plunged into hitherto unknown depths of grief. As Chad Walsh observes, "When he comes up at last into the sunlight and rediscovers, in a convincing but still tentative way, the presence of God, the discovery carries more conviction to the reader than the neatly marshalled ranks of arguments in *Mere Christianity* or even the glowing Christian mythology of the interplanetary novels and Narnia tales."[19] For several years after his wife's death, Lewis was the guardian for her two teenage sons by Gresham. He died on November 22, 1963.

What, then, do we make of this writer's life? What kind of pattern do we see in it? And how do we relate it to his writings? These are the fundamental questions we have to deal with. Given the material that has just been presented, I think we can make several valid generalizations. First of all, we note that throughout his whole life there seems to run a tension between "romanticism" and "logic." Romanticism is the more important of the two and represents an imaginative response of escape to certain threatening realities, e.g., his father, his mother's death, the social life of his various schools, the war. The other sees in romanticism the dangers of narcissism and anarchy, the threat of being totally cut off from the human community. Lewis tried to reconcile these two imperatives by becoming a Christian. Christianity embodied a similar project of escape, but offered Lewis an historical and social sanction for his escape from society. Moreover, it gave him an ethical perspective from which to criticize modern society.

But these two strands were only imperfectly reconciled. Christianity has many meanings, and the dualism in Lewis's personality is reflected once again in the different meanings he gives to his Christianity. At one moment Christianity means "logic" and "philosophy," and is engaged in transforming this world. This meaning of Christianity is expressed in Lewis's polemical writings. At other moments, Christianity means "the Other World" and thereby connects with Lewis's interests in myth and fantasy. Thus Lewis reconciles the dualism but only because "Christianity" is so multivalent and ultimately contradictory in its several meanings. Thus, the dialectic reappears in the differing emphases of his work as a Christian polemicist and his work as a writer of fantasies. Moreover, the dialectic is carried on within the fantasies themselves. No one would ever mistake Lewis's books for the work of anything but a Christian writer. But the two tendencies do not fit together very well. If Lewis's basic strategy is escape, Christianity is the armor and weaponry he dons to cover his escape. But it also slows him down. Lewis's polemics keep him faced toward the enemy, modern society, he would flee. In fact, as a general rule the more explicitly Christian his writing becomes, the less it convinces the reader. But fortunately for Lewis's career as a writer, his polemical voice became less obtrusive as time went on. Gradually he came to write of worlds in which the doctrines of Christianity are often just distant parallels, adding resonance to the imagined situation. In the later work, as in all good literature, the fictional world has a strength of its own, a fullness of imagination, which will sustain the weight of Lewis's ethical concerns.

NOTES

1. Chad Walsh, "C.S. Lewis: The Man and the Mystery," in *Shadows of Imagination*, edited by Mark R. Hillegas (Carbondale, Ill.: Southern Illinois University Press, 1969), p. 1.

2. Clyde S. Kilby, *The Christian World of C.S. Lewis* (Grand Rapids, Mich.: Wm. B. Eerdmans, 1964), p. 13.

3. In *Light on C.S. Lewis*, edited by Joycelyn Gibb (New York: Harcourt, Brace & World, 1965), p. 24.

4. Joy Davidman, "The Longest Way Round," in *These Found the Way*, edited by D. W. Soper (Philadelphia: Westminster Press, 1951), p. 24.

5. What is even more interesting about this narrative is that Joy Davidman later married Lewis. Sometime after the composition of this narrative (as Clyde Kilby notes), Gresham began to drink again, and finally she divorced him. Afterward she went to England where she became Lewis's secretary. In 1956 she became Mrs. Lewis.

6. Nevill Coghill, "The Approach to English," in *Light on C.S. Lewis*, p. 60.

7. Walsh, "C.S. Lewis: the Man and the Mystery," p. 11.

8. Owen Barfield, in *Light on C.S. Lewis*, pp. xi, xii.

9. Ibid., p. xiv.

10. Walsh, "C.S. Lewis: the Man and the Mystery," p. 3. In his introduction to *The Pilgrim's Regress*, Lewis defines the important term "Romanticism": "What I meant was a particular recurrent experience which dominated my childhood and adolescence and which I hastily called 'Romantic' because inanimate nature and marvellous literature were among the things that evoked it.... The experience is one of intense longing" (p. 7). Lewis goes on to say that it is distinguished from other desires by two things: (1) though it is painfully intense, it is desirable in itself, and (2) the object of the desire is a mystery.

11. Richard B. Cunningham, *C.S. Lewis, Defender of the Faith* (Philadelphia: Westminster Press, 1967), p. 141.

12. See Clyde Kilby's *The Christian World of C.S. Lewis* for a survey of Lewis criticism.

13. "Tutor and Scholar," in *Light on C.S. Lewis*, p. 83.

14. *Light on C.S. Lewis*, p. 76.

15. Chad Walsh, *C.S. Lewis: Apostle to Skeptics* (New York: Macmillan, 1949), p. 57.

16. Ibid., p. 59.

17. *Light on C.S. Lewis*, p. 82.

18. Ibid., p. 83.

19. Walsh, "C.S. Lewis: the Man and the Mystery," p. 12.

C.N. MANLOVE

The 'Narnia' Books

Of all post-war English children's books the 'Narnia' sequence is probably one of the most deservedly famous, and *The Lion, The Witch and the Wardrobe*, not merely for its striking title or for the fact of its being the first of the seven books published, has particularly stuck in the public imagination. In these books it is fair to say that Lewis gave back to children's literature some of the 'high seriousness' that—*pace* Kipling, De La Mare and Masefield—it had been without since the work of George MacDonald, Lewis's literary and spiritual mentor, in the nineteenth century. Certainly, appearing as they did when the vogue for the works of Enid Blyton was still at a peak among British children, the Narnia books came as a welcome relief for parents, librarians and educationalists who had long looked for contemporary works of literature for children which would not pander to the 'baser literary instincts': but of course this would have meant nothing and the books would have gone the way of many a tiresome tract for juveniles in the past, had it not been that they actually delighted children themselves. Lewis's particular skill lay in teaching almost 'without meaning to': he tells a 'straightforward' story of children entering a fairyland and meeting all sorts of delightful creatures and exciting adventures, and before the reader knows what has happened he has traversed the central story of the Gospels—not as a story of someone two thousand years in the past, but as one in the

From *C.S. Lewis: His Literary Achievement.* © 1987 by C.N. Manlove.

immediate present of school holidays and railway stations, the recurrence of which makes the reader feel not just that the story is being brought up to date but that it is one that is happening again and again and is everlastingly contemporary.

Why, after his fiction for adults, did Lewis turn to children? In all his work he shows the belief that the child has more clarity and directness—though not more innocence—of vision than an adult. Lewis also valued literature of that character—that is, the fairy tale. Even his last work of the 'space-trilogy', *That Hideous Strength*, he called 'a fairy-tale for grown-ups'. His essay of 1956, 'Sometimes Fairy Tales May Say Best What's to be Said' shows the way his literary temperament had been moving. The innocence of the Lady in *Perelandra* is partly founded on the psychology of a child. Lewis is no sentimentalist regarding the child: he simply regards children as more open to experience, and more open to being changed by experience. In many of his previous books he had described a process by which adult protagonists, without forfeiting their grown-up perspective, stripped themselves of preconceptions, opened themselves more fully to what was before them. John in *The Pilgrim's Regress* must shear away all the modernist, worldly and philosophical clutter that grows around his original childhood desire and vision of an island till he can find the naked truth: after he has done so he makes the return journey to the place of his childhood, which is nearest to God's house and, since the world is round, just the other side of the channel from the point he reached in his full conversion to belief. Ransom in *Out of the Silent Planet* and *Perelandra* learns to undo his adult suspicions and inhibitions and open himself to full experience of strange new worlds; Mark and Jane Studdock in *That Hideous Strength* must rediscover a childlike—not a childish—yielding of themselves to better directors than themselves of their confused lives (which is partly why the term 'director'—the one true, the other false—is used of Ransom and of Wither in that book). In *The Great Divorce* it is precisely that the ghosts shut themselves into themselves, while the 'solid people' want them only open themselves a little to objective awareness of Heaven and to trust, that is the central distinction: the ghosts will not give up their old selves, the defences and lies they have built over time. Even in *Till We Have Faces*, published in the year of the last of the Narnia books, the love of Orual for Psyche (partly 'the soul') was at its best when unthinkingly and freely given in childhood. But we must make no mistake: Lewis is very far from believing children incapable of depravity, as will be seen in *The Lion, the Witch and the Wardrobe* itself: he simply believed that the evil could be more readily isolated, was less hidden beneath long-constructed trappings of adult rationality and evasion, and therefore might be more readily removed. He felt too that children's consciences were more acute, and that a sense of evil done could ultimately work more to cure than to deform: Mark Studdock has to learn what guilt is, while Edmund Pevensie and Eustace Scrubb are quick to feel it (though Eustace has to have the 'adult' mental trappings of his progressive schooling stripped away first).

Lewis vowed that he never 'wrote down' to children, or even that his awareness of them as an audience seriously conditioned his writing: 'I was ... writing "for children" only in the sense that I excluded what I thought they would not like or understand; not in the sense of writing what I intended to be below adult attention.'[1] This is typically precise, but it refers to the state of mind in which the material is presented rather than to the material itself. We are still going to find, given Lewis's own 'child' interests, pages devoted to homely beavers, paw-sucking bears and loyal badgers; descriptions (if restrained) of meals; gifts (Father Christmas enters Narnia in *The Lion*); and an element of protection of the children and a general scaling of the narrative to their taste: so that death and violence where they occur are muted, and reality simplified to its basic constituents. There is nothing intrinsically wrong with this, if it does put a bar between the world of the adult and of the child except via condescension or sentimentality. If there is any problem, it is that we feel the 'adult' Lewis behind it writing what he thinks is appropriate for a child: it does not always seem to come quite naturally. More recently, children's writers have tried to get more of 'everyday' and 'dangerous' reality into their books. In Lewis's time and the fifties generally children were no doubt more amenable to moral instruction. But the problem of writing to the real world that children inhabit, and particularly the urge not to treat them as a separate species, is a perennial one. Lewis wrote to his idea of the child, but there are many others.

The problem lies not just here but inside some of the works too. Lewis, basically, wants his children to behave like adults. They are to grow up spiritually—yes, certainly from the childish to the childlike—but also they are to learn to manage their world. At the end of *The Lion* the children have literally grown up into Kings and Queens of Narnia. The difference is striking if we compare Lewis's work with that of MacDonald or of E. Nesbit, his other literary model in this area. In *At the Back of the North Wind* (1870) and *The Princess and the Goblin* (1872) MacDonald has his child-characters exist among adults: little Diamond in his family or with the great maternal figure of North Wind, Princess Irene with her nurse Lootie and more importantly her 'grandmother' whom she befriends in the topmost room of the castle in which she lives. In such a context the children can exist naturally as children, and, on occasion, something more: and MacDonald has succeeded in creating wonderful child characters. There are semi-adult figures in *The Lion*—the Beavers, or Aslan—and certainly Aslan could be said to 'protect' Edmund from the evil White Witch: but the children are the sole humans in Narnia, being called Sons and Daughters of Eve and Adam. We have to see them at once as children and as 'grown-up' in relation to Narnia: Edmund's yielding to the Turkish Delight offered by the White Witch and his betrayal of his siblings is seen both as the act of a thoroughly naughty boy and as a piece of primal treachery requiring the ultimate sacrifice on Aslan's part.[2] Of course, for Lewis, mere size is nothing, and 'proportion' alien to the Christian view of reality: the smallest act may be of enormous significance. (His use of Reepicheep the mouse as hero in the Narnia books is almost symbolic of this.) But that is not quite the same as viewing the act two ways at once. Constantly throughout the narrative of this particular Narnian book we feel the uneasy juxtaposition of children and child-adults: quite what are we doing except in wish-fulfillment with a child who leads an army into battle? In the work of E. Nesbit, the children 'bounce off' or are shut away from the adult world: in *Five Children and It* they are granted one wish per day which expires at sunset, and the story portrays their crucial inability as children to do other than get themselves into 'scrapes' with them; in *The Story of the Amulet* the children continue, despite their visits in time to a great number of past civilizations, to behave precisely as their normal and very varied child-selves. In asking us to believe in his children both as children and as adults, Lewis is sometimes in danger of forfeiting our belief in them as either.

But these are hard sayings, and in general the Narnia books are a wonderful success, not least because of Lewis's endless fertility of invention—which is not to say that these books are not strongly rooted in past literature. It may be that the child-characters or the scale of the action are not always easy to take at the level required, or that the 'niceness' of the 'animal' characters becomes on occasion a bit cloying, or that the moralizing, for all its integration, is at times oppressive—but what remains most in the mind is the wealth and purity of Lewis's imagination; his ability to create so consistent a world in Narnia, so potent an image of the heart's desire in *The Voyage of the 'Dawn Treader'*, so beautifully handled an utter transformation of reality in *The Last Battle*, so quietly suggestive a narrative as *The Silver Chair*, so much joy and yearning as comes through *The Magician's Nephew*; and even more than this, his power to capture great primal rhythms, Christian and pagan alike, through the fabric of his stories, and to make the whole series together form a total picture of Christian history from the First Things to the Last.

In considering the 'Narnia' books the first issue is their sequence. In order of publication yearly from 1950 to 1956 the books are *The Lion, the Witch and the Wardrobe, Prince Caspian, The Voyage of the 'Dawn Treader', The Silver Chair, The Horse and His Boy, The Magician's Nephew* and *The Last Battle*. So far as the history of Narnia goes, however, *The Magician's Nephew*, which describes the creation of Narnia and its Talking Beasts, comes chronologically first. Then comes *The Lion, the Witch and the Wardrobe*, where we are first introduced to the Pevensie children Peter, Lucy, Susan and Edmund, and Aslan the lion undergoes a voluntary sacrifice to the White Witch for Edmund's sake, after which he rises again. After this is *The Horse and His Boy*, which takes place during the time, briefly summarized at the end of *The Lion*, when Peter and the others reigned as Kings and Queens of Narnia before they returned home. In *Prince Caspian*, the children return to Narnia to restore the rightful king Caspian to the throne of Narnia. In *The Voyage of the 'Dawn Treader'*, Edmund and Lucy, together with their unpleasant cousin Eustace Scrubb, find themselves in Narnia aboard a ship on which Caspian is voyaging to find some of his father's banished friends and perhaps discover Aslan's country far to the east. In *The Silver Chair* a reformed Eustace and his friend Jill Pole have to carry out a task appointed for them in Narnia by Aslan. Finally in *The Last Battle* a battle in Narnia is the prelude to the final destruction of that world by Aslan and a journey by the central characters, via progressively more 'real' Narnias, towards Aslan's country, or Heaven: it is a vision of the Last Judgment.

It might seem perhaps more reasonable to consider the books in this chronological order, rather than that of their publication: but the benefits of reading them in their published order outweigh such ordering.[3] In any case, accidental though the sequence in which the books appeared may have been, for Lewis as for his protagonists 'there is no such thing as chance or fortune beyond the moon' (*Perelandra*, p. 135). But this apart, to read them simply in narrative sequence would impose something of a grid on the series (just as say, it would ruin *Paradise Lost* to read it in chronological order): to open *The Lion* and suddenly come upon the magical world of Narnia and encounter its inhabitants without prior explanation of whys and wherefores quite simply heightens wonder and increases our sense of the sheer 'this-ness' of the world. Mystery and strangeness are of the essence. What would *The Lion* be if the children were not constantly wondering at and gradually having opened to them some of the nature of Narnia? First they have to go through the process of variously doubting its existence; then they encounter its strange inhabitants, find out why it is always winter there, are told of and meet Aslan, and so on. Often the books themselves are structured to heighten mystery. Part of the pleasure of *Prince Caspian* comes from the gradual realization by the children that the island ruin to which they have been transported is the remains of their old castle of Cair Paravel when they ruled in Narnia, and that though they have been absent only a year in their world, a thousand years have passed in Narnia. The whole story of how they came to be called into Narnia is then gradually unfolded for them by a dwarf messenger—so that the narrative sequence is deliberately jumbled, and we stop present events to hear of separate and past ones that led to them. But this desire to interrupt the temporal sequence may have a deeper motive still. In eternity all acts are eternally co-present, and the last exchanges its nature with the first: may not this violation of sequence in the Narnia books be an imitation of precisely that? Not that that has always been so in Lewis's work: the three books of the space trilogy are sequential, developmental and culminative (if the planet we start with, Malacandra, is the oldest; and if we except the fact that Ransom's story in *Perelandra* is told by him after he has returned to Earth, in a kind of temporal loop). But in Lewis's view of reality, arguing from past to present events is futile, where 'All is new': and certainly these children's books mark as radical a departure in literary genre from his space-novels as they in turn did from his allegory, and that from his poetry— and as *Till We Have Faces* (1956) would from everything before it. 'We operate, mostly, in sequence, but sequence is not all.'[4].

THE LION, THE WITCH AND THE WARDROBE (1950)

This book describes the discovery by first one and then three other children of a door into a strange new country called Narnia, through the back of an old wardrobe in an empty spare room of a rambling old country house owned by their uncle, where they have gone for the holidays. Narnia is in the power of a tyrannical White Witch who has caused the country to be gripped in a perpetual winter and has reduced its inhabitants, a variety of Talking Beasts, to servitude and fear. As in fairy tales, there is one way by which the Witch may be overthrown: the enthronement of two 'sons of Adam' and two 'daughters of Eve' on the four thrones in the castle of Cair Paravel; the Witch herself is a daughter of the evil Lilith, Adam's first wife. The arrival of the children, who as humans are sons of Adam and daughters of Eve, threatens to bring this about. The children are as magical to the Witch as she is to them, and to the Narnians they are also magical in being of the human race (which is of far greater antiquity than Narnia). Thus Lewis cleverly suggests that all worlds are in their own way full of magic; though it has to be said that in other books he does not make our world seem so, usually portraying it as a place of tedium, whether going to or stuck at school, from which removal to Narnia is a glad release. The Witch, realizing that the four children threaten to bring about the prophecy, tempts one of them, Edmund, into putting his brother and sisters into her hands. The perceptiveness of Talking Beasts with whom the others are staying forestalls this, and the arrival of the also long-foretold lion Aslan, bringing spring with him, prevents it. But the Witch demands Edmund's life as forfeit to her under the ancient Law, since he has been guilty of treachery. Aslan acknowledges her right in this, but offers to substitute himself for Edmund, and duly dies under the Witch's knife, while she tells him that she will kill Edmund anyway. But Aslan rises again by a 'Deeper Magic' from before the dawn of time, and the powers of the Witch are defeated and the children enthroned at Cair Paravel. After they have ruled for a number of years, a hunt they make one day in pursuit of a White Stag leads them to the forest where they entered Narnia and through the back of the wardrobe once more to their own world at exactly the same time as they left it all that seeming time ago.

The very title of the book, *The Lion, the Witch and the Wardrobe*, suggests that it is a kind of amalgam of different things: and that is indeed the case. There is a sense in which at least three separate crystallizations of the imagination have occurred in it, in the forms of Aslan, the White Witch, and the strange means of conveyance into Narnia.[5] The book is a compendium of different figures and motifs. Even with the children, we deal with them less as a group, as in later books, than in separation from one another. Lucy goes into Narnia first on her own and is not believed by the others. Then Edmund enters and meets the Witch; then all four enter, but soon divide into two sets of adventures, as Edmund leaves the others at the Beavers to tell the Witch about them. The two girls remain near Aslan at his death and afterwards go with him on his risen body to the palace of the Witch to release the creatures of Narnia imprisoned in stone there. Later they return with Aslan to the boys to help them in their desperate battle with the forces of the Witch. We move from a Faun to talking Beavers, from Father Christmas to sacrificial death, from Turkish Delight to Ancient Magic, from snowdrops to resurrection and from fur coats to fir trees. It is as if Lewis delights in the juxtaposition of as many different things as he can, and in refusing us any settled view or position. The book is almost a cornucopia, or, in other terms, rather like a Christmas stocking, full of various and mysterious objects all held together by one container. Indeed the presence of Father Christmas with his diverse gifts, from a sluice-gate for Mr Beaver to a magic cordial for Lucy, may not be the anomaly in the story that some have found it. This is to some extent a story about gifts—the gift of Narnia to the children as an adventure (if later more demanding); the gift of Aslan to Narnia to turn winter to Christmas (always so poignant for children) and then to spring with its flowers; the gift of Aslan's life itself in place of Edmund's; the gift of the four children as the long-promised human rulers of Narnia, topping off the 'unfinished' hierarchy of the Talking Beasts with their natural and supernaturally sanctioned sovereignty. Indeed it is in the light of its being a box of increasing delights that the book is perhaps best appreciated—not that some of the delights are to be won without difficulty or through grace. It is in a sense a story of Paradise Regained.

One of the recurrent motifs of the story is the relation of fiction to reality. What kind of reality does Narnia have that it has a lamp-post in it? Or, for that matter, a Faun whose behaviour when Lucy meets him is distinctly reminiscent of the White Rabbit when Alice first sees him; or a Witch who has evidently come straight out of the pages of Hans Andersen, beasts from Beatrix Potter and Kenneth Grahame, and a Christ-figure from the Bible? For the Narnians, man himself is fictive: the Faun Tumnus has among his books such titles as *Men, Monks, and Gamekeepers: a Study in Popular Legend*, and *Is Man a Myth?*

Edmund and the others think Lucy's Narnia is a fiction at first. At the end, as they become translated into Kings and Queens and described by use of the 'high style' of romance, the children become fictionalized in relation to us. In the book the old prophecies come true: fiction turns to fact in this sense also. In the book Aslan becomes a fictional version of Christ: yet in a world of talking animals is it not right that the image of the King of Beasts should offer himself in sacrifice for man? (In *The Last Battle* the children see that Aslan has other images than that of a lion.) And all of this raises the question of whether our own world is more or less real or fictional than Narnia, a question answered in *The Last Battle* when both are shown to be of equal (un)reality. By reenacting a fiction, that is the pattern of the story in the Gospels, Aslan accomplishes a fact.

Throughout the story we and the children are prevented from settling to any one level of reality: always there is something further beyond what appears. The unprepossessing wardrobe in the bare spare room with the dead bluebottle on the window-sill is a doorway to Narnia. The charming Faun is a deceiver. The Talking Beasts are concealed. The Witch deceives Edmund. The beasts at the Witch's castle seem to Edmund alive but are actually stone—and in one case, vice versa (ch. 9). The winter of Narnia is a false one, though felt as real enough. When Edmund has been rescued from the knife of the Witch and we feel him safe, the Witch returns to claim his life by a 'Law' we could never have supposed. Then, when all seems hopeless,

Aslan offers himself and the Witch thinks *she* has won. And then, by the deepest Law of all, Aslan rises again and overthrows the Witch and her schemes. What seemed dead flesh to the children becomes a miraculously risen lion. Then, after the 'children' have become Kings and Queens they are suddenly returned one day from Narnia to their former selves in their old world. We move through the story, 'farther in' to deeper and deeper levels of reality. In a sense the wardrobe itself is a symbol of this: as the children go into it they find they do not come to its back; Lucy goes through one row of coats, then another, then, wondering at the size of the wardrobe, finds a crunching under her feet which eventually reveals itself to be snow, while the coats become fir trees. The wardrobe, gives something of a smoothness of transition between one reality and another, however: other shifts in the story are to be far more abrupt, forcing us more violently out of previous assumptions and expectations.

Many of the 'Narnia' books have as a theme the awakening of something. In *Prince Caspian* Caspian has to waken the absent powers of the first Kings and Queens of Narnia,[6] and bring the Talking Beasts of Narnia from their hiding places, while Aslan rouses the trees, the gods of water and of nature generally. Part of Caspian's eventual object in *The Voyage of the 'Dawn Treader'* is to wake from their slumber three of the seven exiled lords of Narnia. In *The Silver Chair* the aim of the children's quest is to release Prince Rilian from his imprisonment by the Witch on the silver chair in Underland. The children in *The Magician's Nephew* ignorantly waken the evil queen Jadis on the planet Charn, whence she reaches Narnia; but there too Aslan the lion calls life into being in the sky and on the earth. In *The Last Battle* everything is called to judgment and Narnia is revealed as part of a larger hinterland of Heaven. But this theme of awakening is particularly and fittingly marked in *The Lion, the Witch and the Wardrobe*. There the land is woken from winter to spring. The long frozen stasis gives way to motion: ice and snow turn to water, the hard ground thaws and flowers appear, time moves on in a land that like the Sleeping Beauty or the world of Dickens's Miss Havisham has stood still. And with the overthrow of the Witch the frozen statues of animals in her castle are returned to life by the breath of Aslan:

> I expect you've seen someone put a lighted match to a bit of newspaper which is propped up in a grate against an unlit fire. And for a second nothing seems to have happened: and then you notice a tiny streak of flame creeping along the edge of the newspaper. It was like that now. For a second after Aslan had

breathed upon him the stone lion looked just the same. Then a tiny streak of gold began to run along his white marble back— then it spread—then the colour seemed to lick all over him as the flame licks all over a bit of paper—then, while his hindquarters were still obviously stone, the lion shook his mane and all the heavy, stone folds rippled into living hair. Then he opened a great red mouth, warm and living, and gave a prodigious yawn. And now his hind legs had come to life. He lifted one of them and scratched himself. Then, having caught sight of Aslan, he went bounding after him and frisking round him whimpering with delight and jumping up to lick his face.[7]

This passage, incidentally, shows some of Lewis's strengths. The analogy with the newspaper at once roots the magic in the everyday and literally makes the scene 'come to life' for us. The sentences, short at first, spread in length as, like a flame, life spreads; then they shorten themselves as the lion collects himself before the last longer one in which all of him comes to life and he bounds after Aslan, trying to lick him as he breathed on him. A fine touch is 'all the heavy, stone folds rippled into living hair': the heavy, stone folds feel heavy because each word is separated by comma or consonantal disjunction, and each has a similarly sonorous and weighty stress; the 'rippled into living hair' reads like lyric, with trochaic metre, light, open sounds and a rising rhythm. The whole passage also stands in counterpoise to the earlier passage when Edmund came to the castle and on seeing the lion, thought at first he was alive (p. 88): here what seemed 'dead' comes to life. But of course the great awakening in the story is that of Aslan's resurrection itself, through which these later awakenings are possible: he seemed to be dead, reduced on the slab first to a helpless, bound, static thing and then slain, but the next morning he is there, literally larger than life and twice as natural (p. 147), to dance and romp with the children.

What of other awakenings? The Talking Beasts are roused from their torpor. Aslan returns to Narnia at the same time as the children enter it to change all things. The evening scenes that characterize the first scenes of our visits to Narnia, to Mr Tumnus, and the Beavers, change to morning as time begins to move and winter moves on to Christmas (p. 98); there is to be one other night, the dark night of the soul of Aslan's death, but after that no more, and with these changes the moon imagery associated with the Witch (pp. 85, 125, 136—perhaps symbolic here of coldness and sterility) gives way to sunlight with Aslan's resurrection: 'the red turned to gold along the line where the sea and the sky met and very slowly up came the edge of the sun' (p. 146).

The transformations of the book are also from monotony to variety. The Witch is a tyrant. Her evil is one of selfishness. What she does with it is never clear. She simply spreads herself over all Narnia in the form of a dead white frost, allowing nothing else independent life: the unchanging monotony of winter is her symbol. When she and Aslan talk together (the suggestion of familiar discourse driving them more surely. apart), 'It was the oddest thing to see those two faces—the golden face and the dead-white face—so close together' (p. 128). When her power goes, colour and variety return to Narnia, imaged in the 'zoo' of different creatures brought to life by Aslan in the castle courtyard:

> Instead of all that deadly white the courtyard was now a blaze of colours; glossy chestnut sides of centaurs, indigo horns of unicorns, dazzling plumage of birds, reddy-brown of foxes, dogs and satyrs, yellow stockings and crimson hoods of dwarfs; and the birch-girls in silver, and the beech-girls in fresh, transparent green, and the larch-girls in green so bright that it was almost yellow. And instead of the deadly silence the whole place rang with the sound of happy roarings, brayings, yelpings, barkings, squealings, cooings, neighings, stampings, shouts, hurrahs, songs and laughter. (p. 153)

Corresponding to all this the reigns of the children when they become Kings and Queens are full of variety and activity in contrast to the profitless stasis of the Witch's reign: they root out the remaining evils, drive back marauding giants, make alliances with surrounding nations which enable Narnia to enter from isolation into a community of countries; and at home they make just laws, keep the peace, stop good trees from being unnecessarily cut down and above all promote the freedom of the individual which the Witch has so long suppressed (p. 166).

The Witch, as the daughter of Lilith, is a vampire, a drawer of life from things to herself, and one who lives only with the unnatural and the deformed—with Hags, Werewolves, Minotaurs and the like. She drains the vitality from Narnia, literally 'bleeds it white', and she would with her dagger do the same to Aslan. But where she can only take, Aslan delights to give. The contrast between the two is caught in different passages describing them surrounded by their followers. This is Aslan:

> Aslan stood in the centre of a crowd of creatures who had grouped themselves round him in the shape of a half-moon.

There were Tree-Women there and Well-Women (Dryads and
Naiads as they used to be called in our world) who had stringed
instruments; it was they who had made the music. There were
four great centaurs. The horse part of them was like huge English
farm horses, and the man part was like stern but beautiful giants.
There was also a unicorn, and a bull with the head of a man, and
a pelican, and an eagle, and a great Dog. And next to Aslan stood
two leopards of whom one carried his crown and the other his
standard. (p. 115)

and this is the Witch:

A great crowd of people were standing all round the Stone Table
and though the moon was shining many of them carried torches
which burned with evil-looking red flames and black smoke. But
such people! Ogres with monstrous teeth, and wolves, and bull-
headed men; spirits of evil trees and poisonous plants; and other
creatures whom I won't describe because if I did the grown-ups
would probably not let you read this book—Cruels and Hags and
Incubuses, Wraiths, Horrors, Efreets, Sprites, Orknies, Wooses,
and Ettins. In fact here were all those who were on the Witch's
side and whom the Wolf had summoned at her command. And
right in the middle, standing by the Table, was the Witch herself.
(pp. 136–8)

We start with Aslan; we end with the Witch. Life radiates outwards from
him, but it is all drained and funnelled towards her. It is our first meeting
with him and in a sense he needs no introduction: he is what the children
have long known in their deepest hearts (p. 65), he is *Yahweh*, 'I am'; his name
is an act and he is all the creatures that emanate from him in the passage. The
creatures in the passage have arranged themselves about Aslan in order, 'in
the shape of a half-moon'; in the second passage the Witch's followers are
simply a crowd about the Stone Table; and there is no living centre to their
group, only stone. The creatures in the first passage are portrayed in a
hierarchic order: we move through a chain of being from the Dryads and
Naiads, spirits of the trees, to the centaurs, half man, half-animal, then to a
fabulous animal (the unicorn) and to a man-bull, and soon to the (still faintly
symbolic) Dog; there is some reminiscence of the beasts of *Revelation* 4, 6–7,
here. Then the passage ends as a circle, symbol of perfection, taking us back
to Aslan, who as it were surrounds and embraces the whole. The leopards

who heraldically bear his standard remind us that here to be a beast is to be also far more than a beast, and that hierarchy can also involve equality: the idiom of Narnia is one in which the animal body rejoices to embrace whatever intelligence or spirit it may (in *The Last Battle* the Talking Beasts who do not go to Heaven lose the ability to talk and become mere beasts as they pass into Aslan's shadow). In the passage describing the Witch there is no hierarchy: ogres (level of 'men') are followed by beasts (wolves), then by beast-men, then by spirits of trees, then by plants. What was a beast becoming human, the man-bull, in the first passage, has become a man turning to a beast, a creature with head of brute and body of man, the Minotaur. There is a sense of perversion in the poisonous plants. Finally whatever the reason Lewis politely gives, the effect is of sinking away to evil as nonentity, a matter of obscenities: we know only intermittently anything of that list of 'Cruels and Hags and Incubuses, Wraiths, Horrors, Efreets, Sprites, Orknies, Wooses, and Ettins'. The beasts in the first passage have gathered voluntarily about Aslan; those in the second have been summoned by the Wolf at the Witch's command. She knows nothing of freedom and individuality.

It is not without significance that the 'good' are continually surrounded by a variety of objects—the very detailed description of the interior of Mr Beaver's house with all its furniture and tackle hanging up and even the tea things (pp. 66–72) is an emblem of this—while the Witch in her spiny castle seems to have nothing about her in her empty rooms, apart from the white statues of the creatures she has frozen by her magic. All she can do is reduce things—the living to frozen, life and colour to one dead white, time to stasis, Aslan to a dead corpse, even herself to a mere stump (p. 125). Or pervert them, as she tries to cheat the laws after holding Aslan to them (pp. 140–1). Aslan is treated as more than a lion by the 'good', but as less than one by the followers of the Witch as they cut off his mane before his death and speak to him as a mere cat, '"Puss, Puss! Poor Pussy.... How many mice have you caught to-day, Cat? ... Would you like a saucer of milk, Pussums?"' (p. 139; it will be an ironic undercutting of their ignorant insults that mice will come to bite away Aslan's bonds (pp. 144–5)).

The end of the narrative involves an opening out, a breakdown of the enclosure of evil that previously gripped Narnia. The Witch's castle, hemmed inland between two hills, is invaded and broken open to release the reawakened statues. The castle of the new Kings and Queens is by the wide sea with its wild enchantment: at their coronation, 'through the eastern door, which was wide open, came the voices of the mermen and the mermaids swimming close to the shore and singing in honour of their new Kings and

Queens' (p. 165). The sea looks towards Aslan's land, far to the uttermost east, and the sunrise. During their reign the children open up Narnia to contact with other countries.

It is in keeping with Lewis's portrayal of the good that they have most of the attention in the book. We do not see the evil figures very much, apart from the White Witch. Her dwarf is anonymous. There is a brief vignette of her chief of police the wolf Maughrim, but that is about all. But the characterization of the Talking Creatures is striking by comparison: Tumnus the Faun, superficially the nice furry person asking Lucy to tea, but actually a deceiver, and then a deceiver ashamed of himself; Mrs Beaver, very motherly and so concerned with the little things that she can ignore the large, and even contemplate taking her sewing machine with her when they have to flee from the grasp of the White Witch; the amiable but stupid giant Rumblebuffin; the over-excited lion who has to be 'steadied' when woken by Aslan. And of course Father Christmas, every different flower of awaking spring, the revealed variety of Narnia itself, all add to this sense of diversity.

As for Aslan himself, he is Lewis's finest 'creation' (if he can be called that, since in a way he is 'traditional'[8]), a creation of such quintessential lionhood that he becomes what he is, far more than lion. The Witch we see from the outset, but he is the being long anticipated and heralded through Father Christmas and growing spring. And when he comes and is seen, he is purely himself: 'Aslan stood' (p. 115). No simple, single thing he: he contains and reconciles some of the most energetic opposites: 'People who have not been in Narnia somehow think that a thing cannot be good and terrible at the same time. If the children had ever thought so, they were cured of it now. For when they tried to look at Aslan's face they just caught a glimpse of the golden mane and the great, royal, solemn, overwhelming eyes; and then they found they couldn't look at him and went all trembly' (p. 117). Nor is he a goodness hidden from creatures: he is actively among them, helping, enlivening, fighting, dancing and rolling with the children after he has risen from his death; yet in a way he is the 'farther' also in being the 'nearer'. He can be shamed, his lionhood stripped from him and he for all his divinity, reduced to a bald helpless thing, and yet in his offered shame the glory of his true pride is validated.

The children, too, are quite strongly individuated: Lucy, the youngest, is the kindest and most generous of heart: she wants to help the Faun, she suffers Edmund's early jeering over her 'belief' in Narnia, she is quick, perhaps too quick, to help him when he is wounded in the battle (p. 163). She is the first to find Narnia: she is the most spiritually perceptive; not for nothing is her name Lucy, from lucidity or *lux*, 'light'. Peter often relies on her for decisions: he feels that she has more insight. He himself is brave, considerate, practical and steady—hence with him, too, 'Peter', from 'a rock'. Susan changes during the narrative. She is a slightly impatient teenager, a little concerned to look after herself, and rather unwilling to take things as they come: one of her most frequent questions is '"But what are we to do?"' (pp. 49, 54, 62, 134); she is rather inclined to give up at difficulties (pp. 57, 78); and, less perceptive than Lucy, she thinks at first that the mice about Aslan's dead body are mere vermin (p. 144). But by the end it is she who sees before Lucy how Edmund must be spared the knowledge of how Aslan gave his life for him (p. 163); she has grown, if only for now.[9] Edmund at first is jeering and rather malignant; he finds nothing wonderful in life and disbelieves in Narnia at once until he finds it himself; his greed for the sweets of the Witch expresses something of the insatiable need of evil to fill itself by devouring; and he is to devour others, to draw even his own siblings towards the Witch. Only the shock that is administered to him by his experience of evil, and Aslan's subsequent mercy, save him. He is no simple villain, for his conscience revolts against what he is doing (p. 83): and perhaps the cruel treatment of him by the Witch, and his extraordinarily difficult journey to her castle through the cold and snow (p. 84), express not so much what is being done to him by others as what is being done to him by his own soul, and his gradual movement towards a spiritual change that otherwise might seem rather abrupt. The different characters of the four children—perhaps their moral characters rather than their personalities as such—always come over strikingly. When they first see Mr Beaver beckoning at them from behind a tree in the forest,

> 'The question is,' [said Peter] 'are we to go to it or not? What do you think, Lu?'
> 'I think it's a nice beaver,' said Lucy.
> 'Yes, but how do we *know*?' said Edmund.
> 'Shan't we have to risk it?' said Susan. 'I mean, it's no good just standing here and I feel I want some dinner.' (p. 62)

Always one feels with the 'good' that one is finding out more about the nature of reality. First there is Narnia itself behind our world; then, Narnia itself changes from winter to spring, and at the end from land to seaside. The ground rules seem to alter continually: the story almost depends on continual breaking of expectations. The Witch has only one notion of reality—a frozen world and a threat contained in a prophecy about four humans: she clings to this and her little knowledge of the law myopically. She is shut in her castle,

confined to the limited consciousness of her frozen realm, while Aslan walks
free over many realms, taking many forms, and in Narnia is always seen on
the move, having 'no fixed abode'. Aslan by his death puts down a tap root to
a deeper and more universal reality than she could know. The random, too,
has pattern behind it, and yet is still 'free'. The children come to Narnia 'by
chance' it would seem, simply happening to use the wardrobe as a hiding
place and then finding that they could go through its back. It could have been
any children, surely? And any time? Yet when they are in Narnia they
gradually find out that there is a prophecy concerning two sons of Adam and
two daughters of Eve arriving to overthrow the Witch and take the four
thrones in Cair Paravel: clearly they fit it, children though they are, and their
arrival itself is in one way predetermined. There is another prophecy too,
concerning the return of Aslan: again, only gradually, do we and the children
come to see that the two prophecies are not coming true separately, but are
bound up with one another.

    Yet still, no prophecy is a determinant: acts of choice and will have still
to be made. Aslan finds dying no easy matter: the choice is hard, the pain of
the soul very real, the shame and indignity very great. Nor do we see that his
death will at best do any more than save Edmund—and even this is undercut
by the Witch in her last malicious words to him (pp. 140–1). Later we see the
deeper reality of which Aslan knew but perhaps could not feel; but only then.
Peter and Edmund are nearly overwhelmed in battle and the latter badly
wounded. Death and danger are real enough, however much one may be part
of a pattern of prophecy. This interplay of freedom and the foreseen, of the
random and the patterned, also contributes to the dancing variety that is
goodness in the story. *The Lion, the Witch and the Wardrobe* may have its
uneasy moments, but as a work of full and various vision it is a marvellous
beginning to the Narnia series.

PRINCE CASPIAN (1951)

In this story the same four Pevensie children are at a railway station on their
way back to their various boarding schools when they find themselves
suddenly pulled by a strange force back into Narnia. They are in what they
find to be the ruins of Cair Paravel. They rescue a dwarf messenger who has
been sent to them but intercepted by enemies. He explains to them that they
are in Narnia one thousand years after they left it, since when it has been
invaded by men from the neighbouring land of Telmar. The present ruler is
a usurper called Miraz, who has seized the throne from his nephew Prince
Caspian and forced him to flee for his life. Caspian has succeeded in awaking

many of the long-dormant Talking Beasts of Narnia (warred on and suppressed by the Telmarines, who detest all wild things) and enlisted them on his side in a battle currently being fought about the hill at Aslan's How (a hill cast up above the stone table where Aslan was killed, and honeycombed with tunnels). Caspian has in his possession the magic horn of the High Queen Susan, which she left behind her on her last leaving Narnia (an accident again with a purpose): it is said that when the horn is blown at need, the first Kings and Queens will return to Narnia; and this is what has happened to the children (not through their choice, but who knows?). Caspian knew that they would arrive at one of three places particularly associated with them, of which Cair Paravel was one, and dispatched messengers to meet them.

The rest of the story describes the journey of the children with the dwarf, Trumpkin, towards Aslan's How. The landscape has changed since their time, and though Lucy has a view of Aslan inviting them to follow him, the others decide to ignore it and soon find themselves out of their way. Eventually, however, they reach Caspian, save him and his loyal followers from a *coup* by a renegade dwarf Nikabrik who has leagued himself with evil powers, and overthrow Miraz and his forces. Thereafter Narnia is liberated from various forms of Telmarine tyranny; the Talking Beasts and all the gods and spirits of Narnia are restored to freedom; Caspian is enthroned; the Telmarines are given the choice of returning to the realm (actually on this Earth) from which they originally came or joining with the new Narnian society; and the children once more return home, or rather to the railway station from which their adventure began.

In some ways the story is similar to that of *The Lion, the Witch and the Wardrobe*. The same children are brought to Narnia to save it in its hour of need. A tyrant has usurped rule of Narnia, and the Talking Beasts have long been silenced and driven into hiding. Caspian's struggle with the army of Miraz is going against him until Aslan and the children come, just as happened with Peter and Edmund in their battle against the forces of the Witch. Under the influence of Caspian and Aslan, the Talking Beasts and natural powers of Narnia are roused, just as they were by the children and Aslan in *The Lion, the Witch and the Wardrobe*. The duel between Peter and Miraz is to some extent paralleled by that between Peter and the Witch. The story ends with the establishment of a true King, and a feast.

In a sense this story reiterates at a practical and immediate level what was realized more spiritually in the first book. There, Peter, Edmund, Susan and Lucy were made High King and King and Queens after defeating a force of much more metaphysical evil: the White Witch is categorically different from the fairly bumbling wickedness of Miraz. In becoming Kings and Queens the children as it were established Kingship in Narnia: the prophecy of the Talking Beasts had long looked to the arrival of two Sons of Adam and Daughters of Eve to sit in the thrones at Cair Paravel and complete the unfinished hierarchy of being in Narnia by the addition of men and women. But for the everyday historical necessity of having a succession of Kings, we have to look elsewhere. Narnia is invaded by the men of Telmar and they establish a line, of which Caspian is the tenth of that name in succession. When the children return, Narnia has changed historically and geographically over a thousand years, and they themselves have sunk once more to the status of legends. They return Narnia to something of the spiritual condition it had at the end of *The Lion*, but in this story they are establishing not themselves but another as King. The story has moved from a symbolic context of the establishment of the First Things to the more directly secular levels of politics and sociology. We are in a more everyday world now, where issues are a little more confused.

Confusion is in fact one of the motifs of the story; if not always to reflect realism. Even when the children are first taken to Narnia their sense is one of bewilderment as they are whirled from the station platform. When they arrive they cannot be sure they are in Narnia; and the place where they are is so overgrown and geographically altered that they cannot for long recognize it as Cair Paravel; even more confusing for them is to be the dawning knowledge that they are in Narnia one thousand years beyond the time when they left it a year previously. Meanwhile Caspian has found the world more complex than he supposed. His tutor Dr Cornelius (another 'confusion', for he looks like a small man but is later to reveal himself as part-dwarf) has told him that his uncle Miraz has usurped the throne that is rightfully his; and has disclosed that Narnia is actually inhabited by Talking Beasts, as Caspian's nurse once told him and his uncle punished her for so doing. And later, when Miraz has at last succeeded in begetting a son; Cornelius tells Caspian that his uncle's previous favour to him as eventual successor will now cease and that he must flee the court. In the forest to which Caspian eventually comes in his flight, he loses his way and is stunned when he collides with a tree branch; he wakes to be confused by the appearance of the strange man approaching him, only to realize with a shock that it is a badger. The world is always showing itself more multiplex and disorientating than one might have supposed.

In fact, finding one's true bearings in it is also one of the issues in the book, as the children try to find their way to where Caspian is, and continually lose themselves or become sidetracked. Narnia itself has lost its own true bearings as the Talking Beasts have been suppressed and as the true King has been banished; indeed one can say that general disbelief in the Talking Beasts has clouded reality and made the medium of Narnia one of uncertainty. When Caspian winds Susan's horn to call back the High King and the King and Queens to Narnia, he does not know which of the three possible places in Narnia they will arrive at, even supposing they hear his call. Trumpkin the dwarf finds reality steadily more confusing than his practical commonsense mind would have supposed, and he is eventually forced to accept a larger view of reality—first that there really are 'ghosts' as supposed in these parts, then that what seem to be mere children are in fact the High King and his companion King and Queens, then that Aslan is a real and immediate being. As for the children, they themselves are given only individual or uncertain views of Aslan on their journey, and doubt and disobey him: in the medium of this world it seems, he will not at first appear plainly, though as all clears at the end, he does so. Nikabrik the dwarf is a striking example of confusion: his no-nonsense practicality has changed to a hard-bitten contempt for Caspian's trust in the First Kings and Queens, and that to a readiness to compromise with the evil, even the White Witch, to gain the ends for which they all seek: '"They say she ruled for a hundred years: a hundred years of winter. There's power, if you like. There's something practical.'"[10] Miraz is tricked by his lords into agreeing to a single combat with Peter: he himself becomes involved in an uncertain world, and overthrown by it.

True, at the end, all things are cleared. In a journey that owes much to that of Princess Irene and Curdie and their strange retinue of creatures into the city of Gwyntystorm at the end of George MacDonald's *The Princess and Curdie* (1882), the girls and Aslan and their Bacchic followers enter the Narnian capital Beruna and scour it: in one school a pupil who can see Aslan joins them, while the remainder, including their teacher Miss Prizzle, are driven out; in another (and it is still typical of the book to refuse us simple responses to reality) it is the teacher who is saved and the pupils turned to pigs (pp. 170–3). Then there is a separation among the Telmarines: those who wish to make themselves one with the new Narnia stay, while the others go back to the 'other' country from which they came, through a magic doorway set up by Aslan. Last, there is a separation of one King from others: the children go home leaving Narnia to Caspian. But one feels, despite this general and very real movement from confusion and uncertainty to order and clarity, that the ambiguities of the world as we have experienced them are somehow more native to it than they were in the last book, and that we have been in touch with a 'realer', harder, more resistant Narnia than before.

   This also comes out in the emphasis on the Narnian environment and the much closer contact with it. The first thing the children find when they are transported to Narnia is that they are 'standing in a woody place—such a woody place that branches were sticking into them and there was hardly any room to move' (p. 12). Then when they have struggled out of the wood they find themselves on a seashore with no land in sight: they smell the sea, wade in it, walk on 'the dry, crumbly sand that sticks to one's toes'; then they explore the shore, walking along it till they find another shore opposite them, but though the two grow closer they never meet, and eventually they realize they are on an island. There follows the discovery of a stream, and they walk up it as far as they can until they are forced to 'stoop under branches and climb over branches, and they blundered through great masses of stuff like rhododendrons and tore their clothes and got their feet wet in the stream' (p. 17). And so on, forcing their way through crowding trees into a ruin, making a fire out of sticks and cones, suddenly realizing that they are in Cair Paravel, locating the door of what should be the treasure room behind thick ivy, cutting away the ivy in great dumps with Peter's knife and then, when it breaks, Edmund's penknife, pulling the rotten wood of the door to pieces and exposing the dark, dank and draughty place behind. In *The Lion, the Witch and the Wardrobe* there was less sense of this contact with the environment: one most felt it with the evil, as when Edmund was struggling through the snow and by the frozen stream to the Witch's castle, or the Witch was finding the runners of her sledge stick as the thaw increased. Here it is pervasive. Caspian in his exile goes literally underground, first in being taken to the badger Trufflehunter's sett and then in putting his army inside the hill of Aslan's How. The whole long journey of the children and Trumpkin towards Caspian is a trek over a series of natural obstacles—the sea, a creek, a forest, a precipice along which they wrongly force a way to try to find a route down to a ford over a river before having to return, a difficult descent, a river crossing, a climb up a path over a precipice, and so to Aslan's How. All this makes us have a strong sense of Narnia as a particular and solid place. There is indeed much less sense of perspective over the whole place than there was in *The Lion*: here there are so many forests that we could not have that anyway. Narnia, which seemed a relatively small realm in the first book, has grown into its true size and self as it were, over time: distances have become very real, and the doings and nature of one part can be radically separate from those of another—Beruna here, Caspian there, the children far off there; the narrative describes a convergence of all the participants. What we feel throughout the story is a growing sense of the complex 'personality' of Narnia. And we may note that the personalities of the characters—certainly the children and Trumpkin in their interactive group are even more highly developed in this book than in the last: one is continually noting idiosyncrasies.

Throughout we feel the centrality of nature's power. The civilized castle of Cair Paravel has been reduced to an ivy-covered ruin, surrounded by an orchard gone wild and a forest. What was a promontory on which the castle stood has been turned over time to an island. As we have seen, during the children's journey they are constantly thwarted by natural objects and lost in a changed landscape. Caspian is as it were taken by the earth in the badger's sett. He chooses to lodge his army inside a hill. The Telmarines came to the world bordering Narnia not through an artifice (a wardrobe, a picture), but through a 'natural' cave in a mountain on a South Sea island on Earth (pp. 184–5). Partly this emphasis on nature is thematic. The Telmarines have established the rule of man in Narnia. They have built towns, roads, bridges. They have disinherited the Talking Beasts of Narnia. They will have nothing to do with raw nature: they cut down trees wherever they can and are 'at war with all wild things' (p. 60). They are particularly afraid of the wildness that is Aslan, and, knowing from the stories that he comes from over the sea, they have let the coast become impenetrably wooded so that none may reach it: '"But because they have quarrelled with the trees they are afraid of the woods. And because they are afraid of the woods they imagine that they are full of ghosts. And the Kings and great men, hating both the sea and the wood, partly believe those stories, and partly encourage them"' (p. 53).[11] This is another example of the confusion in Narnia. In a sense the Telmarines have severed themselves from the land itself, which '"is not the land of Men"' but '"the country of Aslan, the country of the Waking Trees and Visible Naiads, of Fauns and Satyrs, of Dwarfs and Giants, of the gods and the Centaurs, of Talking Beasts"' (p. 50).

This is one reason why the 'good' are put so closely in contact with the land, for Narnia is everything that is in it, even its earth and its water (which themselves come to prominence and some life at the end). The children have to struggle with their environment; they have to eat the raw meat of a wild bear. Caspian, taken into the ground, comes to see that as man he has no higher status necessarily than the creatures for which he should care (especially when they are *talking* creatures). Nikabrik refers to him as '"this Human"' and speaks of not letting 'it' '"go back to its own kind and betray us all"' and Trumpkin retorts, '"It isn't the creature's fault that it bashed its head against a tree outside our hole"' (p. 63); 'creature', 'it', 'its own kind'— suddenly Caspian, no longer in control, is being treated like an animal himself. What was a sense of hierarchy with the creatures looking for man in

The Lion, the Witch and the Wardrobe, has become more of a sense of corrective equality here. (In *The Lion* the beasts had no men to 'round them off'; here the men have shut out the beasts.)

And the wilderness that the Telmarines shut out is to return. Aslan, long feared by them, comes back. At his great roar the wildness of Narnia is set loose in the awakened trees, and its very essence returns in the frenzied dance of Bacchus, Silenus and their Maenads (pp. 135–8). The trees smash Miraz's army (pp. 167–8). Then Aslan, the two girls and Bacchus and his Maenads approach the river Beruna and beyond it the town. The river god rises and asks Aslan to loose his chains: under Bacchus's influence ivy spreads over the bridge and pulls it down (pp. 169–70). The town is invaded and most of its inhabitants flee: the dancing crowd go out into the country and break all bonds: 'At every farm animals come out to join them. Sad old donkeys who had never known joy grew suddenly young again; chained dogs broke their chains; horses kicked their carts to pieces and came trotting along with them' (p. 171). All the works of man seem swept away, and his civilization with it. It perhaps may give the impression that bridge or town building are bad ideas, which is unfortunate: the only real intent here is to show wildness reasserting itself, righting the balance of its excessive neglect; we are to suppose that since the direction of the narrative has been to make Caspian king, we are not ending with some primitivist manifesto: the Telmarines built bridges because 'they all hated and feared running water just as much as they hated and feared woods and animals' (p. 179). At any rate all thereafter gather together to feast—men, beasts, dwarfs, trees, gods and Aslan—and Narnia once more belongs, as it did long ago, 'to the Talking Beasts and the Dwarfs and Dryads and Fauns and other creatures quite as much as to the men' (p. 182).

The total journey of Caspian himself has been one to incorporate and bring back with himself all these other levels of being. He has followed the pastoral movement of a departure from the court or city to the wildness of nature and then back again with new and redeeming power, as we see it in Shakespeare's *As You Like It* or *The Winter's Tale*. His journey itself imparts to him a regality he could not otherwise possess: 'To sleep under the stars, to drink nothing but well water and to live chiefly on nuts and wild fruit, was a strange experience for Caspian after his bed with silken sheets in a tapestried chamber at the castle, with meals laid out on gold and silver dishes in the anteroom, and attendants ready at his call. But he had never enjoyed himself more. Never had sleep been more refreshing nor food tasted more savoury, and he began already to harden and his face wore a kinglier look' (p. 76).

The process of the story is one towards increasing meeting and community. At first separated from the court, Caspian meets in the forest with his 'various strange subjects' (p. 76). The children journey to join with him. From being alone he becomes increasingly surrounded by friends (though enemies too). At Aslan's roar all Narnia starts into life. The group of different children and the dwarf Trumpkin form an emblem of relationship and—to some extent—cooperation. What is fighting Miraz is not Caspian or even his army, but the whole tormented nature of Narnia itself. At the end, the harmony of king and country is re-established. Presiding over the whole is the promise contained in the rare conjunction of the stars that his tutor Dr Cornelius shows Caspian one night in Beruna before telling him the truth about Narnia, '"Their meeting is fortunate and means some great good for the sad realm of Narnia. Tarva, the Lord of Victory, salutes Alambil, the Lady of Peace"' (p. 49; see also p. 72). He describes the meeting of the stars as a dance, and dances pervade the narration, from the circling dance of the Fauns in the forest, in which Caspian takes part, to the 'Great Chain' of dancing trees that Lucy sees by night during the journey of the children (p. 122); and from the dancing trees and Bacchic Maenads round Aslan (pp. 136–8), or the dancing invasion of Beruna and its environs (pp. 170–4), to the dance of the trees and the Bacchic crowd that makes both the fuel and the food for the great chain of being that holds all the creatures and beings, even down to the varying earth itself of Narnia (pp. 180–1), in harmony and unity.

There is one other recurrent motif in the book. It concerns faith in the unseen.[12] It is perhaps a symptom of the solidity of the world of Narnia that this should be a central issue. The Telmarines and Miraz refuse to believe in the existence of the Talking Beasts. Trumpkin finds it hard to accept the children as Kings and Queens of Narnia. At the edge of the gorge Lucy sees Aslan beckon her, but the others do not believe her, and all are led out of their way until they trust blindly. Nikabrik the dwarf does not believe in the magic power of the horn Caspian blows to summon the Kings and Queens back to Narnia, and he comes to lose faith in any possibility of success against Miraz except through the use of evil powers. 'Seeing' is the crucial image here: if one looks with 'commonsense', or with sloth or evil, one will not see; only if one's imagination and love are awake and ardent. When Lucy sees Aslan in the forest, 'She never stopped to think whether he was a friendly lion or not. She rushed to him. She felt her heart would burst if she lost a moment' (pp. 122–4). It would seem that during the story Caspian has in a sense had to slough off some of the sin of his Telmarine ancestry, for when Nikabrik brings into his council in Aslan's How two sinister creatures, it is only gradually that Caspian is able to see the evil for what it is, and in doing so perceive plainly the identities of these others: '"So that is your plan,

Nikabrik! Black sorcery and the calling up of an accursed ghost. And I see who your companions are—a Hag and a Wer-Wolf!"' (p. 147). Perhaps even the debate between Caspian's good and bad counsellors here is a debate within his head—certainly the imagery of the closed room in which it takes place is suggestive; and one has felt something of a 'faculty psychology' at times elsewhere in the narrative, in the various relationships of the children and Trumpkin (the gorge they come to and the response to Aslan there reminds us of the allegory of John and Virtue offered the help of Mother Kirk at the gorge in *The Pilgrim's Regress*).

Prince Caspian is in large part an exploration of Narnia, opening it up for us and extending and thickening our awareness of it. At the end of *The Lion, the Witch and the Wardrobe*, Narnia remained a fantastic realm. The children returned in a sudden jerk from their grown-up, Narnian personalities, described in high style, to the colloquial world of holidays in the Professor's house in a country they had for 'decades' forgotten. At the end of *Prince Caspian* the children have been in Narnia for far less time; they know they are going back to their own world before they do so; and they themselves change back into their school clothes in Narnia. When they have arrived back through Aslan's door at the railway station from which their adventure started, Edmund's first words are '"Bother! ... I've left my new torch in Narnia"', as though Narnia were as real as a holiday cottage or a bus—or a home.

THE VOYAGE OF THE 'DAWN TREADER' (1952)

This story introduces a new child character. Peter and Susan at the end of their last adventure have been told that they are now too old to return to Narnia. Edmund and Lucy are staying with their thoroughly unpleasant cousin Eustace Scrubb, who has been brought up by 'progressive' parents. One day they are all looking at a picture in Lucy's room of a Narnian-looking sailing ship, and Eustace is disparaging it, when suddenly the picture comes to life and enlarges about them until they are absorbed into it and find themselves in the sea near the boat, whence they are rescued. On board they find King Caspian, who, after having established his reign, has set out on this ship, the *Dawn Treader*, to sail east to and beyond the Lone Islands to find the seven lords, friends of his father, who were sent away over the sea by Miraz. The fighting mouse, Reepicheep, who has come with him, has larger ends in view: he wants to sail to Aslan's land, which he has long desired. After a series of adventures, during which Eustace's unpleasantness is largely cured by his being turned into a dragon, and it is found that three of the lords are dead and the other four variously enchanted, the ship journeys on to the very end of the world and near to Aslan's land, when Reepicheep leaves and the children also receive an inner prompting to go. Caspian, who wishes to go there also, is dissuaded through a (reported) interview with Aslan from doing so, and returns home to rule Narnia. What happens to Reepicheep is not revealed; but the children come ashore through a great, stationary wave to a flat grassy place where the sky meets the earth. A lamb meets them; it feeds them with fish roasting on a fire. Then the lamb becomes Aslan, and tells them that they will be returning to their own world. Aslan says that now Edmund and Lucy will not return to Narnia because they are too old; and when Lucy wonders how they will live without him, he tells them that he is in all worlds, though in different guises: '"there I have another name. You must learn to know me by that name. This was the very reason why you were brought to Narnia, that by knowing me here for a little you may know me better there."' Then he 'opens' the sky and returns the children to the room from which they started their adventure.

This book is distinctive in the 'Narnia' series for its episodic structure. There is a central line of progress, from Narnia eastwards to the world's end, but along the way a series of incidental adventures occurs, quite separated from one another at the narrative level, and each highly individualized. On an island Eustace suffers his transformation by sleeping on a dragon's hoard (as in *Perelandra*, Lewis is not very fond of 'sleeping' in this book), and has to be helped by Aslan to make a painful repentance and return to human shape. Another island has on it a pool that turns everything that enters it to gold; on another is a collection of bizarre monopods called Dufflepuds, and a magician Coriakin whose spell book tempts Lucy to knowledge and power. On the sea the voyagers encounter a giant sea serpent, and a huge area of darkness in which they discover and rescue one of the seven lost Narnian lords who has been confined on an island there, at the mercy of nightmares. The last island on the journey is that of another magician, Ramandu, where the three remaining Narnian lords are found in enchanted sleep: only a spell brought back from the world's end will wake them. The final part of the journey enters a great sea of clear sweet water which eventually becomes covered by lilies, until the *Dawn Treader* reaches water too shallow for further progress save by rowing boat.

In many ways it would seem that Lewis has exploited the loose structure of his narrative to create little islands of the imagination *en route*. Obviously they are not all simply 'for themselves': the transformation of Eustace into a dragon accomplishes his moral transformation, and the experience of the spell book 'develops' Lucy a little too. There are those who maintain that the whole idea of a directional journey implies a spiritual journey in the book:[13] and it has been argued that Caspian in particular develops throughout.[14] But there is not very much evidence of this. True, he is impractical in going ashore on one island early on with only a few companions,[15] for he is captured and sold by slavers, but an advance in common sense is hardly the same as a spiritual progress. And when he is tempted by greed at the gold-making pool (p. 111), so are the others, for the cause is as much magical as otherwise. At the end he is still impetuous in his—quite natural—desire to go to Aslan's land, and has to be corrected by Aslan himself. These moral moments really do not make much of a connected sequence, nor do they show much development: rather Lewis seems simply to happen on a failing at one point than to have thought in terms of growth.

Is there then any pattern behind the narrative? There is something of a hierarchic movement, after we leave the last known or Lone Islands, where Gumpas the Governor and a crowd of pirates and slavers are overcome: for thereafter we meet first a dragon, then a Sea Serpent, then the stupid dwarfs, the man reduced to terror on the dream-filled island, the sleeping men in Ramandu's land and some sea-people. And as far as magic is concerned, we progress from a transforming dragon's hoard, to an alchemical pool, to the magician-cum-former star Coriakin, who is confined to his island undergoing some kind of purgatory for past sins, to the 'good' star magician Ramandu; and thence to the Great Magician, the Lamb Himself, who has been present throughout the story as Aslan as much as at the end. In parallel with this we move from 'ordinary' to more and more mystical forms of magic action.

Then, in another way, the islands are potential symbols of selfishness, cut off from one another. The ship and its crew provide an image of the relatively cooperative organic body. But on most of the islands life has in some sense degenerated or can be perverted. The slavers on the Lone Islands treat people as beasts; the dragon hoard reduces people to dragons; the magic pool turns people to dead gold; the Dufflepuds are devolved dwarfs whose clumping forms express their nature; the lord on the island of dreams has been worn ragged by his experience; the slumbering lords at the table of Ramandu are covered by their own hair. The sin of selfishness abounds. Eustace for long shuts himself off from the rest of the community of the ship, refusing to co-operate. For love of gold the slavers and pirates of the Lone Islands prey on others. Gumpas, the Governor, has ceased to be responsible to Narnia; Caspian brings the islands back into the Narnian commonwealth. The dragons hoard makes more dragons to protect itself: Eustace finds it when he has got to the centre of an island, remote from the wide and 'connective' sea, and has fallen into a hemmed-in gully, symbol enough of the severed self. The gold-making pool awakens greed and discord in all who see it. The temptations of Lucy by the magician's book all relate to dilation of the self (pp. 131–4). The lord on the island in the darkness has been shut in on the dark self of his dreams; the lords on Ramandu's island are locked in slumber since they quarrelled. Caspian at the end casts aside his duties in his desire to go to Aslan's land.

By virtue of the very journey it makes, the *Dawn Treader* brings connection to the scattered selves of these places; and almost every enchantment is broken or overcome. The effect is one of a general release from captivity of the shut-in self: the slave markets of the Lone Islands (aptly-named) are removed, Eustace is released by Aslan from far inside his dragon body; the *Dawn Treader* itself escapes from the closing coils of the sea-serpent's body; the Dufflepuds are at least able to move off the island to play on the sea, though there is no escape from their stupidity; the Narnian lord is taken from his dark island and the others will be released from their slumber.

And there are other patterns. One is the increasing awareness of the presence of Aslan. He is not seen directly at all until almost half-way through the story, in Eustace's reported dream of him when he is released from his dragon form. He comes to Lucy after she has used the magician's book of spells. In the form of an albatross he saves the *Dawn Treader* from the darkness about the island of dreams, though only Lucy knows this (pp. 158–9). He interviews Caspian directly in his cabin after his wilfulness about going to the world's end. Finally he appears to the three children in his own country. His appearances here are much more restricted than in the previous two books (though there has been a progressive 'wind-down' from *The Lion*, where only he himself could intervene). Here they are journeying 'towards' him (insofar as he is in any place) rather than he coming in to Narnia. They are journeying in effect in a mystic progress towards a clearer and clearer sight of him. The operative text is 'For now we see through a glass, darkly; but then face to face.' As they come nearer to his land, the sea becomes so clear that the bottom is plain many fathoms down; and the sun is far larger and they all seem to move in excess of light (pp. 185–6); this marks a move from the slumber and darkness that characterized the immediately preceding adventures.

But clarity of detail, especially in the bright, elemental descriptions of the *Dawn Treader* and the sea, has been a leitmotif throughout of the almost heraldic world of this book. Failures of clarity are seen as evils from the start:

with Eustace's parents, who blur their identity by allowing him to call them by their first names; with Eustace, who in his diary falsifies his experience aboard the *Dawn Treader* into one of unmixed misery and persists in believing that Narnia is an ordinary place with a British Consul somewhere to whom he can complain; with Gumpas the Governor of the Lone Islands, a man of bureaucratic evasions and verbosity; with the Dufflepuds, who cannot think connectedly but are forever contradicting themselves or uttering tautologies as though they were discoveries, and have therefore fittingly been made invisible, 'unclear'; and even with the Sea Serpent, which is so stupid that it assumes without looking that its tightening coils will have crushed the *Dawn Treader* and is left peering along its body for the wreckage with what appears to be 'a look of idiotic satisfaction' (p. 104).

As befits the character of this book and its creation of so many strange worlds, the accent is on the imagination. Among his other defects, Eustace suffers from a lack of that faculty: 'He liked books if they were books of information and had pictures of grain elevators or of fat foreign children doing exercises in model schools' (p. 9; that word 'foreign' is unfortunate). Characteristically of this book he is going to be thrown into Narnia via a work of imagination, a picture, which comes to life—and a picture, at that, of a wholly 'fictional' ship. (This idea Lewis perhaps got from John Masefield's *The Box of Delights*.) The rest of the adventure he has to live inside a fiction, and he comes to accept it as as much of a fact as the ship that burst out of the picture in the bedroom. During the adventure he is turned into a creature of 'fiction', a dragon. The Dufflepuds are almost totally lacking in imagination; but in themselves they are brilliant creations of the comic imagination of a wizard: there they lie in afternoon slumber on the sunlit grass, each with its gigantic foot over it as a shade. The island of dreams is an island of the tormented imagination. But as we move through the adventures the imagination becomes less purely inventive, and more symbolic: it begins to draw on images of spiritual significance. The sea of lilies over which the *Dawn Treader* glides is an image of dying into a new life, and of purity (seen also through the sunlight and clarity of the water). The lamb who meets the children beyond the upreared wave is the Lamb of God, the same God who divided the Red Sea for the Israelites; when he tells the children, '"Come and have breakfast,"' and offers them fish roasting on a fire, he is the risen Lamb of God appearing to his disciples in John 21, 9–13; and his transformation to a lion calls on those reconciled images of lion and lamb (even Old Testament God and risen Christ) that are long hallowed in Christian tradition. And then, looking back, we begin to see that the whole narrative, in journeying eastwards, has been journeying to the sunrise of the everlasting day (perhaps the boat's name, *Dawn Treader*, coming into its own at last).

Even the landscapes are suggestive. We have left islands and come to a continent. We seem to have come to the increasingly horizontal: the first islands are more or less hilly, but Coriakin's island is flat, that of Ramandu is gently undulating (befitting in part the slumber on it), the sea thereafter is flat with lilies, the place where the children meet the lamb is a flat area of grass. Yet heaven, or Aslan's land, finally defies the imagination: try as we may we cannot put together the pictures of a giant, still wave, a grassy area with the sky coming right to the ground behind it and yet at the same time include those huge far-off mountains that the children see as part of this land. In a sense throughout the book we have moved to the increasingly imaginative—a heroic sea-journey, a dragon, Sea Serpent, Dufflepuds, Ramandu—and beyond, to the point where imagination fails.

The book is shot through with what Lewis called the 'dialectic of Desire', *Sehnsucht*. Every move the boat makes further to the east is a pull on our imaginations, all the more strong for the fact that each stage has put the last totally out of sight, whether by storm or darkness, or by simple endless travelling. (It is only from an immense height that Jill Pole in *The Silver Chair* is to see the various island stages of the journey strung out across the sea from Aslan's land as she is blown across the sky by Aslan towards Narnia.) Before us is the pull of that great name, the World's End (Lewis felt that the title itself of Morris's *The Well at the World's End* was almost enough without the novel[16]). When will we reach it? What will it be like? We join the *Dawn Treader* when it has left most of the known lands east of Narnia and has only the Lone Islands to come. And beyond them—what? The mind ranges freely, tipped off the edge of the world, filled with wonder at mystery. In the first two books the objectives soon became known—the establishment of the first Kings and Queens, the defeat of the White Witch, the restoration of Caspian. But here the goal is mysterious: no one can know of Aslan's land, none along the route have anything but vague hints to give of what lies further to the east from their immediate locations. Every island and experience we come to seems charged with mystery, as a station on the way: how near, we wonder, are we to the end? Will this place provide a key to it? Lewis whets the desire finely with the marvellous variety of the places along the *Dawn Treader*'s route: it was a fine touch, for instance, not to have a simple increase of poignancy but to mix with it an element of the comic and even the grotesque in the picture of Edmund trying to write with his dragonish claws in the sand, or of the stupid Sea Serpent—or best of all, that wonderful mixture of comic fantasy and high seriousness in the Dufflepuds (so surely created) and the dreadful love of Aslan's meeting with Lucy. Even at the end Lewis is still doing this: Ramandu's island is sublime, and the misfortunes of the three lords are real, but their appearance even then is grotesque, with their hair so overgrown that they are 'nearly all hair' (p. 165).

The longing in the story is partly raised by a desire for the unknown, but it also comes from the knowledge that the unknown is the wholly 'other': no simple magic realm or wondrous place lies at the end of this quest; rather these are all passed on the way. Something whose mystery and simplicity transcends and includes them all lies still further, and still beyond the sight of all save a few—and even then what we see is not the heaven that Reepicheep presumably finds. In a sense we learn as we move that though like Tolkien we may have desired dragons with a profound desire, they are not the end, of all desire; and so with all the other wonderful places we visit. Though the breath of the numinous is strong throughout the story, romantic yearning becomes altered to a more mystical longing as Aslan is more in evidence and the magicians more his executives; until finally as the rowing boat crosses the last of the sea of lilies,

> suddenly there came a breeze from the east, tossing the top of the wave into foamy shapes and ruffling the smooth water all round them. It lasted only a second or so but what it brought them in that second none of those three children will ever forget. It brought both a smell and a sound, a musical sound. Edmund and Eustace would never talk about it afterwards. Lucy could only say, 'It would break your heart.' (p. 206)

Here Lewis has realized, if in a romantic context, something of that journey in search of the source of desire that he has portrayed in more self-conscious and explicatory form in *The Pilgrim's Regress*. Of course, the images, and the picture such as we have it, of Aslan's land, are all inventions. The whole story is a fiction, the creation of one C.S. Lewis. How can these possibly touch any reality? But that is the question that Lewis, like George MacDonald, is asking us of the creations of the imagination. Where do they come from? If they move us, are they not more than personal? To confuse the images themselves with the source of the desire is certainly a mistake: that is why Lewis has led us from one to another throughout and still left us with a mystery. But they carry the mystery, as the breeze carried that nameless something to the children. In his earlier Narnia books Lewis made us see and perhaps some of his child readers believe a little in the Deep Magic of God: here, perhaps more surely than anywhere else in his work save

Perelandra, he makes us feel it. He does it without drama, without the heavy romantic cadences of a Dunsany, with his imagination balanced by intellect and common sense, and with those pictures from beyond the world anchored in everyday reality. As the voyagers pass over the clear water on the way to the World's End, Lucy sees a black thing under the boat continually expanding and diminishing in size, and then realizes what it is through a remembered likeness:

> It was like what you saw from a train on a bright sunny day. You saw the black shadow of your own coach running along the fields at the same pace as the train. Then you went into a cutting; and immediately the same shadow flicked close up to you and, got big, racing along the grass of the cutting-bank. Then you came out of the cutting and—flick!—once more the black shadow had gone back to its normal size and was running along the fields.
>
> 'It's our shadow!—the shadow of the *Dawn Treader*,' said Lucy. 'Our shadow running along on the bottom of the sea. That time when it got bigger it went over a hill. But in that case the water must be clearer than I thought! Good gracious, I must be seeing the bottom of the sea; fathoms and fathoms down.' (p. 186)

Later, as the *Dawn Treader* crosses the sea of lilies, we find the practical sailors wondering how lilies could grow in such deep water; and have it explained to us that an 'undersea' girl Lucy saw, and who dropped quickly astern, did so because she was not in a current, about forty feet wide, in which the ship is being driven (pp. 199, 200). No better way could have been found to bring us close to the experience: but that way is part of Lewis's nature.

NOTES

1. 'Sometimes Fairy Stories May Say Best What's to be Said', in Lewis, *Of Other Worlds*, pp. 37–8.

2. There is something of a similar strain put on Tom's greed over Mrs. Bedonebyasyoudid's sweets in Kingsley's *The Water-Babies* (ch. 6).

3. Kilby, *The Christian World of C.S. Lewis*, pp. 116–46, and Walsh, *The Literary Legacy of C.S. Lewis*, pp. 130–57, prefer to consider the stories in their internal sequence. For further arguments for reading them in their published order, see Peter Schakel, *Reading with the Heart: the Way into Narnia*, pp. 143–5.

4. Charles Williams, *He Came Down from Heaven and The Forgiveness of Sins* (London: Faber, 1950) p. 92.

5. The idea of the wardrobe with no back might have come from the backless cupboard, opening on a tunnel, down which a strange shadow comes in George MacDonald's *Phantastes* (1858), ch. VIII (Stephen Prickett, *Victorian Fantasy* (Brighton: Harvester Press, 1979) p. 195 n. 57); however, as Green and Hooper, pp. 250–1, say, a more probable source is E. Nesbit's magic Bigwardrobeinspareroom in her 'The Aunt and Amabel' (1909). One general source of *The Lion, the Witch and the Wardrobe* is Roger Lancelyn Green's unpublished fantasy *The Wood that Time Forgot*, which Green gave Lewis to criticize: see Green and Hooper, pp. 239–40.

6. Actually when we have read *The Magician's Nephew* we find that they are not the first kings or queens or even humans in Narnia after all—for there an Edwardian cab-driver Frank and his wife Helen are made first rulers of the newly-created Narnia after they have 'accidentally' been brought there.

7. Lewis, *The Lion, the Witch and the Wardrobe* (London: Puffin Books, 1959) pp. 152–3. Page references hereafter are to this edition.

8. See Kathryn Lindskoog, *The Lion of Judah in Never-Never Land: God, Man and Nature in C.S. Lewis's Narnia Tales*, pp. 48–60, on the Old and New Testament uses of the lion as symbol.

9. In *The Last Battle*, however, we are to learn that Susan relapsed as she 'grew up' and put away what she considered the childish things of Narnia; so that she does not return with the others at the end of things in Narnia (ch. 12).

10. Lewis, *Prince Caspian* (London: Puffin Books, 1962) p. 145. Page references hereafter are to this edition.

11. Miraz, we learn, 'disapproved of ships and the sea' (p. 54). This dislike of the sea is ironic in view of the very name 'Telmarines', and the fact that these people are descendants of a race of pirates, sea-farers (pp. 184–5).

12. See on this Schakel, *Reading with the Heart*, pp. 36–43; Glover, *C.S. Lewis*, pp. 145–6.

13. Schakel, pp. 49–63; Glover, pp. 149–57.

14. Schakel, pp. 51–2.

15. Lewis, *The Voyage of the 'Dawn Treader'* (London: Puffin Books, 1965) p. 38. Page references hereafter are to this edition.

16. Lewis, 'On Stories', *Of Other Worlds*, p. 18.

JOE R. CHRISTOPHER

The Apologist

Lewis was a Christian apologist in the Latin root meaning of *apologia*: a defender. His training in argumentation under Kirkpatrick had prepared him to argue for his positions. After his return to Christianity in 1931, his turn to logical defenses of that faith is not surprising. Beyond the three books considered below—*The Problem of Pain*, most of *Mere Christianity*, and *Miracles*—in 1942 Lewis accepted the presidency of the Socratic Society at Oxford, which included the "discussion" of the arguments of anti- and non-Christian speakers.

Austin Fatter, in his essay "The Christian Apologist," makes a distinction between an apologist per se, who answers opponents, and an advocate, who advances arguments for a position—in this case, the Christian faith (Gibb, 23). Lewis is both, of course; but much of his writing of this period begins from a defensive position. Even the oddest chapter in *The Problem of Pain*, that on "Animal Pain," begins by saying the suffering of animals is worth discussing because "whatever furnishes plausible grounds for questioning the goodness of God is very important indeed." That is, the topic must be examined because someone might (or, perhaps, someone has) used it to deny an aspect of Christianity. This is a very generalized opponent, but the argumentative position is a defensive one. (One remembers how often the chapters in the latter part of *A Preface to "Paradise Lost,"* two years

From *C.S. Lewis*. © 1987 by G.K. Hall & Co.

later, begin from specific critics; despite the difference in concreteness, the rhetorical position is the same.)

Some of Lewis's essays deal with apologetics or advocacy, rather than just *being* them. The best of these is "Christian Apologetics" (1945) in which Lewis mentions a number of things he has learned from his military audiences—words that do not mean what educated speakers mean by them, and the lack of a sense of sin in the modern world, for example. Lewis also comments that he does not have the ability to give an emotional appeal, but has seen it done effectively by others.

In the last paragraph, Lewis comments that defending articles of faith is dangerous to one's own faith—because, for the moment, the defense "has seemed to rest on oneself" solely, which is a position of pride. He says much the same thing, more thoroughly, in a poem, "The Apologist's Evening Prayer" (1964).

A final point: since these books are apologetics, rather than scholarly or imaginative works, the references to Dante are sparse. In *The Problem of Pain*, one brief reference, listed in the index, and an allusion back to the first passage, not in the index. In *Mere Christianity*, probably due to its aim at a mass audience, no references. In *Miracles*, one minor reference; the index notes two, but it is wrong about the second.

THE PROBLEM OF PAIN (1940)

Lewis was invited to write a book on pain in the Christian Challenge series by a publisher impressed with *The Pilgrim's Regress*. Lewis's volume— or at least individual chapters—was read to the Inklings, and the book is dedicated to them. Dr. R. E. Havard, one of the group, contributes a brief appendix on his observations on patients' reactions to pain. (Charles Williams's *The Forgiveness of Sins* (1942), in the same series, is also dedicated to the Inklings.)

Lewis's book consists of ten chapters, of which the two beginning the second half, the sixth and seventh, are titled "Human Pain" and "Human Pain, *continued*" and sum up his main topic. But Lewis begins, "Introductory," by establishing the background for the intellectual problem: he shows that Christians and other moral theists do not argue from the universe to God, but rather find God in two ways, the experience of the numinous and intellectual apprehension of the moral law, which are then often identified as to source. (Christians add to their belief the Incarnation of God.) Rhetorically, Lewis's opening is arresting—"when I was an atheist"—and it gives substance to his denial of the argument from undesign.

Some of Lewis's antitheistic lyrics in *Spirits in Bondage* show that that argument at one time had been meaningful to him.

It is tempting to see this argument from the numinous to be parallel to Lewis's personal accounts of *Sehnsucht*, just as the emphasis on natural law obviously ties to Lewis's intellectual reasons for conversion to theism. It *may* be, but Lewis here begins from Rudolf Otto's *The Idea of the Holy* (in German, 1917), which assumes that a feeling of awe in the presence of the Wholly Other lies at the core of all religions. This sounds far stronger than the romantic longings that Lewis describes for himself. Certainly, he does not make the claim.

Lewis does not insist that the thesis of the numinous, antithesis of the moral, and synthesis of moral theism is a necessary dialectical development, but only one that the Jews in their religion generally and other great teachers individually have made. Lewis's argument for adding the Incarnation to moral theism is, as usual in his popular apologetics, brief and simplistic. Here he says that, given Jesus's claims for himself, he was either divine (as he said) or a madman. This argument probably goes back to John 10:19–21:

> There was ... a division among the Jews because of these words. Many of them said, "He [Jesus] has a demon, and he is mad; why listen to him?" Others said, "These are not the sayings of one who has a demon." (RSV)

Indeed, when Lewis restates the argument in *Mere Christianity*, he sets up a three-fold dilemma, making a distinction between two terms that the Jews in the quotation do not: either Jesus is divine or he is "a lunatic—on the level with the man who says he's a poached egg—or else (he is) the Devil of Hell" (bk. 2, chap. 3). One remembers that in *Surprised by Joy* Lewis tells of his arguing himself into moral theism but being converted less rationally to Christian belief. Probably he feels that the step from theism to Christian faith is not as presentable in his sort of intellectual terms as the first, and that his main work (explicit in *Mere Christianity*) is to keep a reader from saying Jesus is a great human moral teacher.

It is only when a powerful, moral God is posited that there is a problem of pain in the universe: why, Lewis asks in his second chapter, does the Christian God allow it? He begins with an elaborate syllogism, the major premise consisting of two related conditional statements; the minor premise denying the conclusion of the first conditional statement (and implicitly that of the second statement); and the conclusion therefore denying the first part of either or both the beginning conditions. If God is good, he will want his creatures happy; if He is omnipotent, he can do whatever he wants. But humans—his creatures—are not happy. Therefore .... Lewis goes on to question the popular meanings of the words as used in the syllogism—"Divine Omnipotence" in the second chapter, "Divine Goodness" and true human happiness in the third; in short, to deny the validity of the major premise.

The next two chapters, "Human Wickedness" and "The Fall of Man," open with a statement much like one point in the essay "Christian Apologetics": until modern people realize they are sinful, Christianity has little to say to them. The first of these two chapters attempts to convince the readers of their sinfulness, and the second is a fascinating attempt to establish the doctrine of Original Sin without being literalistic about Adam and Eve. Lewis offers "a 'myth' in the Socratic sense, a not unlikely tale." The myth (or fabulous history) starts with the evolution of mankind as animals to which, at some point in time, God gave the gift of self-consciousness and awareness of the true, the good, and the beautiful—Lewis does not point out the Platonism in the triple awareness. The rest of the account covers the Fall—that is, an act of self-will—and then dwindles into reflections on the event. This is not as concrete or specific as a Socratic myth often is, but the reader of Lewis can turn to the end of the ninth chapter of *The Magician's Nephew* to see Aslan breathing on animals and thus making them talking beasts to see the first part of this account vitalized. What is significant in *The Problem of Pain* is that Lewis does not believe the Adam and Eve story can be taken seriously by his audience at a literal level in a Darwinian age.

The first of the two chapters on "Human Pain" is the more significant one. A few personal touches appear: a brief discussion of sadism as an exaggeration (and hence perversion) of normal love, referring to it as among "the ugliest things in human nature," reminds a reader of Lewis's sadistic daydreams in his teenage letters to Arthur Greeves—Lewis is impersonally denouncing what he once enjoyed; a brief anecdote about his brother and him in their childhood days is a rare foreshadowing of Lewis's accounts of their drawings in *Surprised by Joy*. But Lewis's thesis is that pain awakens mankind to its human limits; he twice uses the image of pain as God's megaphone. Pain keeps mankind from accepting this world as a be-all; it may, but it need not, lead people to believe in God. Austin Fatter, in his excellent essay on this book, comments that Lewis sees the moral half of the truth, but that pain is also "the sting of death, the foretaste and ultimately the experience of sheer destruction" (Gibb, 40).

The chapters on "Hell" and "Animal Pain" are on special aspects of pain—the eternal suffering of the damned, and the suffering of animals in their carnivorous hierarchy. Perhaps four points from these chapters show Lewis's ideas that he displays elsewhere. First, in "Hell," he comments that second and later chances at salvation may be given dead souls, but only if God in his omniscience sees possibilities (certainties?) of salvation. Perhaps this is only a strategic allowance in the argument here, but in *The Great Divorce*, five years later, Lewis shows souls getting another chance—however, most of them are not saved. Second, in "Animal Pain," Lewis has a passage depreciating acceptance of climates of opinion; this is the reversal of his early, pre-Christian chronological snobbery for the present—and Barfield, he says in *Surprised by Joy*, was responsible for his abandonment of it (chap. 13). Third, Lewis's conjecture that the higher animals may gain immortality through their masters—while it drew a letter of objection from Evelyn Underhill, in favor of wild animals—explains the animals who surround Sarah Smith, the saint of *The Great Divorce*. Finally, Lewis's conjectures about some animals' corporate selves may explain why he was so impressed by the first Charles Williams book he read, *The Place of the Lion*, four years before this book. Alternately, the archetypal animals of Williams, including the titular lion, may lead to Lewis's reference to "Lionhood" and "a rudimentary Leonine self" here.

The final chapter, "Heaven," is generally unlike the other chapters in tone. It begins with a description of the emotional appeal of *Sehnsucht* that draws individuals toward Heaven; here Lewis assumes that all people have "these immortal longings." This and "The Weight of Glory," the year after this book, are Lewis's most important statements about *Sehnsucht* between *The Pilgrim's Regress* and *Surprised by Joy*, despite not having their framing works' personal application. Some of Lewis's statements in the middle of the chapter, such as that about the saints being all different since for each the longing has been somewhat different or that about the self-abdication of the saved, are perhaps closer to the previous tone of argument. The emphasis on self-abnegation here explains Owen Barfield's difficulties with the Christian Lewis who seemed to deliberately suppress self-knowledge: Lewis was trying to live by the principles he announced.

Just before the liturgical close of the chapter, Lewis introduces the image of the dance. This image in a limited way ties the book together. In the fifth chapter, Lewis described the universe ("world") as a dance "in which good, descending from God, is disturbed by evil, arising from the creatures." Lewis is here correcting the exaggeration of the implications of God's foreknowledge of the Fall, but the image is important. In the next chapter, in a very brief image, the act of doing good, of obeying God's commandments to do good, is called the "tread[ing] of Adam's dance backward"—in short, learning to obey instead of rebel. At the end of the book, these touches are developed in a seven-sentence image of Heaven as a dance. It is not that the image is used in the same way each of the three times; it is just that a motif is introduced, reintroduced, and then used in some detail. Consciously or accidentally, the celebration in the last chapter has been prepared for. (The best known example of this image in earlier English literature is Sir John Davies's *Orchestra, a Poem of Dancing* (1596), mentioned in *English Literature in the Sixteenth Century*, Lewis elaborates the image as the Great Dance at the end of *Perelandra*, published three years after *The Problem of Pain*.)

MERE CHRISTIANITY (1942–44; REV. 1952)

Due to the publication of *The Problem of Pain*, Lewis was invited to give a series of religious radio broadcasts over the B.B.C. His first series, "Right and Wrong," has been discussed in the previous chapter. The second series, "What Christians Believe," was given in 1942. As stated before, these two series were printed together. The third series, "Christian Behaviour," was broadcast in 1942 and published in an expanded form in 1943. The fourth series, "Beyond Personality: The Christian View of God," was broadcast in 1944 and published later that year. In 1952 Lewis's revised version of these four series appeared as *Mere Christianity*. Very occasionally, his correcting eye missed a reference, as when an "I said last week" appears (bk. 3, chap. 12).

The general movement of these four series of addresses—called books in *Mere Christianity*—is clear. Book 1 argues for moral theism. Book 2 moves through a variety of religious beliefs to Christianity and offers a brief account of the Atonement and the bases for Christian life. Book 3 (to be considered more thoroughly below) is on Christian morality. And book 4 had a different subtitle for broadcast: "Beyond Personality: or First Steps in the Doctrine of the Trinity." It took up these two parts in reverse order: the first four chapters, approximately, consider the Trinity, and the last seven, the individual Christian's need to die to his natural personality and to accept spiritual life from Christ in its place, to go "beyond personality." In short, the volume moves through a preparation for Christian faith, an argument for it, a Christian ethics, and, Lewis suggests (bk. 4, chap. 8), the main—the only significant—further step in the Christian life.

The structure of "Christian Behaviour" can be taken as an example of the smaller-scale structure and can also be discussed in terms of what it reveals about Lewis's approach to his material. When it was first published as a separate work, Lewis indicated on the contents page which chapters were approximately as they were given on the air and which were added for book publication. With the chapter numbers from *Mere Christianity*, the original talks were these:

1. The Three Parts of Morality
3. Social Morality
4. Morality and Psychoanalysis
5. Sexual Morality
7. Forgiveness
8. The Great Sin
11. Faith
12. Faith

In the first chapter, Lewis divides morality into personal, dealing with the inner self; social, dealing with relationships between individuals; and goalistic, dealing with the overall purposes of the adjustments undertaken in the first two. Since Lewis has made his arguments for Christianity in his previous book, "What Christians Believe," the overall purposes are simply assumed to be Christian in the rest of this book. Lewis uses an extended analogy of ships at sea—both a British and a wartime interest—to support his division: the ships must run internally, must not interfere with each other, and must have a port of destination.

The next chapters develop one side of this opening. "Social Morality," as its title indicates, mainly is concerned with society, not the individual. Christianity, Lewis suggests, supplies the principles—such as the Golden Rule—but not the applications for different times and cultures. He then offers three comments on the Christian society: (a) the New Testament suggests one that is leftist in economics and rightist in family hierarchy and manners; (b) the ancient Greeks and Hebrews and the medieval Christians all denounced the loaning of money at interest; (c) the giving to the poor is an essential part of Christian morality. With this Lewis's comments on society are finished, and he turns to the individual.

"Morality and Psychology" eliminates Freudian and other psychoanalytic help as a competitor to Christian morality. In private life, Lewis was hostile to Freudianism (LCSL, 179), but here he quietly distinguishes between Freud's philosophy, which is antireligious, and his psychoanalysis, which helps a person reach a point at which he can make moral choices—at that point, Christian (or some other) morality becomes pertinent. Then Lewis alternates between discussions of evil and good: "Sexual Morality" (the corruption of the modern world, with a delightful analogy of a country in which food is gradually revealed striptease fashion);

"Forgiveness" (opened in terms of forgiving the Gestapo, which in 1942 was attention catching); "The Great Sin" (pride); and two aspects of "Faith" (belief as a virtue, trust in God).

When Lewis revised these talks for publication, he added these chapters:

2. The "Cardinal Virtues"
6. Christian Marriage
9. Charity
10. Hope

Three of these chapters are interesting because they show Lewis the traditionalist in a special way. In the second chapter he begins a discussion of the seven virtues with the four that belong to the general human morality: Prudence, Temperance, Justice, and Fortitude. Then he adds Charity (chap. 9) and Hope (chap. 10) to Faith (chaps. 11–12)—the three theological virtues—to round out a discussion of all seven. Obviously, the three parts of morality (chap. 1) were not, for obscure reasons, satisfactory; he felt a need to add the number and division (4 + 3) of virtues as commonly given in the Middle Ages. The combining of both bases and resulting sequences in one book gives a greater complexity or a poorer organization (or both), as a critic wishes to argue.

"Hope" is of particular interest as another statement by Lewis of his *Sehnsucht* theme. It is here generalized: not put in terms of nature and books, as Lewis experienced it, but in terms of desire for various things—love, foreign travel, learning. Lewis says that, for the Christian, this yearning—never completely satisfied in this world—is meant to arouse a desire for Heaven, the "Hope" of the chapter title.

The chapter of Christian marriage supplements that on sexual morality; in it Lewis argues for the permanence of Christian marriage (not the same as secular marriage) and for masculine headship of the family. Logically, Lewis should have argued just for masculine headship of the Christian, not necessarily the secular, marriage; but, while beginning that way, he seems to drift into a general statement. Obviously, it is chapters such as this that have endeared Lewis to conservative readers. But this is unfair. By the time Lewis wrote *The Four Loves*, about seventeen years later (and as discussed in the last chapter), Lewis was still biblical but he was emphasizing the second half of St. Paul's phrase (Ephesians 5:25), stressing the husband's self-sacrifice. It is still not a position to delight any feminist, but it is also not one to give great comfort to the typical male supremist.

The other two books may be treated more briefly, since their theses were given above. An interesting image that runs throughout "What Christians Believe," no doubt especially effective in World War II when Germany was occupying much of Europe and wanting to invade England, is that of the world as enemy-occupied territory—that is, controlled by Satan. Lewis complicates this by having the rightful king landed in disguise to lead a sabotage campaign—that is, Christ is incarnated to overthrow Satan's rule. "Landed" suggests an invasion from sea, which was not unusual for saboteurs in Europe during that war. This image first appears at the end of the second chapter, is repeated at the opening of the fourth, and reappears in terms of God's invasion (Judgment Day) at the end of the fifth. The close of this book with the latter passage shifts from the usual clear exposition of these radio addresses to a more urgent appeal to make a Christian decision. Lewis uses three rhetorical questions in the last paragraph; four *when* clauses in four consecutive sentences; three *something*'s in one sentence; three *it will be* and one *that will not be* in four sentences; and, in four sentences, *choose, choose, choosing, chosen, choose.*

"Beyond Personality" may be used to mention one of Lewis's personal themes—perhaps paradoxically, given its title. But the same point that was made in the discussion of *The Problem of Pain* can be made here. Lewis's emphasis on dying to a person's own personality, accepting Christ's personality—pretending to be Christ until one becomes a son of God (bk. 4, chap. 7)—is the probable cause of the statement by Owen Barfield that he felt as if he saw two Lewises in the same body after his conversion: Lewis was attempting to suppress his old self, the Old Adam in Christian terms.

In general, *Mere Christianity* fulfills Lewis's statement in his essay "Before We Can Communicate" that it takes ten times as many words to say something in popular speech as it does in a learned vocabulary. Lewis, in these radio addresses, explains matters simply and uses an analogy for every difficult idea. This makes for a delightful book to introduce a person without a theological background to Christianity; the book is worth reading for a minister or other theologically educated person for the freshness of the analogies and the clarity of the ideas; but the wordiness will damage the book's rereadability for someone whose main concern is artistry. In short, Lewis wrote very well for his evangelical purposes, but simplified radio addresses do not make for the greatest nonfiction prose. Better one page of *Walden* (so far as style is concerned) than ten of *Mere Christianity.*

MIRACLES (1947, REV. 1960)

The third of Lewis's apologetic works has a subtitle: *A Preliminary Study*. This is important, for Lewis is producing an argument that miracles are possible—as outside, supernatural interferences to nature—not that they are common or that any particular, non-New Testament ones really happened. Lewis prefaces the book with a 1946 poem of his, untitled here but called "The Meteorite" in *Poems*, in which a meteor, having fallen from the heavens, is worked on by Earth's weather and moss as what is left of it becomes part of Earth's process. It is a clear analogy: a miracle also comes from elsewhere (Heaven, rather than outer space), and, once the supernatural moment is over, whatever has been changed becomes part of the natural processes of the universe.

Most of the controversy about this book has arisen over Lewis's argument in the third chapter (part of a longer discussion, running from the second through the sixth chapter) that a naturalist—that is, one who believes that the naturalistic cause-and-effect chain controls all of life and the universe—cannot defend reason as leading to rational conclusions. Obviously, he believes that the mind and all of its thoughts are the products of causes that did not originate in reason; therefore, he is arguing that irrationality produces rationality. Further, he contradicts himself by assuming that he can use his reason to argue for the universe being controlled by cause and effect.

Is Lewis arguing with a legitimate point of view in this chapter? Yes. Sigmund Freud is one example. Freud, in order to make psychoanalysis "scientific," argued that *all* thoughts and dreams had causes that, at least in theory, could be found. Likewise, B. F. Skinner has assumed this point of view, denying free will, in his behaviorism. Naturalism, as Lewis uses the term, is a widely assumed, if often unexamined, position on the fringes of science: a scientific, cause-and-effect fatalism.

But the controversy over Lewis's third chapter, "The Self-Contradiction of the Naturalist," came from G. E. M. Anscombe, a woman, a Roman Catholic, and a philosopher. On 2 February 1948 she read her "Reply to Mr. C.S. Lewis's Argument that 'Naturalism' Is Self-refuting" to the Socratic Club, and she and Lewis debated the topic afterwards. The primary materials and the significant secondary items can be traced through the notes in Peter J. Schakel's *Reason and Imagination in C.S. Lewis*.[1] Schakel lists Lewis's defeat by Anscombe as one of the four factors that caused him to turn from apologetics. Certainly Lewis revised that third chapter of *Miracles* in the 1960 edition, retitling the chapter "The Cardinal Difficulty of Naturalism."

The longer, second version of the chapter argues not from the previous thesis but from two senses of *because*: the Cause and Effect relationship, and the Ground and Consequent relationship. Lewis says that the former is the basis of science (this produces that) while the latter is the only method of validation of truth (from this is inferred, or on this is based, that). And the two systems cannot be reconciled.

What is certainly true is that the revised version of the chapter is more difficult and less readable as an essay than the first version. Anscombe has driven Lewis to be more rigorous, to the diminution of his ability to communicate. It is a pity that he did not write his revised argument as a third appendix to the book and put a footnote in the original chapter warning the reader about the two senses of *because* and referring him or her to the back of the volume; or that he did not expand his book by a chapter or two if that was necessary to combine rigor and readability. As it is, precision of thought has led to loss of literary merit.

This is an assertion, not a proof. But a reader of the seventh and subsequent paragraphs of the original and the revised chapters—this being their point of variation—will find two paragraphs in the original and eleven in the revised that are completely without illustrations or other concrete language. Of course, the revised chapter is longer, but proportionally not this much longer. Likewise, concrete language is not the whole basis of literary merit; but Lewis made it the foundation of poetry (in the larger sense) in the fifth chapter of *The Personal Heresy*, and it is indicative here.

Miracles is in tone much like Lewis's early philosophic works, discussed in the previous chapter. But the argument here is not on the basis of a morality (with a moral God, whether or not mentioned, behind it); but in terms of a supernatural Reason in which man's reason participates. One remembers that in *The Pilgrim's Regress*, dropping the allegorical images, the three things that Wisdom says were not created by man were logical categories, moral rules, and *Sehnsucht*. *The Pilgrim's Regress* was primarily the account of *Sehnsucht* leading "John" to God; "Right and Wrong as a Clue to the Meaning of the Universe" argued from morality to God; *Miracles* is arguing from reason—logical categories—to God in these early chapters. (Another reason Lewis may have stopped direct apologetics with this book is that he had exhausted his three ways to God.)

Indeed, in chapter 5, "A Further Difficulty in Naturalism," Lewis argues in terms of natural law here also, saying he sees man's moral awareness as part of reason, although others in the natural law tradition do not. Either way, it makes a parallel case: a naturalist (in Lewis's sense) cannot argue for any moral principles because he believes they have nonmoral and nonrational causes. But Schakel comments, in *Reason and Imagination in C.S. Lewis* (135), that Lewis's basic argument leaves open the position of skepticism: perhaps naturalism is the truth—but, if so, one has no rational means of proving it.

At any rate, Lewis, after arguing for man's reason needing a supernatural Reason in order to be valid, later in the book admits that it is easier to argue for the Incarnation in historical terms than philosophical, and he offers a new version of his now familiar disjunction between Christ's claims for himself, which if they are not true suggest madness ("rampant megalomania"), and the sanity of his moral teachings (chap. 14). In short, he argues for rational theism, instead of moral theism, and then tries briefly to shift the theism into Christianity.

But this is advancing too quickly. The latter part of the book does not, at first, give the impression of as tight an organization as the first part. Admittedly, chapters 7 and 8 make a unit, discussing whether or not nature is a system that admits miracles; but the sheer title of 9, "A Chapter not strictly Necessary"—on external nature as a fallen creature that will be redeemed—indicates the pattern. (Lewis's artistic presentation of redeemed nature appears in new Narnia in the last four chapters of *The Last Battle*.) The next chapter, "'Horrid Red Things,'" as Lewis indicates at the end, eliminates rejections of Christian claims based on the imagery involved, but does not touch the miraculous per se. And the next, "Christianity and 'Religion,'" is about an idealistic pantheism—in the philosophy of Bruno, Spinoza, and Hegel; in more popular writings, of Wordsworth, Carlyle, and Emerson—which is Christianity's main religious rival in the modern, Western world. Even here, there is more pattern than appears from the mere topics; in this eleventh chapter, Lewis builds on the discussion of imagery in the tenth. This eleventh, with its emphasis on God being more specific, more factual, than the amorphous pantheistic deity, is the basis for Lewis's imagery in *The Great Divorce of Heaven* as being harder, more specific, than the ghosts who visit it from Hell—as Lewis contrasts ghosts and saints here.

But Lewis is leading toward chapter 14, "The Grand Miracle," which is a discussion of the Incarnation (including, but not limited to, the Resurrection) as being the basic miracle that is asserted by Christianity and by which all Christian miracles should be judged. He leads into this with the twelfth chapter, "The Propriety of Miracles," and the thirteenth, "On Probability." The twelfth turns on an analogy, borrowed from Dorothy L. Sayers' *Mind of the Maker* (1941), between God and creation on one hand and a writer and his book on the other. Arguments from analogy are notoriously fallible, but this one is meant more to indicate the significance of some miracles than prove a point. If a miracle is basic to the type of plot (of the universe), it is artistically included; if it is used deus ex machina or if it is incidental frills, it is not.

The first of "On Probability" turns out to be a refutation of David Hume's essay "Of Miracles" (1748); this, where another philosophical writer might have begun, Lewis includes as preparation for a statement on the probability of the Incarnation. But the more important part of the chapter is Lewis's establishment of a criterion for the judgment of the probability of miracles: "some innate sense of the fitness of things." By itself, this sounds absurd; but Lewis quotes the phrase from an authority of science—Sir Arthur Eddington—who is writing about certain areas of scientific beliefs. As Lewis points out, science often progresses by concentrating on irregularities (things that do not "fit") and explaining how they can be fitted into the overall pattern (or a new, larger pattern). Obviously, this is an excellent debater's ploy: the use of a term from the opponent's camp to support one's own hypothesis. Lewis applies the phrase to miracles and builds his transition to the last three chapters that present, and argue the fitness of, the basic miracle claimed by Christianity and two types of miracles that are related to it.

Thus far, this discussion has been primarily concerned with Lewis's ideas and their disposal, which is appropriate given the philosophical bent of the book. Two comparisons to his fiction have appeared, and more could be made. For example, at one point Lewis mentions the possibility of God having created several natures, several universes, unrelated to each other (chap. 2). Fictionally, the travel to and from Narnia illustrates this concept— or to and from Charn in *The Magician's Nephew*. Even the comment that these universes would seem supernatural to each other is illustrated in the ghostlike appearance of Tirian on Earth (in the fourth chapter of *The Last Battle*.)

Likewise, Lewis's predilection for referring to his friends appears here. Owen Barfield's *Poetic Diction* is praised and used in an argument (chap. 10). Adam Fox, one of the less significant Inklings, is given credit for comparing the imagery of God's appearance to Ezekiel not to nature but to machinery— to a dynamo (chap. 14). And Charles Williams (his name is not in the index) provides the epigraph to chapter 14. Autobiographically, Lewis's brief reference to Kirkpatrick, his one-time tutor, adds a detail about Kirkpatrick's reading to the account in *Surprised by Joy* (not in the index, chap. 10).

Finally, little has been said about the artistry beyond the organization and the lack of imagery in the revised third chapter, and the mentioning of the opening poem. Many other points could be made. Perhaps two illustrative examples will suggest part of Lewis's technique. After establishing man's reason as dependent on God's reason, Lewis compares it, in a separate paragraph, to a water lily whose roots go down to the soil beneath the pond; then he suggests that, for the naturalist, the pond has no bottom (chap. 4). This image does not prove anything, but it does make the naturalist seem foolish. Even more delightful is the discussion of the mystics' use of negatives about God, which Lewis illustrates in a paragraph about a limpet who has a vision of man and describes him as having no shell, not being attached to a rock, and not surrounded by water. The later, nonmystical limpets decide that man (after a step or two) is "a famished jelly in a dimensional void" (chap. 11). There is again satire here, as often in Lewis; but the sheer wit is what is impressive.

NOTE

1. Peter J. Schakel, *Reason and Imagination in C.S. Lewis* (Grand Rapids: Eerdmans, 1984), 148–49, 199–200.

DAVID C. DOWNING

The Recovered Image:
Elements of Classicism and Medievalism

> Humanity does not pass through phases as a train passes through
> stations: being alive, it has the privilege of always moving yet never
> leaving anything behind. Whatever we have been, in some sort we still
> are. —C.S. Lewis, *Allegory of Love*

It is not surprising that the theological orientation of the trilogy is
distinctly medieval in character. Lewis's whole person was drawn to a time
when Western civilization could with some accuracy be called Christendom
and when a predominant literary form was epic romance. The world of
Aquinas and of King Arthur, of Boethius and Boiardo, was the world in
which Lewis the scholar, the Christian, and the lover of heroic adventure
could feel most at home. In his scholarly works such as *The Allegory of Love*
and *The Discarded Image*, Lewis deftly elucidates a world-picture that has
been set aside for centuries; in the trilogy he seeks to recover that image for
modern readers.

The usual paradigm, still found in many history books, is that ancient
Greece and Rome achieved the first apex in Western civilization—the
classical era. Then came a hiatus lasting for centuries, the so-called Dark
Ages and Middle Ages. (Even the term "medieval" means nothing more than
"middle era.") Finally, the cultural stagnation was overcome by the

From *Planets in Peril: A Critical Study of C.S. Lewis's Ransom Trilogy*. © 1992 by The University
of Massachusetts Press.

humanists, who awakened a slumbering glory and began the ascent to a new cultural apex.

Lewis found this common view of Western civilization presumptuous and misleading. He anticipated contemporary post-structuralist historiography by noting that historical events are not self-interpreting; facts must be "read" according to some set of presuppositions, whether acknowledged or unacknowledged. Thus, in his inaugural address as professor of medieval and Renaissance literature at Cambridge, Lewis quoted G.M. Trevelyan approvingly: "Unlike dates, periods are not facts. They are retrospective conceptions that we form about past events, useful to focus discussion, but very often leading historical thought astray" (*SLE* 2).

Lewis went on to argue that historical thought has indeed been led astray by the stratification of Western cultural history into classical, medieval, and Renaissance periods. He denied that the medieval era represented a radical break with the classical era, or that the Renaissance represented a radical break with the Middle Ages. The real break, he argued, came in the intellectual revolution of the nineteenth and twentieth centuries, which separates the modern world from previous eras much more than any of them are separated from each other.

Rather than accepting a fundamental shift between the classical world and the Christian era, Lewis consistently stressed the continuity between the pagan and the Christian. In *The Discarded Image*, for example, he spends two pages showing that pagans and early Christians had far more in common than either shares with the modern Zeitgeist. He concludes that "the modern who dislikes the Christian Fathers would have disliked the Pagan philosophers equally, and for similar reasons" (47).

Pagan is another word that has a specialized meaning and private connotations in the Lewis lexicon. In common parlance, *pagan* and *Christian* are practically antonyms, the first representing a secular, this-worldly attitude, and the second representing its opposite. Lewis saw no such antithesis; he called paganism "the childhood of religion ... a prophetic dream" (*SBJ* 235). For him, paganism was an anticipation, Christianity the fulfillment. He elaborated his view in a letter to Dom Bede Griffiths, his former student: "Paganism does not merely survive but first becomes really itself in the very heart of Christianity. By the way, would you agree that the un-Christening of Europe (much of it) is an even bigger change than its Christening? So that the gap between Professor Ryle [a behaviorist philosopher] and say Dante, is *wider* than that between Dante and Virgil?" (*LCSL* 258). As can be seen here, Lewis defined paganism according to the masters of antiquity—Homer, Plato, and Virgil—not with the self-conscious neopaganism of a Swinburne or a Wilde.

In so defining his terms, Lewis is revealing personal history as well as his reading of cultural history. He associated paganism with myth and romance, and Christianity with the reality that myth and romance point to. Just as his own love of myth and romance was fulfilled when he reaffirmed his childhood faith, he saw the highest strivings of paganism fulfilled with the coming of the Christian era. Soon after his reconversion, Lewis speculated to Arthur Greeves: "I think the thrill of the Pagan stories and of romance may be due to the fact that they are mere beginnings—the first, faint whisper of the wind from beyond the world—while Christianity is the thing itself" (*TST* 430). It becomes clear in this context that when Lewis refers to himself in *Surprised by Joy* as "a converted Pagan living among apostate Puritans" (69), he is not referring to some militant secularism or riotous living in his early years, but rather to his acute responsiveness to "the whisper of the wind from beyond the world."

Just as he stressed the continuity between the classical and the Christian, Lewis also stressed the continuity between the medieval era and the Renaissance. He described the notion of the "medieval" as a fifteenth-century humanistic invention that dismissed "a thousand years of theology, metaphysics, jurisprudence, courtesy, poetry, and architecture ... as a mere gap, chasm, or *entre-acte*" (*EL* 20). He also avoided the term *Renaissance* because he considered it an empty term of self-congratulation invented by the same humanists, one that imposed an illusory unity upon a heterogeneous assortment of cultural events (*EL* 55). Lewis's view is best summed up by his oft-quoted remark that "the Renaissance never happened in England; ... if it did, it had no importance."[1] The influence of Lewis's revisionist reading of Western culture was already apparent in his lifetime, when Magdalene College, Cambridge, created for him the position of professor of medieval and Renaissance literature. In accepting the position, Lewis applauded the title "Medieval and Renaissance," asserting that "the barrier between those two ages has been greatly exaggerated, if indeed it was not largely a figment of Humanist propaganda" (*SLE* 2).

Here again we find interesting correlations between Lewis's reading of cultural history and his reading of his own life. In his discussion of the humanists, he seems to associate them with his traumatic memories of the years he spent in the public schools. He speaks of the "schoolroom severities" (*EL* 21) of the humanists and comments on their strictures concerning syntax and grammar by explaining, "You must not do in English things you were whipped at school for doing in Latin" (22). Lewis also compares the humanists' emulation of the classics to a "desire to be very 'adult'" (24). And when Lewis asserts that the humanists created "a new literary quality—vulgarity" (24), we cannot help but think of his portrait of himself as a schoolboy aping the foppish older lads, and concluding, "a new element entered my life: vulgarity" (*SBJ* 67).

Lewis devoted a great deal of his energy and expertise as a scholar to the task of rehabilitating the medieval worldview, urging his readers to recognize the intellectual and artistic achievements of writers who might otherwise have been considered mainly as precursors. For example, he reiterated in several published works that medieval authors knew the earth to be a globe and that they thought of it as a very small point in comparison to the vastness of the universe (*EL* 2; *Mir* 50; *SMRL* 46–47). (One of the authors whom Lewis faulted for perpetuating the myth of medieval ignorance on these matters was J. B. S. Haldane [DI 97].)

OUT OF THE SILENT PLANET

When Lewis turned his hand to fiction, his task was not to argue for the intellectual vitality of the medieval worldview but rather to show its imaginative beauty. Throughout the Ransom trilogy Lewis tries to suggest, through the vehicle of space fantasy, what the medieval vision of reality might have felt like from "inside."

Early in *Out of the Silent Planet* Lewis serves notice that he does not intend to follow the usual genre conventions about cosmic voyages. While his reading of Wells and others as a boy had impressed upon him the "vastness and cold of space" (*SBJ* 65), his own protagonist discovers just the opposite. Having been drugged by Weston and Devine and hauled toward their spacecraft, Ransom awakens to an invigorating "tyranny of heat and light," which surprises him, since he had expected space to be dark and cold (*OSP* 29). In describing what Ransom feels when gazing at the cosmos from the side of the spacecraft away from the sun, Lewis enthralls the reader with some of the most evocative prose to be found in the trilogy.

> The Earth's disk was nowhere to be seen; the stars, thick as daisies on an uncut lawn, reigned perpetually with no cloud, no moon, no sunrise to dispute their sway. There were planets of unbelievable majesty, and constellations undreamed of there were celestial sapphires, rubies, emeralds and pin-pricks of burning gold; far out on the left of the picture hung a comet, tiny and remote; and between all and behind all, far more emphatic and

palpable than it showed on Earth, the undimensioned, enigmatic blackness. The lights trembled: they seemed to grow brighter as he looked. Stretched naked on his bed, a second Danaë, he found it night by night more difficult to disbelieve in old astrology: almost he felt, wholly he imagined, "sweet influence" pouring or even stabbing into his surrendered body. (31)

Kath Filmer has pointed out how Lewis's choice of metaphors in this passage underscores his attraction to a hierarchical worldview. Quoting Robbe-Grillet's dictum that "metaphor is never an innocent figure of speech," Filmer notes that readers are invited to see the beauty of the scene in terms of earthly monarchs reigning in serene and undisputed majesty.[2] The references to precious stones and to a comet hanging in space like a rich tapestry also suggest a regal setting.

In referring to "sweet influence" and to Danaë, Lewis carries the process a step further. Throughout the trilogy he treats the old astrology and the old mythology as vestiges of lost realities. Our word *influence* derives from astrology, from the belief that a force emanating from celestial bodies "flows into" humans, influencing their behavior.

As well as imagining he can actually feel this force, Ransom also identifies with Danaë, the woman whom Zeus ravished in the form of a shower of gold. Lewis admired a cycle of poems on Danaë appearing in Robert Nichols's volume of poetry *Ardours and Endurances* (*TST* 235). These poems portray her as the infatuated lover of Zeus, breathlessly awaiting his visitation. Something of this same sense of enraptured surrender is suggested in Ransom's willing exposure to the celestial radiance.

As the voyage toward Malacandra continues, Ransom comes to consider the very term *space* a serious misnomer.

But Ransom, as time wore on, became aware of another and more spiritual cause for his progressive lightening and exultation of heart. A nightmare, long engendered in the modern mind by the mythology that follows in the wake of science, was falling off him. He had read of "Space": at the back of his thinking for years had lurked the dismal fancy of the black, cold vacuity, the utter deadness, which was supposed to separate the worlds. He had not known how much it affected him till now—now the very name "Space" seemed a blasphemous libel for this empyrean ocean of radiance in which they swam. He could not call it "dead"; he felt life pouring into him from it every moment.... No: Space was the

wrong name. Older thinkers had been wiser when they named it
simply the heavens—the heavens which declared the glory—the
> "happy climes that ly
> Where day never shuts his eye
> Up in the broad fields of the sky." (*OSP* 32)

Here again Lewis's description invites the reader to set aside the "mythology
which follows in the wake of science" and to reconsider older mythologies,
echoed in Milton's realm of unblinking day (*Comus*, lines 976–78) and the
psalmist's heavens that declare God's glory (Ps. 19:1).

Lewis would not have been greatly disturbed to learn that actual
travelers into space would find more the "black, cold vacuity" than the
"empyrean oceans of radiance" he envisioned. He had little interest in the
scientific side of science fiction. When he wrote *Out of the Silent Planet*, he
knew that there were no actual canals on Mars, and he confessed that
Weston's "scientific" explanation of how his spacecraft flew was "pure
mumbo jumbo" (*OOW* 76, 87). He used the fantasy genre not to depict the
universe as understood in our century but to re-create imaginatively the
medieval cosmology, a vast and magnificent picture that Lewis called "the
greatest work of art the Middle Ages produced" (*SMRL* 62).

Descriptive passages like those quoted above frequently parallel Lewis's
remarks about medieval cosmology in his scholarly works. For example, his
essay "Imagination and Thought in the Middle Ages" is intended as an
introduction to the medieval world picture but serves equally well as a gloss
on *Out of the Silent Planet*. In this essay he explains that when people in the
Middle Ages gazed up at a night sky, they did not think of the spaces they
looked at as silent, dark, or empty (*SMRL* 52). He also discusses the medieval
understanding of "influences" (56) and quotes the same passage from *Comus*
that Ransom had recalled so fondly (53).

In *The Discarded Image* Lewis again underscores the differences
between the ancients' picture of the heavens and our perception of outer
space. He quotes the Latin poet Lucan, who envisions celestial realms bathed
in light: "How dark, compared with the aether, our terrestrial day is" (*DI* 33).
He also contrasts the medieval and the modern in language similar to the
passage from *Out of the Silent Planet* quoted above: "Nothing is more deeply
impressed on the cosmic imaginings of a modern than the idea that the
heavenly bodies move in a pitch-black and dead-cold vacuity. It was not so in
the Medieval Model" (*DI* 111).

Apart from reimagining "space" according to the medieval model,
Lewis also redefines the planets that float in space. When Ransom and his

abductors approach Malacandra, they experience nausea, headaches, and heart palpitations (*OSP* 38). At first one may consider this merely Lewis's (fairly accurate) predictions about the physiological effects of moving from a weightless state back into a gravity field. But soon it becomes clear that he has something more in mind. As the spacecraft descends, Ransom again finds his former conceptions reversed.

> Suddenly the lights of the Universe seemed to be turned down. As if some demon had rubbed the heaven's face with a dirty sponge, the splendour in which they had lived for so long blenched to a pallid, cheerless and pitiable grey.... What had been a chariot gliding in the fields of heaven became a dark steel box dimly lighted by a slit of window, and falling. They were falling out of the heaven, into a world.... He wondered how he could ever have thought of planets, even of the Earth, as islands of life and reality floating in a deadly void. Now, with a certainty which never after deserted him, he saw the planets—the "earths" he had called them in his thought—as mere holes or gaps in the living heaven—excluded and rejected wastes of heavy matter and murky air, formed not by addition to, but by subtraction from, the surrounding brightness. (*OSP* 39–40)

In general, Lewis presents life on Malacandra as very positive, even utopian, so many readers are puzzled to find him describing Ransom's entry into this world in such negative terms. The passage quoted above seems neither "scientific" nor thematically congruent with the rest of the book. Yet again the explanation can be found in Lewis's own discussion of medieval cosmology. In *The Discarded Image*, he explains the hierarchy of created substance developed by the fifth-century author Macrobius: ether, the purest and most limpid form, rose the highest; beneath it came air, less pure and more heavy; then came water, and finally solids. As Lewis sums up: "Finally out of the whole tumult of matter all that was irreclaimable (*vastum*) was scraped off and cleansed from the (other) elements (*ex defaecatis abrasum elementis*) and sank down and settled at the lowest point, plunged in binding and unending cold. Earth is in fact the 'offscourings of creation,' the cosmic dustbin" (*DI* 62–63). According to this order of creation, any planet, even an "unfallen" one, cannot match the glory and splendor of the heavens themselves.

Yet if one must inhabit a world, Malacandra turns out to be a very good choice. Weston and Devine, thinking they have come to offer Ransom as a human sacrifice to the inhabitants of Malacandra, have severely misunderstood the beings they have encountered there. Once Ransom escapes his abductors and meets the three rational species on the planet—the hrossa, the seroni, and the pfifltriggi—he discovers what he had least been expecting: a utopian society. In fact, *Out of the Silent Planet* has been interpreted both as an answer to Plato's *Republic* and as an answer to Wells's utopian novels.[3]

Writers of utopian fiction generally present societies where the author's own cherished ideals have been successfully implemented. Lewis is no exception to this rule: the Malacandrian society he portrays as so attractive is a relatively simple society of hunter/poets, shepherd/philosophers, and artisans. As Ransom comes to know the inhabitants of that world, he learns their ideas about love, art, and spirituality—ideas usually similar to Lewis's own opinions on these subjects. Malacandrian society is also hierarchical, even theocratic, as well as preindustrial and precapitalistic. In short, it approaches the medieval ideal of a well-governed Christian society.

For example, when Ransom recounts the sordid history of earth to a gathering of sorns, they interpret our planet's woes in terms of a breakdown in the Great Chain of Being: "There must be rule, yet how can creatures rule themselves? Beasts must be ruled by *hnau* and *hnau* by eldila and *eldila* by Maleldil" (*OSP* 102). (As shown in chapter 2 this formulation may be translated to mean that beasts must be ruled by rational species, rational species by angels, and angels by God.)

In *A Preface to Paradise Lost* Lewis argues that "the Hierarchical conception" dominated Western conceptions of order—cosmic, political, and moral—from Aristotle to Milton. With God at the top of the great chain and unformed matter at the bottom, everyone and everything had a natural station, ruling over those below, obeying those above. A great many sins, according to this conception, derive from not recognizing one's station, and thus perverting the natural order. In Lewis's reading of Milton, Lucifer sins by rebelling against his natural superiors, while Adam sins by not ruling over his natural subject, Eve.

It is not hard to see that Lewis had a great deal of imaginative sympathy for this view of the cosmic order. In the Ransom trilogy, he pictures a cosmos ordered hierarchically, with only "the silent planet," earth, out of harmony with the natural order. In the Narnia chronicles as well, Lewis portrays the ideal society as a monarchy; those who advocate self-rule in the chronicles are not portrayed as reformers or democrats, but as self-interested demagogues or sullen and insubordinate subjects. Lewis was pragmatic enough to advocate democracy for the contemporary world—not because people are good enough to deserve it, but because they are so prone to abuse power that it needs to be spread out (*OOW* 81). Nonetheless, democracy seemed to him, like so much else about the contemporary world, prosaic and utilitarian, compared to the grandeur and elegance of earlier eras.

Having woven medieval motifs into *Out of the Silent Planet*, Lewis reveals at the end of the story that his own work as a medievalist led him to discover the extraordinary adventures of Elwin Ransom on Malacandra. In chapter 22, Lewis says that he will dispense with literary conventions, drop the mask, and tell his real purpose for writing the book (*OSP* 152). In claiming to abandon the mask of fiction, Lewis thus offers his readers an even more ingenious fiction than the one they have been reading.

At this point, Lewis the author becomes a character in his own story. He explains that he learned of Ransom's voyage after writing to him about the curious word *Oyarses*, which Lewis had run across in the work of Bernardus Silvestris, a twelfth-century Platonist. Another scholar, identified only as C. J., had interpreted the term as a corruption of *ousiarches*, a ruler of a heavenly sphere, or tutelary spirit of a planet. Ransom replied to Lewis's query by inviting him to come over for the weekend, so Ransom could relate his adventures on Malacandra. He felt compelled to do so to convince Lewis that *Oyarsa* was not just a philological oddity but an actual being, a powerful one, known to the ancients but now forgotten on "the silent planet." Ransom convinces Lewis to write up Ransom's cosmic voyage in the form of fiction, arguing that it would be more advantageous to appeal to readers' imaginations than to attack their intellectual presuppositions directly. Ransom explains to the narrator that "what we need for the moment is not so much a body of belief as a body of people familiarized with certain ideas. If we could even effect in one per cent of our readers a change-over from the conception of Space to the conception of Heaven, we should have made a beginning" (OSP 154). Here we see Lewis at once being perfectly candid and perfectly crafty. Of course, he did not really expect readers to believe in a literal Ransom who really had traveled to Mars (though he did receive a number of letters asking if all this had actually happened [*LCSL* 261]). But he really does hope to "baptize the imagination" of his readers, to make them wonder if there are not indeed unseen realities not accounted for by the modern, materialistic worldview. Lewis really is dropping his mask and speaking with sincere conviction when he warns readers of dangers that "are not planetary but cosmic, ... not temporal but eternal" (*OSP* 153).

Throughout the trilogy, Lewis maintains this strategy of intermixing his fictional world with our "factual" world. Besides using himself as character, Lewis's references to the obscure term *Oyarses*, to Bernardus

Silvestris, and even to "C. J." are all taken from "real life." Lewis discusses Bernardus Silvestris at length in *The Allegory of Love* (90–98), where he offers the theory of Prof. C. C. J. Webb that *Oyarses* is a corruption of the Greek *Ousiarches* (362). Here again, as so often in Lewis's books, the ideas discussed in his expository works are given an imaginative embodiment in his fiction.

PERELANDRA

Near the end of *Out of the Silent Planet*, Ransom speaks of having "made a beginning" in re-forming readers' imaginations, and Lewis promises his readers another story (154). *Perelandra* takes up where *Out of the Silent Planet* left off, not only in its use of medieval motifs, but also in its strategy of intermixing Lewis's fictional world with our factual world.

In the second book of the trilogy Lewis again presents himself as a character in the story, and again he refers to an obscure medieval scholar; one who knows more about spiritual beings than his supposedly more sophisticated modern counterparts. In describing his encounter with an eldil at Ransom's cottage, Lewis adds a footnote quoting Natvilcius, who seems to know a great deal about angels, even speculating about their actual, celestial bodies in contrast to the way they are perceived by human eyes. Lewis scholars have searched his other books and pored over many a reference source trying to discover the identity of this Natvilcius. Unable to find any references to him outside of *Perelandra*, some modestly conclude that they do not know if he really existed or not, while others go on record as assuming that Natvilcius is one of Lewis's own inventions.[4]

This second, bolder group of Lewis scholars is correct. Sometimes when Lewis chose to write anonymously, he used the letters "N.W." Most of his occasional poems were published with these initials, and the first edition of *A Grief Observed* appeared with "N. W. Clerk" as its author. "N.W." is short for *Nat Whilk*, Old English for "I know not whom." It is the archaic equivalent of the modern phrase "author unknown."

Natvilcius is simply the latinized form of "Nat Whilk." Unlike his reference to the actual author Bernardus Silvestris in *Out of the Silent Planet*, Lewis has created here a fictional scholar to introduce his idea that eldils exist on a celestial plane and can be perceived only imperfectly by creatures confined to three-dimensional space. Even Lewis's little hoax here is an oblique tribute to a medieval author. In his essay "What Chaucer Did to 'Il Filostrato,'" Lewis notes with seeming delight Chaucer's citation of fictitious sources to lend a greater sense of historicity to *Troilus and Cressida* (*SLE* 30).

Once Ransom reaches Perelandra, he finds that, like Malacandra, it is a hierarchical world ruled by a king and queen. Though these are the first pair, as yet without descendants, they rule the animals and will eventually have authority over the Oyarsa of this world as well. Ransom is confused by this seeming reversal of the cosmic order, but the queen explains to him their world was created after Maleldil the Younger had taken human form. As unfallen humans the king and queen need have no authorities between themselves and Maleldil.

Though it might seem grievous for eldils to serve those whom they once ruled, the queen explains that it is "their glory and their joy" to nurture creatures before whom they would later bow (82–83). Later the Oyarsa of Perelandra confirms this, saying that her relationship with the royal pair is like that of two Perelandran creatures, the dumb dam who suckles the singing beast: "The [singing beasts] have no milk and always what they bring forth is suckled by the she-beast of another kind. She is great and beautiful and dumb, and till the young singing beast is weaned it is among her whelps and is subject to her. But when it is grown it becomes the most delicate and glorious of all beasts and goes from her. And she wonders at its song" (196). In this passage Lewis suggests that a hierarchical social order entails more complex relationships than usually understood in our era, when the only political models we are familiar with are democratic, autocratic, or totalitarian.

Lewis often referred to the medieval metaphor of the dance, both as an image of their social order and their concept of the cosmic order. In *Miracles* he explains that hierarchy itself is more like a dance than a pyramid.

> The partner who bows to Man in one movement of the dance receives Man's reverences in another. To be high or central means to abdicate continually: to be low means to be raised: all good masters are servants: God washes the feet of men. The concepts we usually bring to the consideration of such matters are miserably political and prosaic. We think of flat repetitive equality and arbitrary privilege as the only two alternatives—thus missing all the overtones, the counterpoint, the vibrant sensitiveness, the inter-inanimations of reality. (128)

This is a highly idealized version of hierarchy, one that could succeed only in unfallen worlds. Yet it does show how closely interwoven were Lewis's theological convictions and his love of medievalism. Just after the passage from *Miracles* quoted above, Lewis calls the principle of ascent and reascent "the very formula of reality" (129). God had to descend into human form in order to redeem humanity; Christ had to descend into earth and then reascend three days later in order to complete his atoning work; humans must likewise descend into earth before they are raised up again on some final day.

In this context, it is interesting to recall that Ransom is carried to Perelandra in a casket, which descends and then reascends upon plunging into the seas of Perelandra (34). Later, when he is dragged downward to the ocean's depths by the Un-man, the language describing his descent (171–72) is intriguingly similar to the language Lewis uses in *Miracles*, in which he compares the Incarnation to the descent and reascent of a deep-sea diver (116).

Behind Lewis's principle of ascent and reascent and his metaphors taken from dancing is the medieval commonplace of the Great Dance. Though we have become accustomed since Newton's time to think of the universe as essentially a mechanism, the medieval picture was much more festive. Lewis noted in one of his lectures on medieval cosmologists that their symbol for the primum mobile was a young girl dancing and playing a tambourine. He explains that the orderly movements of the heavenly spheres in the medieval picture "are to be conceived not as those of a machine or even an army, but rather as a dance, a festival, a symphony, a ritual, a carnival, or all of these in one" (*SMRL* 60).

The Great Dance in the closing pages of *Perelandra* summarizes a great deal of theology in poetic form, as well as imaginatively recapturing some of the medieval sense of festival, symphony, ritual, and carnival. As Roland M. Kawano has observed, a central element in the image of the dance is "the reconciliation of order and freedom."[5] In the dance, beasts, humans and spirits all find their place; fallen worlds and unfallen ones, ancient ones and new ones, each participate in the pageant.

The dance also serves as a kind of liturgical answer to the angst produced by positivism, the sense that humans inhabit a vast, dead universe that mocks all philosophy, all desire for justice, all yearning for some larger meaning. As Ransom chased the Weston/Un-man over seemingly illimitable seas, he became overwhelmed by "mere bigness and loneliness" and felt that those vast solitudes were haunted, not by some god, but by "the wholly inscrutable to which man and his life remained eternally irrelevant" (164). Thinking of the even vaster solitudes of space, Ransom was oppressed by what he calls the Empirical Bogey, "the great myth of our century with its gases and galaxies, its light years and evolutions, its nightmare perspectives of simple arithmetic in which everything that can possibly hold significance for the mind becomes the mere by-product of essential disorder" (164). Once

Ransom caught up with the Un-man, the Weston-voice echoed many of Ransom's own anxieties about some fundamental meaninglessness at the core of things (167–69). At the time Ransom had nothing to recommend except to repent and offer a child's prayer.

But the Great Dance offers a whole different cosmic picture. One speaker in the ritual affirms that Maleldil's greatness does not reside in "years to years in lumpish aggregations, or miles to miles and galaxies to galaxies" (214); for all of him dwells in the seed of the smallest flower and is not cramped, yet "Deep Heaven is inside Him who is inside the seed and does not distend Him" (215). Another voice explains that in the Great Dance all is at the center, whether the dust or beasts or hnau species or gods, for "where Maleldil is, there is the center" (216). A third voice, most directly addressing the Empirical Bogey, proclaims, "All that is made seems planless to the darkened mind, because there are more plans than it looked for.... There seems no plan because it is all plan: there seems no centre because it is all centre" (218).

Lewis, the medieval scholar, would revel in such a glad, elegant, and orderly picture of the cosmos. Lewis the twentieth-century Christian would admit that such a picture was not scientifically true, but he affirmed that its theological implications were essentially accurate.

That Hideous Strength

In the first two books of the trilogy, Ransom traveled to other worlds to discover the truth of myth and to find a cosmos more similar to, medieval models than to modern ones. In *That Hideous Strength* Arthurian legend and other medieval traditions prove their relevance, and reality, on twentieth-century earth.

The most prominent Arthurian element in the third novel of the trilogy is the return of Merlin. Bragdon Wood, the ancient garden owned by Bracton College, is the site of Merlin's Well, the reputed resting place of Arthur's wizard. The leaders of N.I.C.E, those who know its real goals, would like to unearth Merlin and awaken him from his enchanted slumber in order to combine his powers with their own.

It might seem highly incongruous to have modern technocrats trying to use magic, but in *The Abolition of Man* Lewis argues that science and magic spring from the same impulse.

There was very little magic in the Middle Ages: the sixteenth and seventeenth centuries are the high noon of magic. The serious magical endeavour and the serious scientific endeavour are twins: one was sickly and died, the other strong and throve.... There is something which unites magic and applied science while separating both from the "wisdom" of earlier ages. For the wise men of old the cardinal problem had been how to conform the soul to reality, and the solution had been knowledge, self-discipline, and virtue. For magic and applied science alike the problem is how to subdue reality to the wishes of men. (87–88)

Since Lewis identifies magic not with the Middle Ages but with the humanists who came afterward, one can see why the words *magic* and *magician* usually have negative connotations in his writings. Magicians in Lewis's fiction (see *The Magician's Nephew*) and his nonfiction are generally depicted as those who abrogate moral laws in order to gain illicit power over nature and over others. Even in *That Hideous Strength* Lewis takes pains to distinguish Merlin's kind of magic, which originated in Atlantis, from Renaissance magic (201).

Once Merlin is awakened from fifteen centuries of sleep, he does not unite his powers with N.I.C.E. but joins the humble company at St. Anne's. Eventually he becomes the instrument by which the conspirators at N.I.C.E. are exterminated. This resolution to the story has troubled some critics. Chad Walsh, for example, complains that Merlin's role in the story comes close to being a deus ex machina and that the victory of Ransom and his followers is based upon the lucky circumstance that they found Merlin before the others did.[6] But this objection overlooks several key elements in the narrative. First, Merlin does not simply stumble into the hands of the good side. Once he awakens, he is guided by some preternatural means, and he rides directly to St. Anne's and Ransom. Second, Merlin does not offer his services to whoever asks. He subjects Ransom to three arcane questions that no one at N.I.C.E. could have possibly answered (272–74). Ransom can speak to these occult matters because he has traveled to other worlds and continues to have contact with lords of other planets. In their conversation, Ransom learns that Merlin, despite his rather druidic appearance, is a Christian—another reason Merlin would never have allied himself with N.I.C.E. Finally, it should be noted that Merlin does not destroy Belbury using his own weapons alone. Ransom arranges to have the powers of the Oyarsas channeled into Merlin (317), powers that the leaders of N.I.C.E. could not have drawn upon.

Merlin submits to Ransom's authority, not just because Ransom can answer Merlin's questions, but because Ransom is the pendragon. In

Arthurian tradition, the pendragon is the head of all the armies in times of war. Though Arthur was only one of many kings in his time, he inherited the title of pendragon from his father, Uther, so he was the chief commander in the wars against the Anglo-Saxons. (Pendragon is from Celtic "head of a dragon," taken from the dragon's head pictured on the standard of the one who held the title.) Lewis imagines that the title has been passed down secretly from generation to generation and that it now rests upon the one appointed to lead the battle against a new type of invasion. As pendragon, Ransom is also the head of Logres. From the Welsh word for "England," Logres traditionally represents the Britain of King Arthur, whose royal court was at Camelot. Though Logres is mentioned in Spenser and Milton with about the same connotations as the word "Camelot," Lewis's friend Charles Williams gave the term a more specialized meaning. In his Arthurian books, Williams used Logres to represent the spiritual side of England, the combination of Christian and Celtic ideals, a force that stands against the tides of worldliness and corruption.

Lewis adopted this usage in *That Hideous Strength*, as seen in Professor Dimble's outline of English history: "Something we may call Britain is always haunted by something we may call Logres. Haven't you noticed that we are two countries? After every Arthur, a Mordred; behind every Milton, a Cromwell: a nation of poets, a nation of shopkeepers; the home of Sidney— and of Cecil Rhodes. Is it any wonder they call us hypocrites? But what they mistake for hypocrisy is really the struggle between Logres and Britain" (369). Lewis's likes and dislikes are certainly made evident here. Mordred is Arthur's nephew (or bastard son in some versions) who betrayed Arthur and brought an end to Camelot. Milton and Cromwell represent the best and the worst of Puritanism. (As an Ulsterman by birth, Lewis resented Cromwell's brutal suppression of the Irish.)[7] Sir Philip Sidney is Lewis's ideal of the poet-statesman, while Cecil Rhodes was the architect of Britain's imperialistic and exploitative policies in the African country that once bore his name.

Besides his title of pendragon, Ransom is also called Mr. Fisher-King. Lewis offers a rather contrived explanation for this, noting that Ransom received a large inheritance from his sister, Mrs. Fisher-King, on the condition that he take her name (114). Despite this unconvincing detail, the name does add another Arthurian dimension to the story and to Ransom's role in it. In the matter of Britain, the fisher-king is the keeper of the grail, a fisherman and king wounded in the thighs who holds court at his castle, Carbonek. The knight-errant Percival (or Parsifal) visits the grail castle and finds the fisher-king in pain, reclining on a couch in front of a fire. During dinner Percival sees a bleeding lance and a radiant golden cup but does not ask about them. The next morning he learns that his fateful silence has serious consequences: the fisher-king cannot be healed, and all his lands will be devastated. This is the beginning of Percival's quest to recover the grail. There are different versions of what happens to Percival. Some versions end happily, some not so. But all present the fisher-king as a wounded godlike figure who is keeper of the grail.

Ellen Rawson has shown that Jane Studdock is a new Percival in *That Hideous Strength*. When Jane first visits Ransom, his chamber seems to her like a throne room, and she finds him reclining in front of a fire with a painful wound, just as the fisher-king appeared to Percival. Ransom reminds her of King Arthur and of Solomon, and for the first time since childhood she could "taste the word *King* itself with all linked associations of battle, marriage, priesthood, mercy, and power" (*THS* 143). Percival became a Christian because of his encounter with the fisher-king, who is a Christ-figure in most versions of the grail legend. Jane too discovers spiritual realities at St. Anne's, coming to suspect that Maleldil is indeed God (234) and finally surrendering her will to Maleldil's (318–19).

Besides his roles as pendragon and fisher-king, Ransom embodies other Arthurian elements as well. In answer to one of Merlin's questions, Ransom explains that King Arthur is not dead but sits in the House of Kings in the land of Abhalljin on Perelandra (274). Later it is revealed that Ransom will be taken to Perelandra to be with Arthur once his work on earth is done. Abhalljin (spelled "Aphallin" on page 368) is taken from the Welsh term *Afallon*, the abode of dead heroes, the Celtic version of Elysium. In Arthurian legend this appears as "Avalon," the mystic isle where Arthur is taken to be healed of his wounds. Since the trilogy suggests that Perelandra is the true source of all myths of paradise, it is only fitting that Avalon should be found there and that Ransom should be healed on the world where he was wounded.

At the end of *That Hideous Strength* Venus herself (the Oyarsa of Perelandra) descends to earth not only to carry Ransom back to her world but also to unite with the other Oyeresu in defeating the dark powers that have gathered at N.I.C.E. Ransom had discovered the reality of planetary "influences" when he traveled through the heavens to Malacandra, though astrology plays only an incidental role in *Out of the Silent Planet*. But in *That Hideous Strength*, all of the planetary intelligences meet with Ransom and Merlin, their very proximity making the rest of the company at St. Anne's successively mercurial, amorous, martial, saturnine, and jovial. This chapter,

"The Descent of the Gods," is a brilliant prose-poem on how planetary influence might be supposed to affect human psyches, but it also sets up the turning point in the story: the passing of their powers into Merlin for the purpose of eradicating N.I.C.E.

Astrology is associated with St. Anne's just as clearly as magic is associated with Belbury. Since Lewis did not approve of magic, one supposes at first that he would not have any imaginative attraction for astrology either. But Lewis explains in his volume of the *Oxford History of English Literature* that magic and astrology were never allied. While the first occult science sought power over nature, the second assumed nature's power over humans (*EL* 6). Lewis also noted that medieval astrologers did not believe that the planets compelled human behavior, only influenced it. The usual view in the Middle Ages, he says, was that a person, assisted by grace, could overcome a bad horoscope just as he or she could overcome a naturally bad temper (*SMRL* 55).

Apart from Arthurian and astrological elements, another medieval motif that figures prominently in *That Hideous Strength* is the image of the enclosed garden. In the Song of Solomon and other books of the Old Testament, the walled garden is a protected place, associated most often with a woman's virginity. In the Middle Ages, the walled garden symbol accrued multiple associations. As Lewis explains in *The Allegory of Love*, the enclosed garden is associated with youth and youthful love in early writers like Andreas Capellanus and Claudius; in Guillaume de Lorris, it includes also the life of the court, the arena for games of love; in later writers it represents allegorically the heart of a woman and the many emotions that reside there. "Deeper than these," concludes Lewis, "lies the world-wide dream of the happy garden—the island of the Hesperides, the earthly paradise, Tirnanog" (119–20).

This summation is perfectly sound scholarship, but it also reveals the man behind the literary historian. The Garden of the Hesperides is the image of joy, or *Sehnsucht*, that Lewis used most often—in *Surprised by Joy*, in *Perelandra*, and in his poetry. The phrase "the earthly paradise" is the title of a romance by William Morris, much beloved and often read by Lewis, which cleverly interweaves classical and medieval motifs. Tirnanog, "land of the young ones," is the Irish equivalent of Avalon.[8] Lewis most likely first heard of Tirnanog from his childhood nurse, Lizzie Endicott, who was full of Irish lore and song. So when Lewis speaks of the deeper meanings of garden imagery, he not only is casting light on the medieval mind but also is revealing his own. Besides the pictures of paradise he mentions, we might add Eden, Perelandra, and a toy garden on a biscuit tin.

In *That Hideous Strength* the sequestered garden first appears in the narrator's description of Bragdon Wood, the ancient copse owned by Bracton College and coveted by N.I.C.E. Indulging a bit too much in elaborate description and historical allusion, Lewis conjures up all the rich traditions of the place, going back to British-Roman times (i.e., the era of King Arthur). The narrator has a sense that he is penetrating a holy of holies as he enters Bragdon Wood (20), and this indeed will turn out to be a kind of sacred ground. After this elaborate spell of history and legend has been woven around Bragdon Wood by the narrator, readers cannot miss the irony when in the very next section of the novel, the bureaucrats at Bracton College treat this hallowed ground merely as a pink rectangle on a map, land to put up for sale.

While Mark Studdock and his colleagues are discussing what to do with Bragdon Wood, his wife, Jane, encounters another walled garden when she goes to visit Ransom and his little community at St. Anne's. As she is led toward the house, Jane passes by a vegetable garden and line of rosebushes that fill her with wistful thoughts: "It was a very large garden. It was like—like—yes, now she had it: it was like the garden in *Peter Rabbit*. Or was it like the garden in the *Romance of the Rose*? No, not in the least like really. Or like Klingsor's garden? Or the garden in *Alice*? Or like the garden on the top of some Mesopotamian ziggurat which had probably given rise to the whole legend of Paradise? Or simply like all walled gardens?" (61–62). The walled garden at St. Anne's evokes in Jane all those images of earthly paradise—from children's stories, to medieval romances, to ancient mythologies. The gardens of *Peter Rabbit* and *Alice's Adventures in Wonderland* are well known. *The Romance of the Rose* is an allegorical love poem begun in thirteenth-century France by Guillaume de Lorris and continued by Jean de Meung. It is discussed at length by Lewis in *The Allegory of Love*; indeed, Lewis's monumental work did a great deal to revive interest in the poem. All of these are enchanted gardens that evoke a sense of paradise.

Nancy Patterson associates "Klingsor's garden" with an exquisite garden described in "Klingsohr's Fairy Tale" by Novalis.[9] However, apart from the difference in spelling between "Klingsor" and "Klingsohr," the garden in Novalis's story is a masterpiece of artifice, with metal trees and crystal flowers. It would seem a more fitting allusion to the garden at N.I.C.E. than at St. Anne's. A better identification, I believe, is the magic garden encountered by Parsifal when he approaches the castle of Klingsor, the magician in Wagner's *Parsifal* (1882). This is another allusion used by Lewis to link Jane with Percival and St. Anne's with the grail castle.

As she continues along the wall, Jane also ponders the sexual connotations of enclosed gardens, remembering Freud's theory that gardens were subliminal symbols of the female body. This reminder of her own unfulfilled sexuality and unhappy marriage changes her mood from one of reverie to one of defensiveness. As she approaches her first encounter with the now-transformed Ransom, she reminds herself that, at St. Anne's, she is on "hostile, or at least alien, ground" (62). But the hostility Jane senses is within her, not around her. She herself will be transformed by her increasing commitment to Maleldil's side.

Jane's husband, Mark, is transformed by the opposite process, by his nearly fatal entanglement with the dark forces who control N.I.C.E. In the closing pages of the novel, once Mark has recovered himself and realized how weary, flat, stale, and unprofitable all his ambitions have been, he discovers also that he really does love his estranged wife. At the same time Mark realizes that his lifelong obsession to be an insider has led him only to "the dry and choking places," he thinks of Jane as one who has within her "deep wells and knee-deep meadows of happiness, rivers of freshness, enchanted gardens of leisure, which he could not enter but could have spoiled" (247).

At the end of the story, Mark contemplates his failure as a husband and lover, and again he conjures up the image of the walled garden and the cloistered rose.

> All the lout and clown and clod-hopper in him was revealed to his own reluctant inspection; the coarse, male boor with horny hands and hobnailed shoes and beefsteak jaw ... stumping in where great lovers, knights and poets, would have feared to tread.... [He] had behaved as if he were native to that fenced garden and even its natural possessor.... He was discovering the hedge after he had plucked the rose, and not only plucked it but torn it to pieces and crumpled it with hot, thumb-like, greedy fingers. (380–81)

Though Mark's mind is full of self-loathing here, he is actually gaining the humility and self-recognition needed to redeem him from moral failure. Remembering that there are no "innocent" metaphors, we sense that in using medieval motifs to describe Mark's thoughts, Lewis implies that Studdock is developing more humane patterns of thought and feeling.

Fortunately for Mark, one of the things that Jane has learned in her time at St. Anne's is forgiveness. So when Mark and Jane are reunited in a kind of honeymoon cottage, we feel assured that their marriage will be renewed. In a suitably medieval ending, it is Venus herself who bids Mark to go in to his wife and who blesses their marriage bed.

NOTES

1. Gibb 61.

2. Kath Filmer, "The Polemic Image: The Role of Metaphor and Symbol in the Fiction of C.S. Lewis" *Seven: An Anglo-American Literary Review* 7 (1986): 64.

3. Norwood 35; Angele Botros Samaan, "C.S. Lewis: The Utopianist and His Critics," *Cairo Studies in English* 1966: 137–38.

4. Gibb 92; Nancy-Lou Patterson, "Anti-Babels: The Images of the Divine Centre in *That Hideous Strength*," in *Mythcon II Proceedings*, ed. Glen Good-Knight (Los Angeles: Mythopoeic Society, 1972) 11.

5. Roland M. Kawano, "C.S. Lewis and the Great Dance," *Christianity and Literature* 26 (Fall 1976): 24.

6. Chad Walsh, *The Literary Legacy of C.S. Lewis* (New York: Harcourt Brace Jovanovich, 1979) 119.

7. Como 111.

8. *The Oxford Companion to the Literature of Wales*, comp. Meic Stephens (Oxford: Oxford UP, 1986) 671.

9. Patterson 8.

KATH FILMER

Masking the Misogynist in Narnia and Glome

If Lewis wished to portray his fictional women as Ladies of the Courtly Love tradition, he must have realised at some point that the image did not sit comfortably with narratives set in the twentieth century. It is hardly surprising, then, that he should select a setting for his Narnian Chronicles which would allow him to establish very clearly the correspondence between chivalric values and those he projected on to his 'ideal' for twentieth-century women.

He achieves the effect by constructing fairy tales, in which chivalric values are the norm. Narnia is a medieval world accessible from the twentieth century; it is a world in which the chivalric notions of honour, loyalty and defence of 'the right' prevail, a fact which implicitly refers to Lewis's own love and admiration for things medieval. It forms a suitable background for fairy stories which double also as romances of the chivalric mode, allowing Lewis to showcase, as it were, particular beliefs and fancies of his own. Interestingly, these are not Christian, except by Lewis's determined association of them with Christianity. In the Narnian Chronicles, as in his own life, Lewis draws under the rubric of Christianity his own idiosyncratic belief system. Nowhere is this more clearly demonstrated than in his treatment of the female characters.

It must be said that Lewis saw feminism as a modern evil. As a man who 'liked monotony' ('Don vs Devil' 65), supported the Society for the

From *The Fiction of C.S. Lewis: Mask and Mirror*. © 1993 by Kath Filmer.

Prevention of Progress (*Letters of C.S. Lewis* 204), and considered himself to be a dinosaur in regard to both literature and personal inclination ('De Descriptione Temporum' 9–25), Lewis detected in what he called 'modernism' (meaning, not the artistic movement but merely everything since the Industrial Revolution) the manifestation of evil and decay. In the passage which deals with a proposal by Prince Caspian to stop the slave trade on one of the Narnian outposts, Lewis gives readers some insight into his attitude to 'progress' generally:

> 'But that would be putting the clock back,' gasped the governor. 'Have you no idea of progress, of development?'
>
> 'I have seen them both in an egg,' said Caspian. 'We call it 'Going Bad' in Narnia ...' (VDT 49)

If 'modernism' is 'going bad', the converse must be true—at least for Lewis. It comes as no surprise then to find that goddess/Earth Mother figures are the kinds of females of whom Lewis approves, and chatty lovers of make-up and frippery are those he dislikes. One worldly wise female (Susan Pevensie) is excluded from the heavenly Narnia; while another, Lasaraleen, is left to her empty life in Calormen. A series of related Witches personifies supernatural evil, while the Headmistress of Experiment House in *The Silver Chair* is a practitioner of modern psychology who dissolves into hysteria at the conclusion of that book. Since at least four of the Chronicles (from *The Silver Chair* 1953) and possibly five (from *The Voyage of the Dawn Treader* 1952) were written after Lewis began his friendship with Joy Davidman, some significant departure from his usual denigratory portrayal of women has been detected by some critics. For example, Maragaret Hannay believes that a passage in *The Silver Chair* provides 'a sign of a [favourable] change in his attitudes toward women' (Hannay 19); but Hannay's search for signs may have resulted in her misreading them.

The passage Hannay cites is, 'Scrubb was quite right in saying that Jill (I don't know about girls in general) didn't think much about points of the compass' (SC 32). However, Lewis's upbringing after the loss of his mother was in an all-male family; his schools were exclusively boys' schools; his Oxford and Cambridge colleges were all male. Lewis is most likely to be stating a simple truth about himself: he did *not* seem to know much about girls in general. Neither his friendship with Ruth Pitter—which many thought might lead to marriage[1]—nor his affection for Joy Davidman seemed to redress this lifelong lack.

In the first Narnian Chronicle, it is Lucy, the youngest of the Pevensie children, who first discovers Narnia. She is intensely feminine, liking 'nothing ... so much as the smell and feel of fur' (12). Upon meeting Mr Tumnus the Faun and having been entertained by him, she is surprised when he bursts into sobs. She comforts him in a motherly fashion, but when the sobs continue, Lucy becomes even more a corrective maternal figure: 'Stop it at once! You ought to be ashamed of yourself, a great big Faun like *you*' (22).

When the Faun confesses that he is about to kidnap Lucy and take her to the White Witch, she cajoles him in a similar way: 'You're so sorry for it that I'm sure you will never do it again' and 'Indeed, indeed you really mustn't' (24). Like Sarah Smith of Golders Green, Lucy is (almost insufferably) virtuous: 'Lucy was a very truthful girl and she knew she was really in the right' (29) when her sister and brothers refuse to believe that she has really been in a strange new world. Moreover, instead of reacting with annoyance when Edmund also stumbles in on her discovery, she is overjoyed: 'Oh Edmund! ... So you've got in too! Isn't it wonderful!' (41).

Lucy's virtue is emphasised at every opportunity. She is the first to acknowledge that the Robin who guides them is a good bird (59) and who decides that the beaver they meet is 'nice' (62). Once established as a Queen of Narnia, Lucy is called 'Queen Lucy the Valiant' (167); she is a healer, receiving healing unguent from Father Christmas, and she remains a nurse or healer in following Chronicles. It is clear, then, that Lucy is an example of the virtuous Lady of Courtly Love, as Queen, she is desired by 'all the Princes in those parts' though of course she does not marry.

Initially, Susan Pevensie is a similar character; but there is in her character a tendency to pseudo-sophistication (apparent in the early pages of *The Lion, the Witch and the Wardrobe*) which the petulant Edmund interprets as 'trying to talk like Mother' (10). But Susan, at the end, is no friend of Narnia, preferring 'nylons and lipsticks and invitations' (129). Like the Green Witch in *The Silver Chair*, Susan chooses the shadow rather than the reality; she also has features in common with the duplicate Camilla Bembridge in the fragment of *The Dark Tower* and Peggy the fiancee in 'The Shoddy Lands'. All represent the modern, self-centred and mindless women of whom Lewis disapproved. Whether all three characteristics invariably go together is apparently an issue which his own logical mind evaded.

Even Mrs Beaver in *The Lion, the Witch and the Wardrobe* is an instance of the Earth Mother. Introduced as she works at her sewing machine, with potatoes and the kettle both boiling away, she is surprised to have visitors, but manages to produce from the oven 'a great and gloriously sticky marmalade roll', although Lewis overlooks the fact that if the kettle is already on the boil, there is no need to fill it to make tea (69). The narrative gives Mrs Beaver no time to prepare the marmalade roll; as a symbol she is rather larger than life. She fusses and bullies Mr Beaver as they prepare to leave the hole, making sure he has clean handkerchiefs and the rest of the party have adequate supplies of tea, sugar, bread and matches (93–95). She is not, however, intellectually well-endowed; she wants to bring her sewing machine on the flight (93–94). Nevertheless, Father Christmas gives her 'a new and better sewing machine' (99), so that it is obvious that Mrs Beaver will return to domestic duties and associated bliss. Mrs Beaver is not a Mrs Fidget; rather, she is close kin to Mother Dimble in *That Hideous Strength*. Both are (apparently) barren but deeply maternal, both are domestic, submissive and amiable.

Jill Pole, introduced as a new character in *The Silver Chair*, experiences what Ransom (in *That Hideous Strength*) describes as 'a shocking contact with reality' which is 'so masculine that we are all feminine in relation to it'. Confronted by the Lion Aslan, Jill asks, 'Do you eat girls?' and is told, 'I have swallowed up girls and boys, women and men, kings and emperors, cities and realms' (27). Although the point here is that all nature is feminine in relation to God, 'girls' come very clearly at the bottom of the hierarchy. Further, while Eustace plans strategies at the Parliament of Owls, Jill sleeps, suggesting that her priorities lie with comfort rather than with battle-plans; indeed this 'feminine' trait causes her to forget the Signs given her by Aslan. She has become preoccupied with the prospect of 'beds and baths and hot meals' in the Giants' house at Harfang (84).

Although Lucy and Susan are prevented from joining in the battles in *The Lion, the Witch and the Wardrobe*, Jill actively participates in the *mêlée*; but this does not mean that her role as woman has been violated. Rather, she moves from Earth Mother to Goddess, the Amazon of Greek mythology or perhaps even more likely, the Camilla of Roman legend, whom Lewis must have admired since he applies the name to characters in both *The Dark Tower* and *That Hideous Strength*. Her Earth Mother role is seen in her befriending of Puzzle, the Donkey, in *The Last Battle*; she comforts and cuddles him while remaining the warrior—she stands between the King and his would-be prey in a courageous defence of the hapless animal. Perhaps when Lewis writes of Joy Davidman that she was 'something of the Amazon, something of Penthesileia [the Amazon Queen] and Camilla' (*A Grief Observed* 39), he reveals that his attraction to her was based upon her substantial conformity with his notion of the ideal female figure rather than (as Hannay suggests) upon Davidman's influence in changing that notion.

The Horse and His Boy is dedicated to Douglas and David Gresham, and apparently dates from after the friendship between Lewis and Davidman began to develop. In this book, one would expect to see some evidence of the change in Lewis's attitudes towards women of which Hannay writes. And yet the contrast between Aravis and Lasaraleen merely reinforces the impression that Lewis's early prejudices remain:

> [Aravis] remembered now that Lasaraleen had always been ... interested in clothes and parties and gossip. Aravis had always been more interested in bows and arrows and horses and dogs and swimming. (HHB 87)

Aravis is Amazonian, with her interest in the weapons of hunting and warfare, and she is clad in armour when first she meets Shasta. She also possesses some of the attributes of the Earth Mother, with her fondness for animals. Lasaraleen, on the other hand, is self-centred, wanting to talk rather than to listen, content to serve the Tisroc (the false god), and believing that Ahosta the Grand Vizier is 'a very great man'. Aravis is more perceptive; she realises that the Vizier is a self-seeking sycophant. Lasaraleen's self-centredness is similar to that of Pam, in *The Great Divorce*, and the mother in *The Screwtape Letters*; she is evil by default in a sense, since although she hardly knows better, she is too self-centred to make an effort to learn.

The talking horse Hwin who appears in the same story (she is, in fact, the 'horse' of the title) embodies all those feminine characteristics Lewis favours. She is maternal, saving Aravis's life with a motherly rebuke (38); she is humble, willingly disguising her own well-bred lines so that her party could travel safely through Tashbaan (29). Though nervous and gentle, Hwin has great courage, and when she is pushed almost beyond endurance, she carries on; 'It's all for Narnia', she tells herself (116–17). Interestingly, although this book was published in 1954, some years before Joy Davidman was to fall victim to cancer, Hwin demonstrates the kind of courage and endurance which Lewis was to so admire in Davidman during the latter's illness. Again, as the fiction suggests, it seems that Lewis's affection for Davidman developed because she embodied so many of the traits with which he endowed the favoured women in his fiction.

All through the Narnian Chronicles, Lewis uses female figures as examples of evil manifested through the corrupting effect of power. Jadis, the White Witch, appears in *The Lion, the Witch and the Wardrobe* and again in *The Magician's Nephew*; the Green Witch rules the Underworld in *The Silver Chair*; and in the same book, the Headmistress of Experiment House uses modern psychotherapeutic methods of promoting evil in the bullying tactics of her favoured pupils. It is safe to assume that, like Pam in *The Great Divorce*, Fairy Hardcastle in *That Hideous Strength*, and the modern duplicate Camilla in *The Dark Tower*, these women embody all those female traits which Lewis abhorred.

The White Witch in the first Narnian Chronicle is a symbol for disease (or dis-ease) by means of her whiteness; she is a sickly white, and associated with her are the sickly sweet images of icing sugar and a surfeit of Turkish Delight (33). And the Witch is certainly a cause of dis-ease; she is responsible for bringing the endless winter; which is (as mentioned earlier), according to Northrop Frye, the archetypal seasonal symbol for the triumph of the powers of darkness (Frye 16); and she is very like Hans Christian Andersen's character the Snow Queen—another evil character whose power is also 'wintery'.

Lewis also exploits the Western convention that children should not accept sweets from strangers, since such strangers are traditionally held to be malevolent. This the White Witch most certainly is; in her Lewis has embodied many devilish features: deception, cruelty, enslavement, and the creation of 'un-creatures' by turning them, with Medusa-like power, into statues of stone.

Because the Witch is white, not black, the usual colour for the wicked witch of fairy tales, her deceit begins from the moment of her first appearance. Moreover, she deceives Edmund into believing she is the true ruler of Narnia, and she deceives herself by imagining that she can defeat Aslan by putting him to death. She may be seen as one of the whited sepulchres condemned by Christ, since she possesses both exterior beauty and inner corruption.

Though the White Witch is cunning, her knowledge is deficient. As an emissary of evil, she is neither omnipotent nor omniscient; indeed, although death does not defeat Aslan, it does defeat the Witch. She is a clear instance of devilry being identified as female. And she is also an example of the 'Great Goddess' figure on which many sinister female literary characters are based—for example, Keats's La Belle Dame Sans Merci and his Lamia; the Arthurian enchantress Morgan le Fay, MacDonald's Lilith and Lewis's own Ungit and Orual in *Till We Have Faces*. The devouring aspect of the goddess was probably based upon the male fear, in mythology, of the *vagina dentata* and resulting castration (de Vries 224–26, 504–5, 490).

Evil enters the Narnian world shortly after its creation in the form of Jadis, who is the White Witch in her identity as the Queen of the dead world of Charn. She is a self-deceived, self-worshipping creature who takes no responsibility for her own actions and who demands from all and sundry their worship and adulation. Her enjoyment of spilling blood and of killing links her clearly with the devouring goddess image, the negative and fearful aspects of femininity which seem to have had a profound influence upon C.S. Lewis.

If the Green Witch is not another manifestation of Jadis—and the textual evidence suggests that she is not—she is certainly of the same *genus* and she shares the same attributes. Like the White Witch, who is 'one of the Jinn' (LWW 76), the Green Witch too is 'of divine origin' (SC 135). Like the White Witch, the Green Witch enslaves the inhabitants of the world over which she rules; she too makes humans into un-humans, and treats Prince Rilian like 'a toy and lap-dog' (143). Rilian's plea, during the moments of lucidity he experiences, is 'to be a man again' (142), which establishes a correspondence between the Green Witch and the devouring Great Goddess, since both are responsible, in some sense, for the loss of 'manhood'.

What is disturbing in the Narnian Chronicles, as well as in the whole range of Lewis's literary corpus is the way in which ultimate good is depicted as ultimate masculinity, while evil, the corruption of good, is depicted as femininity. Lewis was obviously not aware that the biblical image of God incorporates both masculinity and femininity, as in the Genesis text, where both sexes are required to image God (1:27); and again in the book of Job, where the name for God, El Shaddai, has been related to the Semitic word for breast through its primary meaning of mountain (Opope 44). There are also a number of maternal metaphors used in reference to God: 'Can a woman forsake her sucking child?' (Isaiah 49:15), and 'As one whom his mother comforts, so I will comfort you' (Isaiah 66:13). In the New Testament, Christ likens his love for Jerusalem to that of a hen for her chickens (Matthew 23:27, Luke 13:34).

One of the nastiest female characters is the Head of Experiment House, who also appears in *The Silver Chair*. She provides Lewis with the opportunity to hold evil and modernism, not to mention intelligent women, up to ridicule. The Head psycho-analyses her erring students, and if they toady to her, they become her favourites, since she enjoys worship and adulation. Although the Head is a symbol for devilish feminism, she is not so much a figure of fear but of fun. Confronted by Prince Caspian who returns from Narnia with Jill and Edmund, she 'had hysterics' (205). Her title, 'The Head', evokes memories of the demonic disembodied Head of *That Hideous Strength*, but, in what Lewis must have thought of as a humorous gesture, she becomes a school inspector in order to 'interfere with other Heads'—a job at which she is rather less than successful. She eventually enters Parliament through the good offices of her friends, but there, too, she is inept and incapable. Lewis's male characters who exhibit devilish traits become fearsomely powerful; this woman becomes a weak joke. Even in depicting his evil characters, Lewis attributes power to the males and renders his females ineffectual.

It is quite clear, then, that Lewis's attitudes to, and treatment of, his female characters underwent no marked change with the writing of the Narnian Chronicles or with his developing friendship with Joy Davidman. The characterisations typical of Lewis's earlier fiction recur in the Chronicles with the same bitterness and the same slightly sneering and superior authorial tone.

According to Douglas Gresham, the son of Joy Davidman, his mother and Lewis 'worked together' on Lewis's last novel, *Till We Have Faces* in the summer (that is, from June to August) of 1957, and the book is certainly dedicated to her.[2] There is no doubt that Lewis welcomed suggestions from his friends when he was working on his fiction, and there is no doubt, either, that Lewis was profoundly influenced by people close to him. The references to Numinor (a misspelling of Númenor) and Logres in *That Hideous Strength* attest to the influence of Tolkien and especially of Charles Williams on that novel. It is entirely likely that Lewis would have welcomed suggestions and comments from Joy Davidman. Nevertheless, I believe the book is Lewis's own, and, in a sense, an attempt at spiritual autobiography. But there is little evidence in it that Lewis's attitudes to women had changed, despite the so-called 'radical change' in his adopting a new literary form—myth—for this novel.

There is a very real sense in which every novel in his *oeuvre* was a 'radical departure' for Lewis. He experimented with different forms in response to the developments in his life at the time of writing. For example, *The Pilgrim's Regress*—a response to Bunyan's *The Pilgrim's Progress*—came after Lewis had published poetry. Its allegorical nature was possibly prompted by Lewis's interest in allegory as shown in his scholarly book *The Allegory of Love*. And, as previously noted *Out of the Silent Planet* is a response to H. G. Wells's *The First Men in the Moon* (even to a parallel plot line); while *Perelandra* was written at the same time as, and was probably inspired by, Lewis's scholarly study of *Paradise Lost*. *The Great Divorce*, a dream fantasy, and *The Screwtape Letters*, a Swiftian satire written in the episolatory style, were also 'radical departures'—as are the Narnian Chronicles. Indeed, experimentation with genres typifies his writing; in choosing a new form for *Till We Have Faces*, then, Lewis was demonstrating consistency, rather than inconsistency, in his writing practice.

It has also been suggested that Orual, the protagonist of *Till We Have Faces*, was modelled upon Joy Davidman; and it is true that Davidman wrote frankly of her battle with roles and personae in her autobiographical article 'The Longest Way Round'. Nevertheless, Davidman makes clear that she was influenced by Lewis, not he by her (116–17). And Lewis was wrestling with his own masks and posturings twenty years earlier, as his poem 'Postures' in *The Pilgrim's Regress* makes clear. It is with this poem that many parallels exist in *Till We Have Faces*; such parallels show Lewis's cycle of novels ending pretty much where it began—self-consciously and self-analytically; and ending, also, with a celebration of essentially the same beliefs and attitudes that are so much a feature of his early work.

Till We Have Faces is not an easy book to read. Indeed, it was 'the great disappointment of Lewis's career' that the book received 'a cool reception' from the reading public (Green and Hooper 265). There are two distinctive features of the novel: the first is the autobiographical voice, the second the fact that this voice is female. It seems that what Lewis does is to attempt in some way to exorcise the ghosts of his own psyche. Like Mary Shelley with *Frankenstein*, like Charles Dickens with *Great Expectations*, and like Ursula Le Guin with *The Left Hand of Darkness*, Lewis projects himself onto a character who 'completes' himself, who makes, with the author, a kind of androgynous whole.[3] In other words, he confronts what Jung calls the *anima* as it is projected upon the character Orual. Because of this projection and Lewis's use of archetypes in achieving it, there is also a sense in which readers also are drawn in to a similar confrontation. And it is in this fusion of identities—of author, of protagonist, of reader—that this novel develops and maintains an emotional intensity which repels many readers. But to those who accept the deeply mythical and metaphorical nature of the book, there is a sense in which the novel works as both mask and mirror—concealing Lewis behind the mask of Orual, but vividly revealing him through her enactment of his spiritual quest. It is a quest to shed the spiritually fallen Self, its masks and postures, so that at last Orual—or Lewis—can be real.

Lewis's name for the pagan state and its capital city in which the novel is set is Glome. This is a word designed to evoke a sense of gloom, for which the name is a near-homophone. There is, also, a resonance with the Scottish word for twilight, 'gloaming'. And Glome is a twilight world; it has not had the 'light' of Christianity, and its inhabitants are self-centred and self-serving. There may be a further allusion to the words of the Pauline epistle: '... now we see through a glass, darkly, but then face to face: now I know in part; but then shall I know even as also I am known' (1 Cor. 13:12).

The two principal characters, Orual and Psyche, enact the quest suggested by the title—the quest for the true self. But there are other female characters in the novel who clearly indicate that Lewis never significantly changed his views about the nature of women. They are still either saints or sluts, either goddesses or devouring devils.

Orual and Psyche's middle sister, Redival, is wanton and sensual, embarrassing the girls' tutor, the Fox, with her lack of modesty:

> 'Heigh-ho,' yawns Redival, lying flat on her back in the grass and kicking her legs in the air till you could see all there was of her (which she did purely to put the Fox out of countenance, for the old man was very modest). (36)

Redival also flirts with a young officer, Tarin; but her tyrannical father witnesses the event and gelds the young man. But Redival desires only to marry 'a young king, brave, yellow-bearded, and lusty' (37). Excluded during her childhood by Orual's preoccupation with the Fox and later with Psyche, Redival is jealous and lonely; in maturity, with a family of her own, her life is completely centred on her own small world. As a character, she is not unlike Susan Pevensie of the Narnian Chronicles, or the modest ghost who worries about her attire in *The Great Divorce*, or the worldly Camilla in *The Dark Tower*, or—finally—Peggy in 'The Shoddy Lands'. All are examples of the worldly, self-centred woman who demands attention and admiration.

In Batta, the slave, Lewis achieves a denigration of the female equalled perhaps only by Fairy Hardcastle in *That Hideous Strength*. Batta is drunken and spiteful, jealous and gossiping. She is also treacherous: she callously betrays Psyche to the Priest when Psyche has been chosen to be sacrificed. She dominates the Glomish royal household until Orual has her hanged, and even the name Batta connotes dark places, vampiric evil and bats, which, according to Cirlot, were associated in Western alchemy with the dragon or satanic figure; their wings in particular are also an infernal attribute (23). Even Batta's attempts at maternal comfort are smothering and sinister. She is in some ways the darkest picture of femininity Lewis draws, and yet she is a creation of his own imagination, an attempt, perhaps, to face the dark *anima* within his own psychological identity. Was Lewis trying to come to terms with the mother who was too ill to comfort him when he was suffering agonies of toothache as a very young child? Did he feel in some ways betrayed by her so that women were to be avoided, and above all never to be trusted, in the course of most of his adult life? It is not possible to attribute biographical verity to the characters Lewis creates; but it is possible to see these warped women as products of Lewis's own monstrous imaginings and projections of the dark aspect of his own *anima*.

By contrast, Pysche and Orual exhibit those characteristics which Lewis always found admirable in women. Before she is sacrificed, Psyche, the healer, the Earth Mother, is a character cognate with Sarah Smith of Golders Green; but she is still bound by her natural affections until she completes the quest for the Water of Death on behalf of Orual. Lewis is careful to show Psyche as a flawed character, despite her beauty and charm. She evades Orual's questions about accepting tokens of worship, and her own response when Orual elicits the truth—'Is it wrong?'—seems more than a trifle disingenuous (35–36); Psyche seems to be well aware that she was accepting a role which she should not. Further, there seems to be a touch of pride and ambition to Psyche's dream of the Grey Mountain:

> 'When I'm big,' she said, 'I will be a great, great queen, married to the greatest king of all, and he will build me a castle of gold and amber up there on the very top.' (31)

This insistence upon greatness indicates a lack of humility; but Psyche's most serious flaw is her enslavement to her natural love for Orual.

It is an enslavement of which Psyche is only too well aware: 'I felt like a bird in a cage when the other birds of its kind are flying home' (82); it is, moreover, an enslavement which results in her rejection of the god, the ultimate reality, when she disobeys him at Orual's request. But Psyche is fully responsible for her own actions: 'I know what I do,' she admits at the moment when she stands to lose her lover and her happiness (175–76). The god punishes Psyche by exiling her so that she can finally choose between the natural and the spiritual realms, between the natural love and surrender to the ultimate reality and individuation offered her by the god.

Throughout the novel, Psyche is shown in a sympathetic light; but what is generally overlooked is that Psyche is seen (as indeed are all the characters) through the eyes of the first-person protagonist, Orual. The perceptions recorded by Orual are often quite clear, such as when she describes the tyrannical selves of her father, King Trom, Batta, and Redival; but the characteristics she describes with most clarity and revulsion are those which are mirrored in her own personality. As Jungian psychotherapist June Singer explains:

> If, when an individual speaks of another person whom he hates with a vehemence that seems nearly irrational, he can be brought to describe that person's characteristics which he most dislikes,

you will frequently have a picture of his own repressed aspects which are unrecognised by him though obvious to others. (Singer 192)

This psychological truth is evident in *Till We Have Faces*: Orual presents the cruel face of her father as when Psyche attempts to soothe Orual's rage when the people turn against the younger girl: 'There, don't be angry. You look just like our father when you say those things' (48). Again, confronting Psyche on the mountain, and unable to see Psyche's spiritual world, Orual experiences 'fury—my father's own fury' (127). But does the psychological truth hold for author as well as protagonist? Are the monstrous selves he depicts images of the unrecognised monsters within himself?

Orual shows to her readers, if not to others, the sensuous face of Redival in the fantasies where Bardia has become her husband (233); more often she reveals a Batta-face, deceiving the Fox about the palace on the Grey Mountain, allowing him to think it is merely the gold and amber castle of Psyche's childhood dreams—and this despite the fact that Orual has glimpsed the real castle (141). Orual also misleads Psyche in her account of how Bardia and the Fox regard the Shadowbrute, and justifies the lie by suggesting that it would help her towards truth (170). On learning that Orual has shared her confidences with the Fox and Bardia, Psyche observes, 'It was more like Batta than you' (170).

Deception, cruelty, anger and gossip all distort Orual's personality and her perceptions of reality, but at the heart of these manifestations of the self-aggrandising self is a consuming jealousy. Orual loves Psyche, but it is a love which demands total possession and enslavement. It is a love corrupted by the assertive self, the *meum* of theology which chooses itself over God, demands worship and gratification and which corrupts human affections by imprisoning the beloved. Orual's behaviour is an illustration of what Lewis calls Affection, the most natural of the four loves (affection, erotic love, friendship and agape love) of which humanity is capable (*The Four Loves* 33–54).

Again Lewis has chosen to exemplify the possessiveness and the domination of others to which possessiveness leads, through a female character. Humphrey Carpenter suggests that the novel is 'a self portrait of Lewis' (245), while Peter Schakel believes that Lewis's growing relationship with Joy Davidman allowed him 'to give attention to himself and to write about himself' (151). Schakel goes on to say that the distancing technique of allegory which Lewis used to write *The Pilgrim's Regress* was overcome, that the influence of Joy Davidman allowed Lewis a subjectivity which is apparent in both *Surprised by Joy* and *Till We Have Faces* (151); but *Surprised by Joy* is a restrained and guarded account of carefully selected incidents, an account of conversion distanced from emotion, and the personal element veiled by long passages which reveal more about the influences upon Lewis than about Lewis himself.

Till We Have Faces also allows Lewis distance and restraint—or, metaphorically, a mask through which to peer into the mirror. By using a female character behind which to conceal the author's own self, Lewis follows in this novel the same patterns set in his earlier fiction. Orual is yet another mask; it is perhaps ironical that she functions also as perhaps the clearest mirror reflection of Lewis's own tormented spirit in all his fiction.

Orual's besetting fault is jealousy. She is jealous of Psyche's beauty, but finds some satisfaction in being, for a time, the centre of Psyche's world. When Psyche seeks to widen her world, Orual is desperate. The warped nature of her affections is seen in a passage where the older woman tries to define her love: she wants to be mother and male lover and sister and slave, and her love is seen to be full of misplaced eroticism, masochism, and sadism (31).

What distorts affection into a quasi-incestuous, punishing and devouring emotion is the need to be totally in control of another person's life. This, Lewis recognised, is devilish; and in his portrayal of this most human weakness undoubtedly has caused many readers grave discomfort. It is a natural development of human affection, and Glome is a world which is set very firmly in the natural world—that is, among the appetites and cravings of human beings who aspire to nothing higher than nature, to whom the supernatural is a force to be appeased and avoided. Lewis seems to have recognised this aspect of himself. In a poem written for his wife shortly before her death, he reveals his personal difficulties upon finding his world in ruins:

> All this is flashy rhetoric about loving you.
> I never had a selfless thought since I was born.
> I am mercenary and self-seeking through and through:
> I want God, you, all friends, merely to serve my turn.
>
> (*Poems* 109–10)

Like Lewis, Orual must achieve self-knowledge, she must she herself as she truly is. The god tells her in the moment of solemn judgment, '... know yourself and your work. You also shall be Psyche' (182). But this is painful. Orual tries to hide from herself by adopting poses and personae; she even wears a black veil to hide her face completely from the world.

Her roles are Amazonian, following the pattern of womanly behaviour which Lewis admired; she is a Camilla when she dons armour and fights with men, learning to kill in battle. She is a wise Queen, releasing slaves, treating the workers in her mines fairly, and encouraging education and learning. But the Queen is haunted by Orual, and images of herself are introduced into the narrative through a series of mirrors both actual and metaphorical.

The first and most important of these is the text of the novel itself. Orual's complaint against the gods is echoed in the story told by the priest of Essur who presents a version of the Cupid and Psyche myth from Apuleius, emphasising the element of jealousy in the relationship between the sisters. Orual 'sees' herself in this mirrored tale, but denies what she sees. Next, she meets the eunuch Tarin, who shows Orual how her possessiveness towards the Fox and Psyche alienated Redival, who had been lonely and who felt unloved. Again, Orual refuses to recognise herself (266). The visit of Bardia's wife, Ansit, functions in the same way. Ansit tells Orual that the latter is a vampire who drains dry all those who love or serve her: 'Faugh! You're full fed. Gorged with other men's lives; women's too. Bardia's; mine; the Fox's; your sister's; both your sisters' (275). Again, Orual denies the allegation; it takes a visit to the dark and bloody temple of the ancient goddess of Glome to waken her to self-realisation.

The goddess, Ungit, is a squat stone; a faceless lump of rock. And yet Orual discerns in the rock thousands of faces, thousands of masks (281). Orual, veiled, is also faceless, yet her roles as man, friend, Queen and warrior supply faces. As she gazes at Ungit, she is reminded of Batta's smothering affections: in that instant Batta and Ungit melt into one mirrored reflection of Orual's own self.

Finally, an image of Orual's father appears and leads her down through many levels of ground—a Jungian archetype for journeys into the depths of the unconscious. She is at last able to come to terms with what and who she is. 'I am Ungit', she confesses to the mirror in which she sees herself (287); she is Trom, Batta, Redival, the Fox, Ansit and Bardia, but not yet Psyche.

Despairing, Orual tries to suicide, but a warning voice prevents her. Finally, armed with her grievance against the gods (the text of the book is her complaint against their injustices to her), she appears in the Deadlands before a mystical judge. She hears in her complaint her real voice, sees in herself the real self, and at last, revulsed by both, she is able to surrender. She becomes, like her sister Psyche, redeemed and glorious; there are 'two Psyches, the one clothed, the other naked ... both beautiful ... beyond all imagining, yet not exactly the same' (319). The Amazon has become a goddess in the act of spiritual individuation.

The novel relates the same process which is the subject of Lewis's early poem, 'Postures':

> Because of endless pride
> Reborn with endless error,
> Each hour I look aside
> Upon my secret mirror
> Trying all my postures there
> To make my image fair.
>
> (*PR* 184)

The poem ends with the declaration that self-love must die, bringing forth a reborn personality, a spiritually and psychologically whole individual. The themes of the novel are very close to those of the poem—postures, masks and poses, all of which must be acknowledged by facing their reflections in a mirror, and which then must be put to death so that the new soul can be reborn.

These correspondences cannot be mere coincidence: it is clear that Lewis is tackling in detail and depth in his last work of fiction the same concerns which confronted him in his earlier work.

And in the same way, those feminine attributes which receive Lewis's approval in the early novels recur in his last. The Amazon, the goddess, the Earth Mother are all acclaimed; while Ungit, Batta and Redival, and the character Orual's jealous and possessive, unredeemed state, are consistent with those female characters and characteristics which Lewis denigrates. It seems, then, that Joy Davidman's role for Lewis was to bring to life the Lady of Courtly Love tradition so that Lewis could love and admire her in person. Nevertheless, despite Lewis's admiration for her, and his long friendship with Ruth Pitter, his attitudes to women generally were little affected. He chose for his wife that woman who could fulfil in his life the role of earth mother and warrior-goddess. His choice of the character Orual through which to relate a spiritual autobiography is consistent with his former restraint in revealing himself without the security of a mask of some kind. It is, moreover, entirely consistent with his belief that God is utterly Masculine, and that all else, in relation to God, is necessarily feminine.

Till We Have Faces is, I believe, Lewis's most compelling and powerful novel. But the Lewis it reveals beyond the masks and through the mirrors in this his final novel is the same Lewis to be found in his first.

NOTES

1. It is said that Lewis confided to his friend Hugo Dyson, 'I am not a man for marriage, but if I were, I would ask R P' (uttered by Dyson to Miss Pitter and quoted in the editorial introduction to her 'Poet to Poet' contribution to *In Search of C.S. Lewis*, ed. Stephen Schofield (South Plainfield, NJ: Bridge, 1983) 111.

2. In an address at the Seminar held by The Inner Ring, Saturday, August 11, 1985, at The University of Queensland and later published in *The Ring Bearer* from tapes made of the proceedings. He has made an error with the date; the book was in the hands of the publishers by February 1956, three months prior to Lewis's marriage (Green and Hooper, 261, 268).

3. The relationship between Le Guin and Genly Ai in *The Left Hand of Darkness* has been discussed by Robert Scholes in his book *Textual Power: Literary Theory and the Teaching of English* (127). The relationship between Mary Shelley and the character Frankenstein and his monster has been discussed by Barbara Johnson in 'My Monster My Self' (in her *A World of Difference*, 151ff). A summary of these treatments, and detailed discussion of Dickens's relationship with Pip in *Great Expectations*, including the 'feminine' aspects of Pip, are to be found in my article 'The Spectre of Self in *Frankenstein* and *Great Expectations*', in *The Victorian Fantasists: Essays on Culture, Society and Belief in Victorian Mythopoeic Literature*, ed. Kath Filmer (London: Macmillan, 1991).

LIONEL ADEY

Children's Storyteller

Of all the books by Lewis, the Chronicles of Narnia have attracted and retained the largest readership. Critics have explored their plots, characters, and genre, religious and moral teaching, language, biblical and literary sources, structural devices, symbols, and motifs, not to mention the geography of their imagined worlds.[1] Just as it seemed that nothing new could be said about them, I read David Holbrook's *Skeleton in the Wardrobe*.[2] After so many encomia on the stories, this book acted as a shot of adrenalin, but when a Leavisite critic attempts assassination by psychoanalysis, no friend of Narnia can stand by and do nothing.

Holbrook gives two reasons for thinking the tales unfit for children. The first is that Lewis was insufficiently mature to handle the "deeply disturbing material" (Holbrook, 173) that welled up from his unconscious as he wrote. Queen Jadis the White Witch (*Magician's Nephew, The Lion, the Witch and the Wardrobe*) and the Witch of the Green Kirtle (*Silver Chair*) emanated from Lewis's mother, who had not only rejected him by dying but had earlier failed to confer a secure identity through creative play. Aslan, the Christ of Narnia (whose name Lewis derived from the euphonious Turkish word for lion),[3] bounded into Narnia "out of Lewis's own unconscious" (Holbrook, 55), originating in Rev. Robert Capron, the flagellating principal of Wynyard School ("Belsen"). Having identified with the aggressor, the

From *C.S. Lewis: Writer, Dreamer and Mentor.* © 1998 by William B. Eerdmans Publishing Co.

"unhappy child" (Holbrook, 11) surviving within the distinguished academic turned Capron into a punitive deity.

Holbrook goes on with the happy freedom of an amateur psychoanalyst to convert Mrs. Lewis's "cheerful and tranquil affection" (*Surprised by Joy*, 9) into maternal coldness and inadequacy, and her nine-year-old son's grief into a castration complex (Holbrook, 36, 48–49). He infers a presumption that her cancer had resulted from marital intercourse (Holbrook, 65), that her "Bad Breast" is represented in the spires and turrets of the White Witch's castle (Holbrook, 36, 68, 73), and that a Narnian lamp-post represents the paternal penis (Holbrook, 67). In response to such an interpretation, the uninventive scholar can only protest that from at one time daily readings of Wordsworth's *Prelude* Lewis was fully conscious of the maternal role in forming a child's identity, and that he nowhere wrote of being thrashed at Wynyard, only of his unsought status as Capron's "pet."[4]

Admittedly the most convincing villains in the tales are female, and the heroes include three orphan princes. Compared to Queen Jadis, King Miraz (*Prince Caspian*) is a paper cutout of Hamlet's wicked uncle, and Uncle Andrew (*Magician's Nephew*) a clown. Since Jadis the Queen-Witch existed from before the creation of Narnia, her name probably derives from the French word *jadis* ("formerly," "once upon a time") rather than from "jade" ("nightmare") as Holbrook suggests (Holbrook, 65). She brought about the ruin of the ancient city of Charn, introduced evil into the world on the day of Narnia's creation (*Magician's Nephew*), and practiced "Deep Magic from the dawn of time" (*The Lion, the Witch and the Wardrobe*, chap. 13). As I have argued, Lewis's antifeminism and need of a surrogate mother did result from his childish perception of being abandoned by his mother and the added shock of being sent so soon to boarding school. But this does not license conjectures about his babyhood for which neither *Surprised by Joy* nor the letters of Mrs. Lewis offer any support, so as to turn her into a witch. Nor will supposed parallels with psychiatric patients prove much about Lewis.

There is more to support Holbrook's belief that Capron's cruelty inflicted lasting damage. Lewis describes with horror seeing a classmate caned (*Surprised by Joy*, 28), an experience I recall as being more distressing than being caned in person. But Lewis's own attribution of his first religious convictions—and terrors—to the faith of clergy at the Anglo-Catholic church near the school (*Surprised by Joy*, 33) implies an identification with them rather than with the clerical sadist Capron.

As regards the "minatory" (Holbrook, 34 et al.) figure of Aslan, it is important to note that punishments in the tales usually involve religious symbolism. Thus the metamorphosis of Eustace into a dragon (*Voyage of the*

"*Dawn Treader*") alludes to a biblical image of the devil (Revelation 12:3–9). The peeling of the dragon skin down to the boy's heart, which Holbrook converts from singular to plural (Aslan "lacerates and unpeels people": Holbrook, 30), represents conversion and repentance. Its good effects can be seen in Eustace's satisfaction in helping his fellow voyagers while still a dragon and in his newly developed sense of humor once restored to human shape. Aslan's mauling of Aravis (*The Horse and His Boy*) is also an external sign of a need for inward change, for it brings home to her the punishment of the slave-girl she deceived into abetting her escape. When Shasta comes to her defense, Aslan at once departs. In the same book, Prince Rabadash's transformation into a donkey is reversed on condition of good behavior, a fact that Holbrook conveniently ignores. Like the dwarf's taunting of Edmund, "'Turkish delight for the little prince'" (*The Lion, the Witch and the Wardrobe*, chap. 11), it represents reform by ridicule. To call Aslan a "minatory figure" is to miss much that children love about him: the golden mane and silky fur, the playful rolls and graceful steps.

Holbrook's second major criticism is that Lewis acts duplicitously in presenting his own nightmares as fairy tales, his own misogyny and paranoid view of the world as Christian teaching. If, as Lewis maintained, his fictions grew out of mental images[5] (as Holbrook adds, from his unconscious), he had no hidden agenda. If he found the world a cruel place through which his characters needed guidance, so do many children in tough schools or adults outside the secure enclaves of the prosperous. On Lewis's own submission, the win-or-lose situation of Britain in the 1940s was what his experience had led him to expect (*Surprised by Joy*, 32), but that says as much about his battle experience in 1918 as about his schooldays at Wynyard. By combining his antipathy to "coarse, brainless" boys at Malvern who had inflicted "abject misery, terrorism and hopelessness" (*They Stand Together*, 47, 55) with his tirades about homosexuality between "Bloods" and "tarts" (*Surprised by Joy*, chaps. 7–8), one might guess at sexual abuse that an adolescent would be too embarrassed to report yet surely too grownup to repress into his unconscious, but that would be only conjecture.

Although Lewis was worried by a headmistress's prediction that his *Lion, the Witch and the Wardrobe* would confuse and terrify children,[6] in fifteen years of teaching the stories to students who mostly read them first as children, I recall not one complaint of their inspiring fear or hatred. Some objected to talking animals and some, justifiably, to the strictures on coeducation in the *Silver Chair*, a book dated by its author's prejudice against "progressive" schooling and parenting, not to mention the absurd headmistress of Experiment House. Such, however, is often the case with children's classics. Consider the Victorian idea of a healthy diet in *The Secret Garden*: eggs, butter, and lashings of cream. Or compare the "delight and joy" that Isaac Watts's *Divine and Moral Songs* gave eighteenth-century children with their denunciation by a twentieth-century historian appalled by their images of hell.[7] Indeed, that Lewis himself received countless enquiries from both children and adults is a tribute in itself.

To judge the Chronicles of Narnia from figures and symbols taken out of context is to distort them. To read the tales as wholes, whether individually or in sequence, is to realize the equal importance of symbols that originated in mid-twentieth-century life, in medieval and Renaissance literature, and in Lewis's own past.[8] Captain Maugrim the wolf (*The Lion, the Witch and the Wardrobe*) may embody a castrating mother-figure, as Holbrook claims (Holbrook, 65), but as head of a tyrant's secret police he signified a very real threat when Lewis began the tale (1939), or even when he published it (1951). The medieval swords and arrows of Narnian warfare are even less likely to terrify or brutalize children than the six-shooters of old-time westerns. As with the final slaughter in Homer's *Odyssey*, obsolete weaponry and the written word filter violence through the reader's imagination. It may be of interest to note that the villainess of Morris's *Water of the Wondrous Isles* is also called a "Witch," and the heroine addressed as "Daughter of Adam" (Morris, 469). In the case of educational or racial prejudices, as in the portrayal of dark-skinned, garlic-smelling Calormenes (*Last Battle*), such elements risk provoking protest and so spoiling the illusion for adult readers, but whether they annoy or puzzle the young one must vary with the individual.

It may be useful to consider the Chronicles' probable meaning, influence on, and attraction for young readers. Details noticed by young readers may depend on whether the books are read at random, as must often happen, or in a deliberate order: either the order in which the books were completed (*The Lion, the Witch and the Wardrobe*; *Prince Caspian*; *Voyage of the "Dawn Treader"*; *Horse and His Boy*; *Silver Chair*; *Last Battle*; *Magician's Nephew*); the order of their publication (*The Lion, the Witch and the Wardrobe*; *Prince Caspian*; *Voyage of the "Dawn Treader"*; *Silver Chair*; *Horse and His Boy*; *Magician's Nephew*; *Last Battle*); or the order of chronology from the creation to the end of Narnia (*Magician's Nephew*; *The Lion, the Witch and the Wardrobe*; *Horse and His Boy*; *Prince Caspian*; *Voyage of the "Dawn Treader"*, *Silver Chair*; *Last Battle*).[9]

Those who read in the order of writing are more likely to perceive the progression from early childhood to old age in the protagonists and in the Narnian landscape.[10] Having briefly begun writing *The Lion, the Witch and the Wardrobe* late in 1939, Lewis resumed in the summer of 1948. From that point, the whole series took him six years, long enough for some changes of perspective to emerge. In *The Horse and His Boy*, written in 1950, the Calormene sovereign, Prince Rabadash, and the Grand Vizier use the rhetorical formulae of the Arabian Nights. In *The Last Battle*, written two years later, the worshipers of Tash bow to the ground like Muslims, yet the Calormene officer Emeth uses plain English and is welcome in Aslan's country because he has obeyed the universal moral law that Lewis elsewhere called "the Tao." Imagination and, no doubt, reflection on the author's own *Abolition of Man* have modified a stereotype and a dogma. The continuing concern in the Chronicles with the effects on children's values of positivist conditioning has been very fully explored by Myers.[11]

In *The Lion, the Witch and the Wardrobe*, the four Pevensie children are evacuated from London during the war to the house of an old bachelor known as "the Professor." While hiding in a wardrobe to escape a tour of the house led by the housekeeper, they find it to be a passage into another world and so stumble into Narnia by seeming accident. Yet in Aslan's good time they find themselves to be Narnia's long-expected sovereigns.[12] The youngest of the children, and the first to enter Narnia, is named after Lucy Barfield, to whom the book is dedicated, whose first name has the root meaning "light."[13] Lewis concluded the book by anticipating "further adventures" in Narnia, and at once began *Prince Caspian*. As that book opens, the Pevensies are waiting at a junction for the trains that will take the girls to one school and the boys to another, when they are summoned back to Narnia by a horn blast. The horn signals a cross-over not only from childhood to pubescence but also from present time to the author's inner journey, for Prince Caspian's medieval education is analogous to Lewis's own development from predilection for folklore and romance to rejection of modernism and secular humanism. When finally returned to the station platform, Peter and Susan have grown too old to visit Narnia again.

The past in the enchanting *Voyage of the "Dawn Treader"* is more cultural than personal. The two youngest Pevensies, Edmund and Lucy, are spending the summer with their aunt and uncle. Their cousin Eustace has had a modern, permissive upbringing by parents who taught him to call them by their first names instead of "Mother" and "Father" and has attended a school resembling Summerhill or Dartington Hall. While discussing a picture of a Narnian ship that is hanging in a back bedroom, all three children suddenly find themselves aboard the ship, which is called the *Dawn Treader* (a name signifying discovery and enlightenment). Once at sea, Eustace is reeducated by experience in a world that is predominantly symbolic and mythological. Transformed in the "Lone" Isles into a dragon, he suffers the isolation that awaits a spoilt child, then has his dragon skin peeled off down to his heart, so as to become a caring and sharing person. Lewis attributes the boy's greed and egoism to his permissive upbringing. The more spoiled the child, the deeper and more painful his reformation.

Following Eustace's transformation, the voyage takes us even further into a timeless world of myth and symbol. The finding of a Narnian lord's corpse on the isle called Goldwater by King Caspian but Deathwater by the idealist Reepicheep (chap. 8) doubtless originated in the Midas myth but represents opposed values. A psychological symbol, the rescue from Dark Island of an exiled Narnian lord nearly driven mad by the terror of nightmares coming true (chap. 12) implies a lack of trust remarked by Bacon: "Men fear death as children fear to go in the dark."[14] When the *Dawn Treader* approaches the Utter East to set Reepicheep down near Aslan's country, Caspian's lust to follow recalls Sir Percival's obsessive quest for the Grail in Tennyson's *Idylls of the King*.

In the next tale Lewis wrote, *The Horse and His Boy*, which features an adolescent boy and girl who break free of wicked stepparents, discover their true identities, and eventually become King and Queen of Archenland, Lewis juxtaposed three cultures. In the southern empire of Calormen, the ruler, crown prince, and Grand Vizier address each other in the language of the *Arabian Nights*. In Archenland, law and custom rule even its king, who hunts like a medieval monarch. The free-spoken Narnians who accompany their Pevensie sovereigns from the north seem idealized Vikings.

The ensuing *Silver Chair* draws upon the medieval quest-romances, and beyond them the myth of Orpheus. The "Underland" inhabited by the Witch's inhibited and silent subjects blends elements from the Greek Underworld, the Judaic Sheol, and the modern totalitarian state. Once liberated, Prince Rilian experiences a compulsion to descend to the still lower region of Bism, a desire compounded of curiosity about an alien world and a momentary death-wish. This overcome, his ascent to Narnia blends liberation from confinement by a possessive foster mother with joyous awakening to life and freedom. His confinement explains both his outbreaks of violence[15] and the general rejoicing at the Green Witch's death. His relief resembles that of Lewis when Mrs. Moore died, shortly before he began this book.[16]

At the beginning of the book, Eustace Scrubb and Jill Pole have entered Narnia from a shrubbery where they hid from Jill's tormentors at Experiment House. The sea voyage in the *Dawn Treader* that has changed Eustace forever took place during the recent school holidays, so he is still about nine years old. At first, his classmate Jill behaves like a schoolchild, posturing at the cliff edge until Eustace tries to rescue her. When Eustace falls off himself, Aslan blows him down to Narnia (21–22).[17] Unaware that the lion is Aslan, Jill is terrified of him. She tries to excuse herself for her part in Eustace's fall but soon bursts into tears. Isolated and thirsty, she has no choice but to follow Aslan's direction to drink from the only stream. Humbled and submissive because of her recent fear and guilt, she accepts the quest to search for the lost Prince Rilian and listens carefully to Aslan's explanation of four signs to follow. Jill and Eustace mature quickly during the journey and adventures that follow. Imprisoned in the giants' castle, Jill simulates childish giggles and behavior to deceive the Queen and attendants into allowing her to explore the castle and find an escape route.

Since even children so mature for their age could not have coped alone with the Queen-Witch in Underland, Lewis gave them a mentor. The transformation of his gardener Fred Paxford and perhaps his old tutor Kirkpatrick[18] into Puddleglum the Marsh-wiggle was a stroke of genius. As with Dickens's Mark Tapley, Puddleglum's demeanor varies with his circumstances. He is pessimistic when all seems well, soberly confident in Aslan's instructions when the children are bewildered, and prompt and courageous in stamping on the Witch's fire as its hypnotic fumes begin to lull the Prince and children into acquiescence. Already the drug has made them deny the sun's existence, just as secularism and materialism dispose moderns to deny God. In that sense, Underland signifies the post-Christian culture.

The remaining books have both theological and personal meaning, the latter more affecting for young readers. Having ended his first story with the resurrection of Aslan and the defeat of the Witch, Lewis relates Narnia's apocalypse in the most fully theological story, the *Last Battle*, which he began last and finished in the summer of 1953. In the next few months he finished *The Magician's Nephew*, begun in 1949 and resumed for part of 1951. He probably wrote the central chapter of *Magician's Nephew*, relating Narnia's creation and fall, before starting the *Last Battle*. The opening and closing episodes of *The Magician's Nephew* are saturated in his personal history, from the attic passage and "end room" of Little Lea and the magic rings of Nesbit's *Amulet*,[19] through the occultism of the "adept" Uncle Andrew, which recalls the "Great War" against Steinerism (though the would-be magician also combines the ruthlessness of Weston with the greed of Devine),[20] to the poignant episode of Digory healing his mother by feeding her the apple. The last fulfills a wish not granted Lewis in childhood. Was he right to grant it to Digory, whom Aslan has prepared to live without his mother? Yet child-readers might be depressed by a conclusion so inconsistent with the mercy of Aslan, who has invited the prayer he grants. Her death would, moreover, make nonsense of the quest for the apple of life or, as the Witch claims, eternal youth. Lewis concluded the tale as Nesbit concluded her *Amulet*, for no sooner has Digory healed his mother than his father returns rich from the East.

Thus the Chronicles take the Pevensies from Lucy's first entry into Narnia in *The Lion, the Witch and the Wardrobe* to their final entry into the "real Narnia" in Aslan's country in *The Last Battle*, via a stable that alludes to the Nativity. After the final destruction of the old Narnia, the creatures who love Aslan enter the new Narnia through the doorway, while the others disappear into Aslan's dark shadow. Among those who enter the door are a Calormene and many creatures from folk-literature, all of whom have in common good hearts and the power of speech. But only three of the four Pevensie children join the rush "farther up and farther in," for Susan has succumbed to the lure of teenage pleasures and fashions and is "no longer a friend of Narnia." After their first adventures in Narnia, the only collective undertaking by all four is the rescue of Prince Caspian. This completed, the adolescents Peter and Susan can no longer return to Narnia. At the end of *The Voyage of the "Dawn Treader,"* Edmund and Lucy are told that they will not visit Narnia again, and Eustace and Jill take the central roles in *The Silver Chair* and *The Last Battle*. Aslan's explanation to the three Pevensies at the end of *The Last Battle* that they and their parents left the "Shadowlands" of earth by means of a railway accident may have been suggested to Lewis by a pile-up of three trains at Harrow on 8 October 1952 in which more than a hundred passengers died.[21]

In representing puberty as closing the door to Narnia, Lewis seems to have had in mind the teenager's rejection of fairy tales as "kids' stuff."[22] Narnia resembles the worlds of myth and fairy tale in which everything, whether Narnian or English, is alive and existentially meaningful for the central figures. Aslan's country includes a "real" Narnia but also a "real England," thus uniting imagination and reality as in the Platonism Professor Digory Kirke commends in his old age, or the Neoplatonism of Steiner and Barfield.[23] When the creatures of Narnia enter Aslan's country with their human visitants, all distinction between fact and imagination disappears.

Looking at the tales in the order of the chronology of Narnia, one begins with its creation in *The Magician's Nephew*, continues with its redemption in *The Lion, the Witch and the Wardrobe* and its golden age under the four Pevensie sovereigns in *The Horse and His Boy*, and proceeds through the quest-voyages to its decay and apocalypse in *The Last Battle*. In keeping with Lewis's principle of smuggling in Christian doctrine, this sequence approximates the Christian mythos,[24] beginning with the creation and fall (*Magician's Nephew*), continuing with the sacrifice of Aslan on the Stone Table and his resurrection (*The Lion, the Witch and the Wardrobe*), followed by the Narnian equivalent of Exodus (*The Horse and His Boy*),[25] then by a mission to retrieve lost lords and journey toward heaven (*Voyage of the "Dawn Treader"*), a descent into Sheol (*Silver Chair*), and the apocalypse (*Last Battle*). This order would self-evidently put more weight on Lewis's theological overthought than on his personal underthought. How much of it is gathered upon a first reading must vary with the reader's age, education, and acquaintance with the Bible.

Only readers well-versed in English literature and recent history will discern some sources and allusions. To illustrate from his creation and apocalypse narratives, in the *Magician's Nephew* the Deplorable Word of Jadis, a female equivalent of the Dolorous Stroke in Malory's *Morte d'Arthur*, turns the city of Charn into a charnel house and is the antithesis of God's creative word "Let there be light." The story proceeds from the undoing of creation within the Witch's world to her failure to tempt Digory to disobey Aslan and take an apple to revive his mother with the forbidden fruit. As Aslan later explains, this would have been giving it to her "at the wrong time, in the wrong way" (chap. 14). After eating the apple, Digory's mother falls into a sweet, drug-free sleep, but she is pronounced cured only after Digory has buried the apple core in the garden (chap. 15). To understand why Digory would have brought disaster upon himself by eating the apple we must combine several passages, from the rhyme over the golden gates (chap. 13) to Aslan's explanation. According to the rhyme, those who enter the garden over the wall to "steal" apples will find their "heart's desire" but also "despair." This implicitly echoes the contrast in *Paradise Lost* between the Devil's climb into Eden over the wall and a pilgrim's entry into Heaven through the golden gates. The injunction breached by the Witch, "Take of my fruit for others or forbear," helps Digory resist her temptation to eat an apple himself and share eternal youth and power with her, as king and queen of Narnia or Earth. Digory prefers to "go to Heaven" after his allotted span. The Witch then tempts him to steal an apple and take it immediately to cure his mother. If he does not, she argues, he will always feel guilty for having failed her—the charlatan's argument to a cancer patient's relative. Though hesitantly responding that his mother has taught him to keep promises and not to steal, Digory finally refuses when urged to abandon Polly (his Eve).

Aslan's "Well done" (as to the faithful servant in Matthew 25:21) remains Digory's sole reward until he has planted the apple that will protect Narnia and seen the misery of his Uncle Andrew, the would-be magician, who has endured being planted and watered by animals who think him a type of tree. As the astonished boy sees a perfumed tree grow from the apple, Aslan explains that its smell nauseates the Witch, just as long life and power bring misery upon the evil-hearted. Had someone plucked the fruit and sown the seed unasked, he would have made Narnia into a cruel world like Charn. In the same way, it is the apple Digory plucks at Aslan's direction from the new-grown tree that heals his mother. The text both upholds religion against amoral magic and implicitly contrasts the divine order with slave empires from the Egypt of the Pharaohs to the Soviet Union under Stalin.

The framework of the *Last Battle* consists mainly of theological symbols. We may dismiss as gothic machinery the thunderclap when Shift assures Puzzle that 'Aslan never turns up nowadays'" (chap. 1), yet the figures of the ancient ape and his ass combine a glancing blow at Darwinism with an allusion to the bestiary characterization of the ape (simius) as deceitfully imitative.[26] The name "Shift" connotes a fraudulent stratagem, a change of clothing, and the shifts of front Lewis thought characteristic of evil. Shift is often referred to as "the Ape" to emphasize both his subhuman status and the pretense implied in our verb "to ape." Shift's announcement that "true freedom" consists in obedience to him is his version of the "glorious liberty of the children of God" (Romans 8:21). It is also comparable to the enslavement by the Pigs in Orwell's *Animal Farm*.[27] The context becomes unambiguously theological when jewel the unicorn calls on seven adherents of Aslan to proclaim the truth at Stable Hill and King Tirian commands the Narnians to make a stand by the "great Rock" whence they drink refreshing water (Isaiah 32:2).

The dream of Tirian, who is the seventh in descent from King Rilian, in which he sees the seven friends of Narnia dining together, is meat and drink to the numerologist. Since the Pevensies had been told that they cannot return to Narnia, they realize that they must have entered Aslan's country. The final entry to the "real "Narnia through the stable door, Aslan's "Well done!" to Tirian, the giant squeezing the sun that has swallowed the moon, and Aslan's order "Now make an end" complete the apocalypse.[28]

Why the Chronicles have attracted so many readers is a question best considered with regard to individual books, but first we should note two reasons evident from reading them in the order of their writing. The first is the progression from childhood to old age noted earlier, which would obviously extend the age-range of readers and reward rereading. The second is an increasing subtlety in narration.

Lewis uses the narrator most explicitly in the first book completed (*The Lion, the Witch and the Wardrobe*). The narrator warns readers of the foolishness of shutting oneself in a wardrobe, explains the White Witch's descent from Lilith, announces Edmund's desertion, partly blames his bad behavior on his schooling, hopes readers will not suffer the misery of Lucy and Susan after Aslan's death but will understand the quiet that follows their storms of tears, asks them to imagine the jubilant rides on Aslan's back, and promises further adventures in Narnia.

The events of *Prince Caspian* are conveyed by more varied means and with less use of the narrator. By describing Prince Caspian's childhood, education, and escape from King Miraz from Trumpkin's view point (chaps. 4–8), Lewis compels the reader to contrast the dwarf's skepticism with Lucy's faith that the trees might speak again, as in Narnia's "good old days" (chap. 9). Conversely, Trumpkin displays alertness and promptitude in shooting the bear who would have eaten the contemplative girl. Yet Lucy and her convert Edmund wisely counsel the group to take Aslan's suggested way, while the practical Peter decides on the wrong one. All this is accomplished without authorial comment. Not until the thirteenth chapter does the narrator intrude, by explaining that it was stranger for the Prince to meet the great kings out of the old stories than for them to meet him. The narrator becomes omniscient only later in that chapter when reporting King Miraz's manipulation by his advisers into accepting Peter's challenge to single combat.

In *The Voyage of the "Dawn Treader"*, "the narrator explains "port" and "starboard" and blames Eustace's "greedy, dragonish thoughts" for his transformation into a dragon, but otherwise merely adds details, as in the brief conclusion. Apart from the beauty of its imagined scenes and the intense longing communicated by the description of the sea near Aslan's country, the delight of this tale largely results from skillful use of Eustace as diarist, of Edmund as interpreter of Eustace's encounter with Aslan and transformation back into human form, of the magician Coriakin as cartographer, and of Ramandu's daughter as exponent of festal symbols and the means of disenchanting the sleeping lords.

The reader is expected to exercise judgment in reading the two portions of Eustace's diary. In the first portion, the "facts" he notes are always negative and the other voyagers always at fault. In the second, though Eustace still complains of his "unanswerable" arguments being ignored by Caspian, he records attempting to steal water and later receiving some from Lucy. Even young readers should see through her face-saving excuse that boys get thirstier than girls.

After his restoration to human shape, Eustace conforms to Todorov's theory of fantasy as "hesitation," wondering whether his nightmarish experience had been real or a dream, until Edmund assures him of its reality and identifies the lion as Aslan. Like Lucy, he saves the boy's self-respect by confessing his own treason in Narnia.

By unobtrusive shifts of viewpoint—to those of Eustace on Dragon Island and Lucy in the magician's library—Lewis provides constant variety without sacrificing clarity of outline. But the chief pleasure of the Voyage lies in the marvelous descriptions of the scenes through which the ship journeys and in Lewis's unobtrusive use of motifs by Malory, Tennyson, and Morris.[29]

In the next completed tale, the *Horse and His Boy*, Lewis makes skillful use of viewpoint. After the overheard conversation between the Tisroc and Ahoshta he departs from this well-worn convention by recording the very different reactions of the eavesdroppers. Implored to abandon her plan of escape, Aravis shakes her panic-stricken companion, threatens to rush screaming from the room to ensure their capture, and declares she would rather "be killed" than marry Ahoshta (chap. 9). As they part, that superficial socialite Lasaraleen, who might be any "flapper" of the 1920s, urges her to change her mind now that she has seen "what a very great man" her prospective husband is. In calling him a "grovelling slave" who has encouraged the Tisroc to send his son to certain death, Aravis articulates the likely response of young readers not bemused by rhetorical formulae.

Lewis is most inventive when using the Hermit to narrate the battle by interpreting its shapes reflected in his pool and the questions or comments of his listeners to flesh out his report. As he describes "a tall Tarkaan with a crimson beard," Bree interjects, "My old master Anradin!" When the Hermit says he sees "Cats" rushing forward, Aravis repeats, "Cats?" and the Hermit hastily explains, "Great cats, leopards and such" (159). His illustration of Edmund's "marvelous" swordplay, "He's just slashed Corradin's head off" (161), is too insensitive from the Hermit in his present way of life. Lewis regresses to his soldiering days in his commentary:

> Oh, the fool! ... Poor, brave little fool. He knows nothing about this work. He's making no use at all of his shield. His whole side's exposed. He hasn't the faintest idea what to do with his sword. Oh, he's remembered it now. He's waving it wildly about.... It's been knocked out of his hand now. It's mere murder sending a child into the battle; he can't live five minutes. Duck, you fool— oh, he's down. (160)

When the breathless listeners cry, "Killed?" the Hermit replies, "How can I tell?" and continues to relate what he sees of the rest of the battle, leaving us in suspense until the narrative resumes with the words "When Shasta fell off his horse, he gave himself up for lost" (161). When last in Shasta's viewpoint, we shared his realization "If you funk this, you'll funk every battle all your life" (157). In a rare intrusion warranted by personal experience, Lewis justifies the switch to the Hermit's viewpoint by pointing to the futility of describing a battle from that of a single combatant.

The award-winning *Last Battle* shows Lewis at his best and worst as a storyteller. Introduced as the "last King of Narnia," Tirian is soon bound to an ash tree by Calormenes in league with the Ape. Watching the goings-on in front of the stable from afar, even Tirian wonders whether the stiff, silent creature shown to the frightened Narnians might after all be Aslan, until he recalls the Ape's "nonsense" about Tash and Aslan being identical (42). He recollects Narnia's past glories, recalling how children from another world had appeared in Narnia at every crisis. His reverie, amounting to a brief retrospect of the Chronicles, leads him to call out a plea for help for Narnia, even at the cost of his own life. Dawning hope prompts his appeal to all "friends of Narnia," upon which he is plunged into his dream or vision of the Seven Diners. When Peter challenges him, "If you are from Narnia, I charge you ... speak to me," Tirian finds that he is unable to speak (45). Tirian's disillusionment as he wakes at dawn stiff with cold is among Lewis's subtlest touches; his misery is relieved almost at once by the appearance of Eustace and Jill, who untie him.

Peter's self-announcement as "High King" contrasts with the colloquial speech of Jill and Eustace and with Tirian's medieval salutation of Jill as "fair maid" (46). The ash tree and King Tirian's pronouncement "Narnia is no more" (85) on hearing of the death of Roonwit the Centaur link the Christian and pagan mythologies; in the Norse sagas the world is supported by an ash tree, and Tirian's pronouncement recalls the death of Baldir. The reporting of Roonwit's death by Farsight the Eagle echoes another Norse motif.

Too often, however, Lewis indulges in personal and contemporary intrusions. We can accept the children's entry to Narnia via the railway accident, which Eustace perceives as a "frightful jerk" (51) and later identifies as a collision (89), but when Jill says she would rather be killed fighting for Narnia than to "grow old and stupid at home ... and then die in the end just the same" and Eustace replies, "Or be smashed up by British Railways!" (88), Lewis's apparent allusion to the Harrow accident has no place in the fantasy. In addition, at times his word choices can be misleading. As a working-class term for colored immigrants, the Dwarf's epithet "Darkies" for the Calormenes (116) has unintended overtones of racism.

An odd feature of *The Last Battle*, the Ape's retreat into alcoholism and his replacement as leader by the Ginger Cat, at first seems a mere contrivance for using his sad experience of Warnie's dipsomania and a mental image of a cat bolting from a stable. The cat motif, however, probably originated in the talking animals of the Boxen tales, for the surname of a pleasure-loving bear, the rakish Lieutenant James Bar,[30] was reused in *The Horse and His Boy* for the lord who set Shasta adrift. The motif involving the Ginger Cat shows a subtle irony in that the Cat agrees with the Calormene captain Rishda that Aslan and Tash are only figments of the imagination, tells the Narnians that Aslan has swallowed up King Tirian, cynically persuades the dwarfs that there is no real Aslan (73–74), coolly offers to enter the stable, stalks in with feline primness (99), then moments later bolts into oblivion when confronted by Tash (100). Disbelief evaporates in the presence of evil.

While occasionally involving uncertainty (Todorov's "hesitation") as to the reality of an event or person, the fantasy more often uses reversal of ground rules, or what Manlove calls "upset expectations."[31] Thus Tirian, who talks and thinks as a medieval monarch, is struck by the strange, drab garments of the twentieth-century children. Combining reversal with word-play, Aslan explains that the hard-bitten dwarfs are so anxious to avoid being taken in that they cannot be taken out of this world and brought into a better one (135).[32] Their satisfaction that "the Dwarfs are for the Dwarfs" is more than a simple takeoff on communism or the triumphalism that accompanied the Labour landslide in the 1945 election. In contrast to Edmund, who attained "a kind of greatness" when breathed on by Aslan in Prince Caspian (153), these godless dwarfs, having forsworn the means of growth, must remain forever dwarfish.

A more fundamental reversal takes place in the final chapters. In "Night Falls on Narnia" (chap. 14), the falling stars, red moon near the sun, and creatures heading for the doorway to Aslan's country echo Revelation and the Flood myth. As in pagan myths, the falling and vanishing stars are people. As in what Lewis called the "myth" of evolutionary progress,[33] dragons and lizards inhabit Narnia—but at the end of time, not the beginning.

In chapter 15, as in his *Great Divorce*, Lewis endeavors to reverse the stereotype of heaven as a state of eternal torpor. Having reversed the dark and lonely cosmos of post-Newtonian astronomers by encountering warmth and daylight beyond the stable door, the children find themselves caught up with creatures factual and fabulous in a westward, not eastward, rush when the Unicorn calls them "farther up and farther in" (*Last Battle*, 155), a refrain that one critic has suggested might otherwise connote returning to the womb.[34] The refrain is repeated and the rush intensified in the final chapter, called (with Platonic implication) "Farewell to Shadowlands." Here Lewis reverses the image of heaven as a city, for the voyagers pass waterfalls and climb mountains. The self-reflexive image that ends the Chronicles of Narnia, the story in which every chapter is better than the last, suggests that heavenly stasis is a conclusion never to be reached.

In these stories a childless academic managed to communicate with children throughout and beyond the English-speaking world. What proportion of child readers belong to his own social class has never been determined. Nor to my knowledge has reader research established why the Chronicles have been found such compulsive reading. For that matter, we do not know whether more children have first heard them read by parents or read them independently. The following suggestions, therefore, are merely speculative.

First, the attraction may derive from the narrator's identification with children. In *The Silver Chair* the narrator presumes that his readers attend better-disciplined schools than Experiment House, where the need for just authority is appreciated. Presuming impatience with discipline near the end of term, he presents in *The Last Battle* the entry into Aslan's country, where life resembles an everlasting holiday, as a joyous running and bounding akin to the end-of-term fever at a hard-working school. Second, the narrator assumes agreement on principles that do not need to be justified to children: loyalty to schoolmates, brothers, and sisters; dislike of bullies or tyrants, sycophants or flatterers. Many an impoverished author must wish that to uphold such principles would automatically guarantee sales in the millions.

Looking for inducements to read on, we find some in elements common to all the cafes. Two or more children of both sexes enter an enchanted world via a door, or its equivalent—a picture that comes alive, or magic rings they must learn to manage.[35] In each tale, the children depend upon a nonhuman counselor, perhaps mythical, but always full-grown: a beaver, raven, horse, or centaur. Sometimes they depend on an observer, but—whether eagle or hermit—not one they would meet at home. Notably, apart from Aslan, the animal companions change with the implied reader's age. In the first tale Mr. Tumnus the faun and Mr. and Mrs. Beaver are roughly the same size as the children, who can eat and converse in the Beavers' cozy home. In the *Horse and His Boy*, Bree and Hwin require riders well into their teens; and the owl, eagle, or centaur who advise the protagonists of later books are clearly distanced by their size and/or mythological associations. In the first tales the children meet no parents, teachers, or other adult humans they can respect in the enchanted world, but only the witches, magicians, or sovereigns of fairy tales; in the later tales they begin to encounter good human adults, such as the Hermit and the large-hearted King of Archenland in *The Horse and His Boy* or Drinian and Lord Bern in the *Voyage of the "Dawn Treader."* In war, they use medieval weapons and tactics. They depend immediately on signs and omens but ultimately on Aslan the lion-god, a figure derived partly from Christ the Lion of Judah and perhaps partly from Richard the Lion-heart, but also from Lewis's dream of a lion. As in medieval romance, the stories always involve a quest, which takes them to an island, a castle, a subterranean prison, and ultimately a stable.

The enchanted world differs from their real one in its time-frame. During a school vacation, centuries of Narnian time can pass, a dynasty can rise and fall, children can function as adults[36]—kings or queens, generals or discoverers—yet never attain independence. In seeking self-sufficiency, Eustace finds loneliness and misery on Dragon Island, his precursor death. The enchanted world of Lewis offers escape, not only from childhood subservience to parents and teachers and from city life in an industrial country, but also from the whole notion of carving out one's own path in life. So in the author's view do myth, literary fantasy, and the Christian life. Yet the boy or girl character drawn into Narnia finally depends on Aslan, who with one exception[37] will interpret only his or her own life story.

In other ways the fantasy depends on reversal of normal distinctions between humans and animals, reality and imagination. Folklore becomes practical, and the folly or wickedness of practical people—Uncle Andrew, King Miraz, Nikabrik, the bureaucrat Gumpas, or the wily Tisroc—is sometimes cruelly exposed. The outdated education by Dr. Cornelius stands Prince Caspian in good stead, while Eustace has to unlearn his "progressive" education at Experiment House. The key elements of Narnian education are ethical and ecological: courage in battle, comradeship, cooperation with other species, and care of trees and plants threatened by commercial exploitation. The approaching end of Narnia is signaled by religious uncertainty or disbelief and a ruined environment.[38] Above all, the child characters play a crucial role in the enchanted world; instead of being marginal because of their inexperience and simplistic view of life, children affect the whole future of that world by making plans or decisions at places adults would consider marginal, historical, or imaginary: animal lairs; islands; castles; a subterranean, real, or remote wood.

The moral ground rules are those of the child reader's normal world, in that actions are always right or wrong, information trite or untrue. At times, Lewis appears to share that simplicity. In this sense, his much-remarked immaturity enabled him to communicate with children. Consider, for example, Professor (Digory) Kirke's reasoning on Lucy's account of her first entry to Narnia:

> Either your sister is telling lies, or she is mad, or she is telling the truth. You know she does not tell lies and it is obvious that she is not mad. For the moment then and unless any other evidence turns up, we must assume that she is telling the truth. (*The Lion, the Witch and the Wardrobe*, 47)

Elsewhere Lewis used a similar argument to justify belief in the divinity of Christ. Further alternatives—daydream, wish-fulfillment, hallucination—would have taken him beyond the child reader's register and the context of the episode.

The increasingly subtle switching between viewpoint characters, as compared with the obtrusive switching in *That Hideous Strength*, may blind us to the fact that the viewpoint character is nearly always a juvenile extending his or her experience. The principal learner is Lucy, followed by Edmund, Eustace, and Jill. We enjoy the viewpoints of Narnian characters within single novels, *Prince Caspian*, the *Horse and His Boy*, or the *Last Battle*. Save for occasional passages in the viewpoint of Susan or Peter—or gap-filling by Trumpkin, the Hermit, or a nonhuman observer—the viewpoint character is of the child reader's presumed age. Thus, as Doris Myers remarks, the reader vicariously experiences life at different stages: young childhood with Lucy, middle or late adolescence with Shasta, the consciousness of age and impending death with King Tirian and Jewel.[39]

In one sense, the Narnian Chronicles are the medievalist's revenge upon the modernist; in another, as Kath Filmer notes,[40] they anticipate a civilization that still lies ahead. As in medieval stories, events and situations often conform to literary patterns or analogues. We have noticed the parallel between Caspian's urge to follow Reepicheep into Aslan's country and the Grail obsession. What is acceptable in a mouse or hermit would be neglect of duty in King Caspian. In his boyhood, Caspian, like Hamlet, disliked his usurping uncle, but without knowing why. Lewis departs from Shakespeare by making the Queen a wicked stepmother and the birth of her son the incentive for the now-redundant Prince to flee the court.

Near the end of *Prince Caspian*, Aslan, Bacchus, and the Maenads disrupt a dull history lesson. After transforming the girls' school into a "forest glade," its ceiling into tree branches, and the teacher's desk into a rose bush, they put to flight the teacher and all the pupils except for the inattentive Gwendolen, whom two Maenads whirl in a dance and help remove the "unnecessary and uncomfortable" parts of her school uniform (171). Lewis told Greeves of the joy and vitality he found in pagan mythology.[41] Though rightly condemning the ridicule of the woman teacher and schoolgirls, David Holbrook misses the point of the episode. Less convincingly than D. H. Lawrence, Lewis exposes the lifelessness of a culture bereft of the gods who infused pagan societies with energy and joy in life. To avoid the appearance of misogyny, in the following episode "pig-like" schoolboys are unconvincingly put to flight.

Lewis shows originality in blending derived with invented incidents. The baptismal bath of Eustace is preceded by the unpeeling of his dragon skin, and Lucy's magical restoration of the Dufflepuds to visibility takes place only after she eavesdrops on her schoolmates' conversation about herself. Mystery or enchantment attaches to figures and incidents drawn from literature or mythology, while invented elements are literal, even prosaic. Turkish Delight makes far more sense literally, as an inducement to betrayal at a time when candies were rationed in England, than in Holbrook's gloss of it as a disguised form of breast milk.[42] When Prince Rilian laments his ten-year subjection to the Witch as surrogate mother, surely any autobiographical reference is much more likely to involve Lewis's subjection to Mrs. Moore than the maternal inadequacy presumed by Holbrook.

Will the Chronicles continue to be relevant to the lives of children? A case can be made either way. Whether future generations of children will enjoy battles with swords and bows and arrows may be doubted, but they will unquestionably condemn clear-cut logging and slavery. The influence of Tolkien's readings to the Inklings from the *Lord of the Rings* is patent in episodes of *Prince Caspian* and the *Last Battle* that feature trees as combatants.[43] The popularity of Tolkien's trilogy at the dawn of the ecological movement was by no means coincidental. As yesterday's protest becomes tomorrow's orthodoxy, more and more stories are likely to involve preservation of the natural environment.

Whether instant and miraculous answers to prayers will endear the Chronicles to tomorrow's children is again doubtful. In alluding in *The Last Battle* to Aslan's nonappearance "nowadays" Lewis acknowledges the declining influence of religion. C. N. Manlove remarks that Lewis "was unusual among Christian writers in admitting the draught from outside [Christianity]."[44] In order of completion, the Chronicles show Aslan a central figure in the first two (*The Lion, the Witch and the Wardrobe*; *Prince Caspian*), absent for long periods in the next three (*Voyage of the "Dawn Reader"*; *Silver Chair*; *Horse and His Boy*), and returning to center stage in the conclusions of the final two (*Magician's Nephew*; *Last Battle*). In their christological reference, they begin with the crucifixion and resurrection, continue with discipleship, the following of Aslan's path, the baptism and conversion of a modern spoiled child, and the renewed vision of eternal life, and end with the routing of secular magicians and gurus, Aslan's second coming, the ridicule of godless class-consciousness, and (skeptical Dwarfs excepted) the general entry into Aslan's country. There is no mention of Hell, for Calormenes killed in battle simply vanish. In the finale, the lost simply disappear into Aslan's shadow, while the saved from all seven books undergo no Last Judgment but a kind of evolution. Their eternal life perpetually unfolds, the root meaning of "evolve."[45] The metaphor of a book that improves chapter by chapter implies design by an Author warming to his subject matter. In this way Lewis marries an age-old Christian metaphor with a conception of divinely planned evolution common in his childhood[46] and extends to eternity the progressive revelation evident in the Old Testament.

As regards the moral "upshot" of the Chronicles, isolated incidents or phrases can be used to demonstrate antifeminism and a veneer of male toughness covering the unhealed wounds, but it is sounder to note the purport and emphasis of a whole story or major episode. The child reader cannot but condemn the willingness of Edmund to betray his brother and sisters to the Witch in *The Lion, the Witch and the Wardrobe*, still more his pretended disbelief in Narnia, from which he has just returned. The virtues of family loyalty and sincerity require no huddling together of schoolmates at Wynyard to explain them. Again, readers attuned to Lucy's love of Aslan will understand her pity at his humiliation and delight in his resurrection without recourse to Lewis's grief for his mother.

The upshot of *Prince Caspian* is less clear. Arguably, Caspian's love of old Narnian folklore and his happiness when with animals could promote an immature response to the troubles of adolescence. In a wider perspective, Dr. Cornelius saves Caspian's life both literally in urging him to flee the palace and metaphorically in nourishing his imagination with a cultural tradition that forearms him against the withering reductiveness of the commercially minded Telmarines, whose very name connotes both marring of earth (*tellus*) and skepticism ("tell it to the marines"). If the youngest readers see how the courtiers of the vain King Miraz manipulate him into accepting Peter's challenge, or even decipher the meaning of "Sopespian," the name "Glozelle" (liar) will surely escape any readers unfamiliar with medieval or Renaissance English. If death seems too harsh a judgment on Nikabrik for wishing to use the White Witch as an ally against Miraz, the author surely asserts principle against expediency. But nothing in the behavior or feelings of characters in *Prince Caspian* is so morally compelling as the treason of Edmund or the faith and love of Lucy.

In the *Voyage of the "Dawn Treader"* the reformation of a spoilt child and the assertion of common sense against excesses of chivalry and self-centered mysticism carry more conviction than any moral "upshot" in the *Silver Chair*. Instead, the latter story sheds light into the mind darkened by positivist conditioning against religion. In fact, later stories show a distinct shift in emphasis, for the practical sagacity commended in Puddleglum appears in Jill, Shasta, Aravis, and Lucy. What is rebuked is lack of empathy—by Aravis with the deceived slave girl, or by Jill when her posturing draws Eustace to the cliff edge. Yet Jill's devising of an escape from the castle of the giants (*Silver Chair*) and her shrewdly compassionate treatment of Puzzle (*Last Battle*) rebut Holbrook's charge of authorial misogyny based on passing references to tears spoiling bowstrings and blood wiped from swords.[47]

The final issue between hostile and sympathetic readers of the Chronicles concerns the quality of the writing. In condemning a passage on the pleasure of eating freshly caught fish as being insensitive to children's feelings (*The Lion, the Witch and the Wardrobe*, 70), Holbrook puts his finger on the central difficulty of an Edwardian-reared adult writing for mid-twentieth-century children of any class.[48] The problem may be highlighted with his contrast between Lewis's "paternal respect" and "admiration of the children's energy and courage" when describing their regal appearance in fur coats and his "prep-school language"[49] when Peter calls the treasonous Edmund a "poisonous little" beast and Edmund thinks the others "stuck-up, self-satisfied prigs" (*The Lion, the Witch and the Wardrobe*, 55). Both use the Edwardian public-school argot perpetuated in magazine stories up to the Second World War. Reared in an era and class that wore fur coats and used such terms (as he sometimes did to Greeves), Lewis could not plausibly have employed the diction of children from any class in the 1940s. Instead, he kept author-to-reader address to a minimum by staying within viewpoints. For example, this description follows Peter's suggestion to the others that they spend the rainy morning exploring the house:

> Everyone agreed to this and that was how the adventures began. It was the sort of house that you never seem to come to the end of... full of unexpected places. The first few doors ... led only into spare bedrooms, as everyone had expected ... but soon they came to a very long room filled with pictures and there they found a suit of armour; and after that there was a room all hung with green, with a harp in one corner; and then came three steps down

and five steps up, and then a kind of little upstairs hall and a door that led out on to a balcony, and then a whole series of rooms that led into each other and were lined with books—most of them very old books and bigger than a Bible in a church. (*The Lion, the Witch and the Wardrobe*, 11)

This atomistic account of a house conceivably inspired by Little Lea sets the tone of medieval romance and ends with an illustration that all readers can picture.

A little later, as Lucy enters the wardrobe, advice is given from her viewpoint. She leaves the door ajar "because she knew that it is very foolish to shut oneself into any wardrobe" (12). When Edmund goes in, he closes the door, "forgetting what a very foolish thing this is to do" (30). Lewis uses advice probably drawn from experience with evacuees at The Kilns to suggest prudence in the girl with second sight and willfulness in the skeptical boy.

In the stories the narrator sometimes takes sides, with unfortunate results. In *Prince Caspian*, Lewis's forgivable hit at a modern materialist history lesson contributes nothing to the story; in addition, as Holbrook says, the partial stripping of Gwendolen may strike readers as indelicate, while the transformation of disorderly schoolboys into pigs (172–73) is pointlessly petulant. The same may be said of Polly's aspersions upon Susan:

> I wish she *would* grow up. She wasted all her school time wanting to be the age she is now, and she'll waste all the rest of her life trying to stay that age. Her whole idea is to race on to the silliest time of one's life as quick as she can and then stop there as long as she can. (*Last Battle*, 124)

A far more important aspect of Lewis's writing, one unremarked by Holbrook, is Lewis's use of a repertoire of styles to fit incidents and speakers. He shifts at will from plain speech for Peter to Morrisian medieval language for Reepicheep or Tirian ("Hast any skill with the bow, maiden?" [*Last Battle*, 55]) or *Arabian Nights* rhetoric for the Tisroc and Grand Vizier (*Horse and His Boy*). The array of styles is most dazzling in the *Voyage of the "Dawn Treader"*, "which shifts within a page from hierarchic-feudal language to announce King Caspian "come to visit his trusty and well-beloved servant the governor of the Lone Islands" (51) to mumbled bureaucratese by the porter ("No interview without 'pointments 'cept 'tween nine 'n' ten p.m. second Saturday every month") to stage cockney ("'Ere? Wot's it all about?")

at Bern's Shakespearean reproof "Uncover before Narnia, you dog" (51). In the next few pages (52–57), the bureaucratese of Gumpas ("Nothing about it in the correspondence.... Nothing in the minutes.... All irregular. Happy to consider any applications"), laced with economic jargon in support of the slave trade, alternates with plain but increasingly abrupt orders from Caspian. The slave auctioneer's sales-pitch swings sympathy away from the unseated governor, no longer "His Sufficiency."

Eustace's record of the resumed voyage, written in a plain style, betrays egotism in every "I" and self-righteousness in every account of a disregarded suggestion. When Caspian dismisses his idea of rowing back to Doorn on account of the water shortage, Eustace writes, "I tried to explain that perspiration really cools people down, so the men would need less water if they were working. He [Caspian] didn't take any notice of this, which is always his way when he can't think of an answer" (65–66).

Near the end of the *Voyage*, the style shifts to the plain but solemn phrases of the ancient star Ramandu, recalling those of the "Great Dance" episode in Perelandra:[50] "And when I have become as young as the child that was born yesterday, then I shall take my rising again ... and once more tread the great dance" (177), punctuated by the chivalric speech of Reepicheep. As the ship nears the world's end, the style changes to the romantic, northern expressions of Lucy, exhilarated by the sea's "fresh, wild, lonely smell" (201).

How long children will continue to read the Chronicles of Narnia may depend on considerations unrelated to their artistic merits: reception of stories via electronic media rather than books; the religion or irreligion of parents and school librarians; social or educational changes rendering some episodes less comprehensible. Already schoolchildren must find the animus against coeducation difficult to understand. While at present Holbrook's view of the tales as unfit for children seems as perverse as Eliot's judgment of *Hamlet* ("an artistic failure"), many incidents or passages that Holbrook finds morally or stylistically objectionable do show a lack of restraint in the author. Lewis's achievement as a storyteller was limited by over-hasty production and unwillingness to take his fiction as seriously as his major critical works. As novelists, the perfectionist Tolkien and the boyishly eager Lewis represent opposed extremes.

While the images and values of the Chronicles had been in Lewis's mind for decades, the energy that enabled Lewis to complete the Chronicles within seven years (1948–54) may well have been generated by personal stresses: Mrs. Moore's senility, his entanglement with Joy Davidman, the denial of promotion at Oxford, and the campaign to defeat his ill-judged candidacy for the Professorship of Poetry. Undoubtedly anxiety or anger from these stresses as well as his bereavement and exile in childhood affect a number of episodes. What I have tried to show is that, so far from distorting or blurring the impact of a story, such "speaking pictures" (to quote Sidney) and moral attitudes at times enhance it. Even Holbrook appears moved by Digory's anxiety to heal his mother and finds the *Silver Chair* a well-told tale of adventure. Yet of all the stories the latter is most susceptible to the now dated academic game of psychoanalytic reductionism: the Witch as Mrs. Lewis turned nasty, or Prince Lewis unable to mate because he never got over the Queen's death. As Freud maintained, most if not all works of art spring from some trauma—in Edmund Wilson's phrase, a creative "wound." The only issue that should concern a critic is the quality of craftsmanship evident in the resultant works. The late John Peter, himself a Leavisite critic and Pulitzer Prize-winning novelist, once told me that while he detested Lewis and "everything he stood for," when reading the stories with his children he discerned "quality." For all their imperfections, they constitute a body of fiction worthy of their immense and sustained readership.

NOTES

1. Among others, Donald E. Glover, *C.S. Lewis: The Art of Enchantment*, and Evan Gibson, *C.S. Lewis: Spinner of Tales*, discuss plots and characters; Michael Murrin, "The Multiple Worlds of the Narnia Stories," in Peter J. Schakel and Charles A. Huttar, eds., *Word and Story*, 232–55, examines the Narnia stories in connection with German art fairy-tale genre; and Dabney A. Hart, *Through the Open Door: A New Look at C.S. Lewis*, discusses Lewis's use of myth. Among those writers who examine religion, ethics, and language in Lewis are Doris T. Myers, *C.S. Lewis in Context*, 112–81; Jim Pietrusz, "Rites of Passages"; John D. Cox, "Epistemological Release in *The Silver Chair*," in Peter J. Schakel, ed., *The Longing for a Form*, 159–70. Charles A. Huttar, "C.S. Lewis's Narnia and the Grand Design," in Schakel, ed., *Longing for a Form*, 119–35, and Kathryn Lindskoog, *The Lion of Judah in Never-Neverland*, examine Lewis's use of motifs, especially biblical motifs. More comprehensive studies of the Chronicles include C. N. Manlove, "'Caught Up into the Larger Pattern,'" in Schakel and Huttar, eds., *Word and Story*, 256–?6; Paul E Ford, *A Companion to Narnia*; Hooper, *Past Watchful Dragons: The Narnian Chronicles of C.S. Lewis*; and Peter J. Schakel, *Reading with the Heart: The Way into Narnia*.

2. David Holbrook, *The Skeleton in the Wardrobe*. Page references will be given parenthetically in the text.

3. Letter to W. L. Kinter, 28 October 1954.

4. See *Surprised by Joy*, 26; *Letters to an American Lady*, 117 (6 July 1963).

5. Lewis, "Sometimes Fairy Stories Say What's Best to Be Said."

6. Letter to Ruth Pitter, 28 November 1950.

7. Frances Hodgson Burnett, *The Secret Garden*; Isaac Watts, *Works*, I:xix; Esmé Wingfield-Stratford, *A Victorian Tragedy*, 57–58.

8. In *C.S. Lewis: His Literary Achievement*, 120–86, C. N. Manlove traces allusions in the Chronicles to literary sources in all periods.

9. All information concerning the order and dates of the stories is taken from tables in Ford, *A Companion to Narnia*.

10. Myers, *C.S. Lewis in Context*, esp. 125.

11. Myers, *C.S. Lewis in Context*, 112–81.

12. On the blurred distinction between accident and design, see Manlove, "'Caught Up into the Larger Pattern,'" 262.

13. Manlove, *C.S. Lewis: His Literary Achievement*, 135.

14. Francis Bacon, "Of Death," in *Essays*, 4–6.

15. Cf. the violent outbreaks of Knight in William Morris, *Water of the Wondrous Isles*, 258. It may also be noted that in Morris's book as well as in *Silver Chair* the villainess is called "Witch" (Morris, 343, etc.) and the heroine is addressed as "Adam's Daughter" (Morris, 469).

16. George Sayer points to Lewis's inviting friends to stay at Kilns again, resuming exercise, and improving in health (*Jack: C.S. Lewis and His Times*, 203–4).

17. Page references given parenthetically in the text for all of the Narnian Chronicles refer to the editions cited in the bibliography.

18. Respectively, Hooper, *Past Watchful Dragons*, 81–83; Myers, *C.S. Lewis in Context*, 151.

19. Cf. Manlove, *C.S. Lewis: His Literary Achievement*, 170.

20. Myers, *C.S. Lewis in Context*, 171.

21. Armin Schneider and Ascanio Mase, *Railway Accidents of Great Britain and Europe*, 67–73. The enquiry into the accident resulted in the installation of automatic signaling.

22. In "On Three Ways of Writing for Children," Lewis blames modernist critics for promoting this attitude.

23. On Platonism in the Chronicles, see Myers, *C.S. Lewis in Context*, 151, 180–81, and Murrin, "The Multiple Worlds of the Narnia Stories," 232.

24. Cf. Manlove, *C.S. Lewis: His Literary Achievement*, 124, where he describes the Chronicles as "Christian history."

25. Manlove, "'Caught Up into the Larger Pattern,'" 267.

26. Myers, *C.S. Lewis in Context*, 177.

27. Manlove, *C.S. Lewis: His Literary Achievement*, 182.

28. Manlove provides a list of apocalypse signs that appear in *The Last Battle* in *C.S. Lewis: His Literary Achievement*, 182.

29. For example, compare the Isles of Nothing, Kings and Queens, Young and Old, and Increase Unsought in Morris, *Water of the Wondrous Isles*, with the islands in *Voyage of the "Dawn Treader"*, and Utter Hay in Morris's book with the Utter East in the *Voyage*.

30. In "Littera Scripta Manet" (unpublished) and "The Sailor" (in *Boxen*, 153–94).

31. Manlove, "'Caught Up into the Larger Pattern,'" 262.

32. Manlove (*C.S. Lewis: His Literary Achievement*, 136) mentions changing ground rules in *Prince Caspian* and fantasy as paradox plus reversal (185), but he sees this within extraterrestrial episodes rather than between real and imagined worlds.

33. Lewis, "The Funeral of a Great Myth," in *Christian Reflections*, 110–23.

34. Glover, *C.S. Lewis: The Art of Enchantment*, 56.

35. On entrances, see Murrin, "The Multiple Worlds of the Narnia Stories."

36. Manlove points out that the child-heroes of MacDonald and Nesbit remain children (*C.S. Lewis: His Literary Achievement*, 122).

37. The one exception Aslan makes to this rule is telling Digory what would have happened had he given his mother the forbidden apple (Myers, *C.S. Lewis in Context*, 168).

38. Myers, *C.S. Lewis in Context*, 132–33; Lindskoog, *The Lion of Judah in Never-Never Land*, 46.

39. Myers, *C.S. Lewis in Context*, 125.

40. Kath Filmer, *The Fiction of C.S. Lewis: Mask and Minor*, 73, 83–86.

41. E.g., *They Stand Together*, 433 (Dec. 1931) Lewis writes of Morris: "his treatment of love is so undisguisedly physical and yet so perfectly sane and healthy—real paganism at its best, which is the next best thing to Christianity."

42. Holbrook, *The Skeleton in the Wardrobe*, 42.

43. Cf. Manlove, *C.S. Lewis: His Literary Achievement*, 142.

44. Manlove, *Christian Fantasy from 1200 to the Present*, 261.

45. A. Owen Barfield, *History in English Words*, 190.

46. The popularity of this concept of divinely planned evolution is attested to by a *Daily Telegraph* reader survey of 1904, cited in Hugh McLeod, *Class and Religion in the Late-Victorian City*, 155, 229–31.

47. Holbrook, *The Skeleton in the Wardrobe*, 248.

48. Holbrook, *The Skeleton in the Wardrobe*, 39.

49. Holbrook, *The Skeleton in the Wardrobe*, 45–46.

50. The similarity was pointed out to me by Dr. Edwards.

DON W. KING

C.S. Lewis, Poet

Although C.S. Lewis is best known as a prose writer for his clear, lucid
literary criticism, Christian apologetics, and imaginative Ransom and Narnia
stories, he actually began his publishing career as a poet. His first two
published works, *Spirits in Bondage* (1919) and *Dymer* (1926), were volumes
of poetry published under the pseudonym of Clive Hamilton. In addition, he
wrote many other poems that were later collected by Walter Hooper and
published as *Poems* (1964). Hooper also published *Narrative Poems* (1969), a
volume that reprints *Dymer* as well as three other narrative poems. Most
recently Hooper has published *The Collected Poems of C.S. Lewis* (1994), a
work that reprints *Spirits in Bondage* and *Poems*, but includes for the first time
"A Miscellany of Additional Poems," a supplement of seventeen other short
poems (eleven previously unpublished). With one exception, the previously
unpublished poems date from the time Lewis was seventeen to nineteen
years old. In addition, a recent essay, "Glints of Light; The Unpublished
Short Poetry of C.S. Lewis," has published another ten poems and
fragments.[1]

Despite this body of work, Lewis has not achieved acclaim as a poet.
While Thomas Howard calls *Poems* "the best—the glorious best—of
Lewis,"[2] other critics view his poetry less favorably. Chad Walsh refers to
Lewis as "the almost poet,"[3] and Dabney Hart believes that Lewis "will

From *C.S. Lewis, Poet: The Legacy of His Poetic Impulse*. © 2001 by The Kent State University
Press.

never have a major place in the canon of ... poets."[4] Charles Huttar says that, given current critical taste, Lewis as a poet is viewed as a "minor figure" and, "barring a revolution in taste, he will never be accorded a higher position."[5] On the other hand, George Sayer's brilliant study of *Dymer* argues "the time may come when it will be ranked higher than much of Lewis's prose work."[6] W. W. Robson, a Lewis colleague and friend, has published an article, "The Poetry of C.S. Lewis," in which he reevaluates his own earlier negative view of Lewis's poetry, arguing that in some of Lewis's poems he "touches greatness."[7] Luci Shaw has celebrated Lewis's poetic "ability to see and probe reality and express it in vivid and illuminating metaphors."[8]

ASPIRATIONS AND INFLUENCES

While critics debate the quality of Lewis's poetry, anyone interested in Lewis as a writer should become aware of the important role poetry had in shaping his literary life, particularly his aspirations to achieve acclaim as a poet, and the literary influences that shaped him. Owen Barfield remembered Lewis when he first met him as one "whose ruling ambition was to become a great poet. At that time if you thought of Lewis you automatically thought of poetry."[9] Tracing these aspirations and influences as he moved from boyhood to mature adult is fascinating and sheds significant light upon the prose for which he later became best known. His autobiography, *Surprised by Joy*, letters (particularly to Arthur Greeves), diaries, and journal entries provide ample chronological evidence of his early enthusiasm for poetry, the writers most influencing him, and his sustained desire to achieve acclaim as a poet. Furthermore, throughout we see his attempt to establish his own theory of poetry, something he pursued throughout his life via a number of different forums culminating in his published debate with E.M.W. Tillyard, *The Personal Heresy*. What all these sources make clear is how integral poetry was to Lewis's life. He did not sip or taste poetry in a casual, off-handed manner; rather, poetry was a stream intricately threaded through his life that fed a literary well—a nourishing reservoir almost without bottom—one from which he drank deeply and passionately.

In *Surprised by Joy* he recalled how his imagination developed from the ages of six to eight, in part through his writing about Animal-Land. At first there was an absence of poetry: "I was training myself to be a novelist. Note well, a novelist; not a poet. My invented world was full (for me) of interest, bustle, humor, and character; but there was no poetry, even no romance, in it. It was almost astonishingly prosaic" (15). Yet during this same period he says his "third glimpse [of joy] came through poetry" specifically the lines "I heard a voice that cried, / Balder the beautiful / Is dead, is dead," from a translation of Tegner's *Drapa*. The impact of these lines was electrifying: "I knew nothing about Balder; but instantly I was uplifted into huge regions of northern sky, I desired with almost sickening intensity something never to be described" (17). While it may be argued that this example is less about poetry's role in his early life and more about his awakening to the pangs of joy around which much of Lewis's life came to revolve, poetry was in fact the primary vehicle by which this intense longing was felt.

Still, prose, not poetry, demanded Lewis's attention in these early years. Whatever interest in poetry the reading of Balder may have prompted remained dormant through Lewis's early education. The critical years 1908–10, which he spent under the tutelage of Robert Capron at Wynyard School—"Oldie" and "Belsen"[10] in *Surprised by Joy*—effectively squelched almost all his literary interests. Lewis says that while at Wynyard, "the only stimulating element in the teaching consisted of a few well-used canes which hung on the green iron chimney piece of the single schoolroom."[11] Lewis speaks volumes in this regard by naming the chapter covering these years in *Surprised by Joy* "Concentration Camp." In a diary he kept while at Wynyard, Lewis provides additional insight into his life there:

> It was on a bleak November morning in the year of grace 1909 that I pulled myself from my bed in an uncomfortable corner of the dormitory at the abominably early hour of 7:30 a.m. Mindful however that a half-penny fine awaited me if I was late, I began to wash in icy water with all reasonable despatch [*sic*].... I had a shop egg for breakfast, today being Sunday; for breakfast most weekdays we have bad ham. We ... marked to Church in a dismal column. We are obliged to go to St. Cuthbert's, a church which wanted to be Roman Catholic but was afraid to say so. A kind of church abhorred by all respectful Irish Protestants.... In this abominable place of Romish hypocrites and English liars, the people cross themselves, bow to the Lord's Table (which they have the vanity to call an altar) and pray to the Virgin .... [For dinner the next evening] we had enormous helpings of boiled beef with thick, sickening yellow fat, and little grey puddings known as slime balls, not to mention an adjoining complement of black, adamantine parsnips.[12]

While some of this may be dismissed as adolescent sarcasm, clearly such living conditions did little to nurture literary, much less poetic, sensibilities.

Still the diary entry itself is remarkably mature, an early indication of his writing potential.

Mercifully, Lewis's father sent him to Campbell College, Belfast, in September 1910, and while there only through December, for the first time he experienced poetry in a profoundly significant way through reading Matthew Arnold's *Sohrab and Rustum*: "I loved the poem at first sight and have loved it ever since. As the wet fog, in the first line, rose out of the Oxus stream, so out of the whole poem there rose and wrapped me round an exquisite, silvery coolness, a delightful quality of distance and calm, a grave melancholy.... Arnold gave me at once (and the best of Arnold gives me still) a sense, not indeed of passionless vision, but of a passionate, silent gazing at things a long way off" (*SJ*, 53). He goes on to use this occasion to describe "how literature actually works." To those who argued that only classicists could enjoy a poem such as *Sohrab and Rustum* for its Homeric echoes, he counters: "[I] knew nothing of Homer. For me the relation between Arnold and Homer worked the other way; when I came, years later, to read the Iliad I liked it partly because it was for me reminiscent of *Sohrab*. Plainly, it does not matter at what point you first break into the system of European poetry. Only keep your ears open and your mouth shut and everything will lead you to everything else in the end" (53). This commendation, that readers practice an unfiltered, objective reading of great literature, especially poetry, was one Lewis held throughout this life. Moreover, it is important to note he did not say we should read poetry uncritically, but instead that we should use great poetry to find great poetry. It is not literary criticism that should capture our attention; instead, we should give our full attention to great literature itself.

Beginning in January 1911, now enrolled at Cherbourg House, Malvern, Lewis had an even more important encounter with poetry, perhaps the defining moment in his literary life.[13] While idling in the school library, his "eye fell upon a headline and a picture, carelessly, expecting nothing. A moment later, as the poet says, 'The sky had turned round'" (*SJ*, 72). In the passage that follows, Lewis connects his reading of the words *Siegfried and the Twilight of the Gods* and Arthur Rackham's illustrations for that volume with birthing in him a zeal for Norse literature: "Pure 'Northernness' engulfed me: a vision of huge, clear spaces hanging above the Atlantic in the endless twilight of Northern summer, remoteness, severity ... and almost at the same moment I knew that I had met this before, long, long ago (it hardly seems longer now) in Tegner's *Drapa*, that Siegfried (whatever it might be) belonged to the same world as Balder" (73).[14] What has not been sufficiently noted before is how profoundly Lewis was drawn to Wagner's music through this event. He relates how fortuitously his father's purchase of a gramophone gave him ample opportunity to indulge his new passion. Indeed, he connects for the first time his love of poetry with his growing interest in music: "Gramophone catalogues were already one of my favorite forms of reading; but I had never remotely dreamed that the records from Grand Opera with their queer German or Italian name could have anything to do with me" (73–74). Only several weeks later he says he is "assailed from a new quarter" when he begins reading a magazine that contains synopses of Wagner's *The Ring of the Nibelung*.[15] Lewis was completely overwhelmed: "I read in rapture and discovered who Siegfried was and what was the 'twilight' of the gods. I could contain myself no longer—I began a poem, a heroic poem on the Wagnerian version of the Niblung [*sic*] story.... I was so ignorant that I made Alberich rhyme with *ditch* and Mime with *time*" (*SI*, 74).[16] Although he never completed the poem, Lewis comments on the powerful effects it had on him as a writer:

> Since the fourth book [of his poem] had carried me only as far as the last scene of *The Rhinegold*, the reader will not be surprised to hear that the poem was never finished. But it was not a waste of time, and I can still see just what it did for me and where it began to do it. The first three books (I may, perhaps, at this distance of time, say it without vanity) are really not at all bad for a boy. At the beginning of the unfinished fourth it goes all to pieces; and that is exactly the point at which I really began to try to make poetry. Up to then, if my lines rhymed and scanned and got on with the story I asked no more. Now, at the beginning of the fourth, I began to try to convey some of the intense excitement I was feeling, to look for expressions which would not merely state but suggest. Of course I failed, lost my prosaic clarity, spluttered, gasped, and presently fell silent; but I had learned what writing means. (74)[17]

That Lewis engaged in such an effort at age thirteen clearly reveals how deeply poetry gripped him. What makes this more surprising is he that tells us he still had never heard a note of Wagner's music, though the composer's name became to him "a magical symbol." Upon first hearing a recording of the *Ride of the Valkyries*, he remembers it came "like a thunderbolt," and all his pocket money went toward purchasing Wagnerian records: "'Music' was one thing, 'Wagnerian music' quite another, and there was no common measure between them; it was not a new pleasure but a new kind of pleasure, if indeed 'pleasure' is the right word, rather than trouble, ecstasy, astonishment, 'a conflict of sensations without name'" (75). In addition, he says that, at this time, "Asgard and the Valkyries seemed to me incomparably more important than anything else in my experience," so "I passed on from Wagner to everything else I could get hold of about Norse mythology" (76, 78).

In September 1913 Lewis moved to Malvern College, still nurturing his discovery of Wagner and Norse poetry. Here he encountered the first of his two greatest teachers, Henry Wakelyn Smith (Smewgy in *Surprised by Joy*) who is discussed in more detail later.[18] Of note is Lewis's gratitude to Smith for teaching him Latin and Greek poetry, especially Horace's *Odes*, Virgil's *Aeneid*, and Euripides' *Bacchae*: "I had always in one sense 'liked' my classical work, but hitherto this had only been the pleasure that everyone feels in mastering a craft. Now I tasted the classics as poetry.... Here was something very different from the Northernness. Pan and Dionysus lacked the cold, piercing appeal of Odin and Frey. A new quality entered my imagination: something Mediterranean and volcanic, the orgiastic drum beat" (113). The other great contribution to his developing poetic sensibility was the school library where he discovered "Milton, and Yeats, and a book on Celtic mythology, which soon became, if not a rival, yet a humble companion, to Norse." Together these influences led him to begin "an epic on Cuchulain and another on Finn, in English hexameters and in fourteeners respectively. Luckily they were abandoned before these easy and vulgar meters had time to spoil my ear" (114).

A year later, in September 1914, Lewis went to live with his greatest teacher, W. T. Kirkpatrick.[19] Kirkpatrick's influence on Lewis's intellectual development is everywhere present and need not be recounted here; however, noteworthy is what Lewis said about Kirkpatrick's teaching: "Homer came first. Day after day and month after month we drove gloriously onward, tearing the whole *Achilleid* out of the *Iliad* and tossing the rest to one side, and then reading the *Odyssey* entire, till the music of the thing and the clear, bitter brightness that lives in almost every formula had become a part of me" (145). However, by far the most important poetry at this time is Lewis's *Loki Bound*.[20] Because his primary literary interest centered upon Northernness, he modeled *Loki Bound* after an ancient literary form: "Norse in subject and Greek in form ... as classical as any Humanist could have desired, with Prologues, Parodos, Epeisodia, Stasima, Exodus, Stichomythia, and (of course) one passage in trochaic *septenarii*—with rhyme. I never enjoyed anything more" (114–15).[21]

Concurrent with Kirkpatrick's influence, Lewis began a lifelong correspondence with Arthur Greeves, an amazing record of his developmental years with particularly rich material about Lewis's consuming love of poetry. In his letters to Greeves (*They Stand Together*, hereafter *TST*), we find him freely sharing his latest poetic discoveries. For instance, in a letter dated June 1914, he writes: "I have here discovered an author exactly after my own heart, whom I am sure you would delight in, W.B. Yeats. He writes plays and poems of rare spirit and beauty about our old Irish mythology.... His works have all got that strange, eerie feeling about them, of which we are both professed admirers" (*TST*, 47–48). Many letters further reveal the important literary influences shaping his poetic sensibilities. For instance, we find he enjoyed reading Homer's *Iliad*, Malory's *Morte D'Arthur*, Spenser's *The Faerie Queene*, the Pearl Poet's *Sir Gawain and the Green Knight*, Milton's "Comus" and *Paradise Lost*, Shelley's "Prometheus Unbound," Wordsworth's "The Prelude," and the poetry of Tennyson, Morris, Arnold, Swinburne, and Yeats. About reading aloud in Greek the *Iliad*, Lewis writes to Greeves on September 26, 1914: "Those fine, simple, euphonious lines, as they roll on with a roar like that of the ocean, strike a chord in one's mind that no modern literature approaches" (50).[22] Of the *Morte D'Arthur*, he notes on January 26, 1915, "It has opened up a new world to me" (*LL*, 63). A month later he says, "It is really the greatest thing I've ever read" (Feb. 2, 1915, 64).

However, the most profound early influence was Milton.[23] Lewis tells Greeves that "Comus" is "an absolute dream of delight" (Sept. 27, 1916, *TST*, 130) and that "it is agreed to be one of the most perfect things in English poetry" (Aug. 4, 1917, 198). His praise of *Paradise Lost* was more frequent and sustained. For example, he writes Greeves after reading the first two books of *Paradise Lost* that "[I] really love Milton better every time I come back to him" (Feb. 7, 1917, 165). A month later he adds: "I have finished 'Paradise Lost' again, enjoying it even more than before.... In Milton is everything you get everywhere else, only better. He is as voluptuous as Keats, as romantic as Morris, as grand as Wagner, as weird as Poe, and a better lover of nature than even the Brontës" (Mar. 6, 1917, 176). In reading of Lewis's early delight in poetry, we are struck by the depth of his enthusiasm; his passion for poetry was visceral, and it fed and nourished his aesthetic taste. Letter after letter communicated his love of literature, music, and art, but especially poetry. He consumed it greedily, and his appetite was perhaps never sated.[24]

Lewis's deep affection for the poetry he read stimulated his own aspirations as a poet. Once again, his letters and diary entries are filled with these longings. He frequently writes Greeves about the poems he is writing. Concerning *Loki Bound*, he wrote seven letters between June 1914 and

November 1916. In one, he writes: "I was very glad to hear your favourable criticism of 'Loki.' ... Your idea of introducing a dance after the exit of Odin etc, is a very good one, altho' it will occasion some trifling alterations in the text" (Oct. 14, 1914, 54). Twelve letters were written about his efforts to write "The Quest of Bleheris."[25] Apparently Lewis struggled throughout as he composed this prose romance: "I think Bleheris has killed my muse—always a sickly child. At any rate my verse, both in quality and quantity for the last three weeks is deplorable" (June 6, 1916, 107). He adds later that he regrets he "began Bleheris in the old style [as opposed to a modern style]: I see now that though it is harder to work some effects in modern English, yet on the whole my way of writing is a sort of jargon" (July 4, 1916, 118). Eventually he records the death of Bleheris: "As to Bleheris, he is dead and I shan't trouble his grave" (Oct. 12, 1916, 136). In addition, several letters concern his effort to write "Medea": "The subject [of the poem] is 'The childhood of Medea,' & it will leave off where the most poems about her begin—shortly after her meeting with Jason. It will describe her lonely, frightened childhood away in a castle with the terrible old king her father & how she is gradually made to learn magic against her will" (Feb. 15, 1917, 167). In a later letter he records the fate of this poem: "'Medea's Childhood' after struggling on for 300 turgid lines has been quietly made into spills for my 'tobacco pipe'—all those fine landscapes and vigorous speeches, devoted to real use at last!" (Feb. 28, 1917, 173).

Other early letters to Greeves revealed Lewis devoted himself to writing lyrics, many later published in *Spirits in Bondage*. Consciously turning away from writing narrative poetry, he confesses to Greeves: "I begin to see that short, slight stories & poems are all I am fit for at present & that it would be better to write & finish one of such than to begin & leave twenty ambitious epic-poems or romances" (Oct. 4, 1916, 133). However, he did not abandon narrative poetry; instead lie began work on a prose version of *Dymer* late in 1916 or early in 1917, after matriculating at University College, Oxford. Yet in April 1917, while involved in officer training, he found it easier to focus upon short lyrics rather than narrative poetry. He tells Greeves: "I am in a strangely productive mood at present and spend my few moments of spare time in scribbling verse. When my 4 months course in the cadet battalion is at an end ... I propose to get together all the stuff I have perpetrated and see if any kind publisher would like to take it" (June 10, 1917, 192). In addition, he continued his interest in Wagner, writing Greeves about a performance he saw: "Now will I make you envious. On Friday night I went to Drury Lane to hear 'The Valkyries.' The dream of years has been realized, and without disillusionment: I have had thrills and delights of the real old sort, I have felt as I felt five years ago" (June 17, 1918, 221). Despite Macmillan's rejection of this collection, Lewis was not dejected, writing to Greeves: "I am determined not to lose heart until I have tried all the houses I can hear of. I am sending it off to Heinneman [*sic*] next" (Aug. 7, 1918, 227).

Happily, William Heinemann accepted this work less than a month later, and Lewis's letters show his increasing ambition to achieve acclaim as a poet. For example, he writes his father: "This little success gives me a pleasure which is perhaps childish, and yet akin to greater things" (Sept. 9, 1918, *LL*, 88). To Greeves he says: "You can imagine how pleased I am, and how eagerly I now look at all Heinneman's [*sic*] books and wonder what mine will be like" (Sept. 12, 1918, *TST*, 230). Several weeks later he gives his father a qualified evaluation of the poems: "I am not claiming that they are good poems—you know the schoolboys' definition—'prose is when the lines go on to the end of the page; poetry is when they don't'" (Oct. 3, 1918, Warren Lewis, unpublished "C.S. Lewis: A Biography," hereafter *WLB*, 73). When asked by John Galsworthy for permission to publish one of the poems from *Spirits in Bondage*, "Death in Battle," in a war poetry anthology, Lewis writes his father that "I naturally consented because it is pleasant *laudari laudato viro*" (Oct. 27, 1918, *LL*, 94).[26] He tells Greeves later when recalling his first meeting with the publisher: "You will understand well how pleasant it was to walk in under a doorway ... feeling I had some right to be there" (Nov. 2, 1918, *TST*, 237).

Spirits in Bondage was eventually published in March 1919. Once a published poet and enjoying the first taste of fame, however modest, Lewis continued his poetic maturation. In a series of letters to Leo Baker, Lewis reflected upon the classical poets he so admired and the role and function of poetry. In April 1920 he confides in Baker: "All poetry is one, and I love to see the great notes repeated. Homer and Virgil wrote lines not for their own works alone but for the use of all their followers. A plague on these moderns scrambling for what they call originality—like men trying to lift themselves off the earth by pulling at their own braces: as if by shutting their eyes to the work of the masters they were likely to create new things themselves."[27] In September 1920 he writes Baker and thanks him for his theory of poetry: "The most valuable part of it, and the part which should be insisted on is that 'a poet who is only a poet is not the greatest poet': the assumption that a great poem must have nothing in it but poetry has 'worked like madness in the brain' of too many of us" (*LKB*, 0092). A poet, Lewis suggested, cannot afford to be a poet only; he must be involved in the lives of men and women. In addition, Lewis intimated how longing to achieve acclaim as a poet can interfere with writing poetry. That is, as he worked to write great poetry, the focus had been too much upon *him* and too little upon poetry.[28]

Later in the same letter Lewis attempts to describe the peculiar function of poetry as compared to other arts: "What we want to find is—that which is proper to poetry alone: what is the method by which poetry *and no other art* [Lewis's emphasis] performs the duties shared with all art? Doubtless you would answer that in the same way as I wd. & come to a definition something like this: 'Poetry is the art of utilizing the informal or irrational values of words to express that which can only be symbolized by their formal or conventional meanings.' These values include chiefly sound & association: also of course their—'group'—sounds or rhythms which are above and beyond their individual sounds: here is the meaning & justification of metre. Hence the value of the test 'could this be said as well in prose?': if the answer is in the affirmative the poem is condemned" (*LKB*, 0093). Here Lewis reflects a workman's view of how poetry happens. That is, he implies that the poet uses language in a particularly structured and precise way to produce a desired emotional effect. Form, therefore, becomes a central interest for Lewis.[29] His interest in form may explain why Lewis eventually turned his attention back to narrative poetry. Having finished a prose version of *Dymer* in 1917, Lewis finished a verse version in December 1918.[30] However, still not content, from 1920 to 1926 Lewis pursued a final poetic version with intensity and deliberate singlemindedness. His diary, *All My Road before Me: The Diary of C.S. Lewis 1922–1927*, contains over seventy-five direct references to this effort. In these entries he recounts an almost daily obsession with both his progress on the poem and his ambition to achieve fame as a poet. A study of the diary shows that he completed initial drafts of the first two cantos by the end of June 1922; Canto III by the end of July 1922; Canto IV by the end of August 1922; Cantos V and VI by the end of June 1923; and Cantos VII, VIII, and IX by mid-April 1924.[31] Of course during this process he went back and forth between one canto and another, revising here and there as he saw the need. Often he was assisted in this process by the sympathetic but frank criticism of colleagues, including Leo Baker, Owen Barfield, Alfred Hamilton-Jenkin, Cecil Harwood, Rodney Pasley, and Arthur Greeves. He completed a final version in the summer of 1925.

At times he wrote about his struggles. For instance, early on he notes that "I am very dispirited about my work at present.... I have leaned much too much on the idea of being able to write poetry and if this is a frost I shall be rather stranded" (*DCSL*, Apr. 15, 1922).[32] Three months later he is rewriting Canto IV, "with which I am finding great difficulties" (July 30,

1922, 77). Eighteen months later he is at his most dissatisfied: "[I am] discontent with the whole plan of 'Dymer': it seems 'full of sound and fury, signifying nothing'" (Jan. 6, 1924, 281). When revising the proofs just prior to publication, Lewis shares a feeling many writers have as they look over their labors: "I never liked it less. I felt no mortal could get any notion of what the devil it was all about. I am afraid this sort of stuff is very much hit or miss, yet I think it is my only line" (July 6, 1926, 422). Yet, more often than not, he is at least upbeat if not jubilant about his progress. Many entries include comments such as "made some progress," "pleased myself fairly well," "felt fairly satisfied," "pleased myself with it," and "with considerable satisfaction." After several months of work, he writes: "After supper I worked on 'Dymer,' bringing it to the end of the storm. I was so transported with what I considered my success that I became insolent and said to myself that it was the voice of a god" (Sept. 30, 1922, 111). A week later he adds, "I read the whole thing through and felt fairly satisfied with the general movement of the story" (Oct. 9, 1922, 115). The following summer Lewis says that Harwood "covered me with enough praise to satisfy the vainest of men" (July 8, 1923, 255).

It is a mistake, however, to think that Lewis's only poetic preoccupation during this time was *Dymer*. While it is true he published no poetry between *Spirits in Bondage* in 1919 and "Joy" in 1924, *All My Road Before Me* contains over fifty references showing him at work on several other poems. For instance, apparently he spent a good deal of time working on two poems that have not survived, "Misfire" and "Offa," submitting them for publication to the *London Mercury* (Apr. 4, 1922, 16). While he waited to hear their fate, he asked his friend William Stead how he managed to get his poems published by the *London Mercury*. Lewis wrote in his diary that Stead called on the editor, John Squire, and said: "'Look here Mr. Squire, you haven't taken these poems of mine and I want to know what's wrong with them!!' If the story ended there, it would be merely a side light on Stead, but the joke is that Squire said, 'I'm glad you've come to talk it over: that's just what I want people to do' and actually accepted what he'd formerly refused. Truly the ways of editors are past finding out!" (Apr. 5, 1922, 17). After this, several entries chronicle his work on "Joy."[33] "Nimue," first mentioned in a letter to Greeves of June 2, 1919, was the subject of eight entries (*TST*, 254).[34] When it was eventually rejected by the *London Mercury*, Lewis despairs: "I was thinking seriously of how I could face the prospect of having to give up poetry, if it came to that" (May 10, 1922, *DCSL*, 32). Six months later Lewis refers to "a new poem on my old theme of Alone in the House. I soon found that I was creating rather too well in myself the creepy atmosphere wh. I was trying to create in the poem, and gave it up" (Jan. 3, 1923, 169).[35] Lewis also recalls Owen Barfield's comments after reading several poems sent him for review: "He said it always surprised him that my things were as good as they were, for I seemed to work simply on inspiration and did no chipping. I thus wrote plenty of good poetry but never one perfect poem. He said the 'inspired' percentage was increasing all the time and that might save me in the end" (Jan. 26, 1923, 186).

Lewis took such criticism to heart as he revised one poem: "Worked as hard as I have ever done on a poem, trying to resist all my cliches, shortcuts and other original sins" (Feb. 11, 1923, 195). Still, self-doubt plagued his efforts at poetry: "I am haunted by fears for the future ... and whether I shall ever be able to write good poetry" (Feb. 15, 1923, 200). Yet, a year later when "Foster," a poem he spent considerable effort writing, was rejected by the *London Mercury*, he was not crestfallen, seeing in the rejection a silver lining because "an unknown publisher called Stockwell wrote saying that 'a mutual friend' had told him I would soon have enough poems for a book and telling me he would be pleased to see them" (Jan. 28, 1924, 286).[36] One particularly ambitious project was a sequence of sonnets "which was to be put in the mouth of a man who is gradually falling in love with a bitch, tho' quite conscious of what she is. I don't care for sonnet sequences and it is not the sort of thing I ever imagined myself writing: but it would be jolly if it shd. come off" (May 29, 1926, 403).[37] However, and unexplainably, after several weeks, he abandoned the sequence. Other poems he worked on during this period were "Wild Hunt," "The King of Drum," "Sigrid," and variations on the myth of Cupid and Psyche.[38]

However, the most penetrating insights into Lewis's poetic aspirations are found in his diary entry of March 6, 1926. Here Lewis is brutally honest in analyzing his feelings when *Dymer* was rejected by Heinemann (it was later published by Dent in 1926). As he analyzed his reactions to the rejection, he posited five reasons for why he was so disturbed.[39] In a process reminiscent of his logical parry-and-thrust apologetic dialectic, he at first discounted each motive. But as he probed deeper, he finally admitted that he did desire fame as a poet: "I desire that my value as a poet should be acknowledged by others" (*TST*, 383). What follows is one of Lewis's longest passages of self-analysis:

> As far as I can see both these are manifestations of the single desire for what maybe called mental or spiritual rank. I have flattered myself with the idea of being among my own people when I was reading the poets and it is unpleasing to have to stand down and take my place in the crowd.... The completion of the

poem, Coghill's praise of it, and the sending off to a publishers [*sic*] (after so many years) threw me back into a tumult of self-love that I thought I had escaped.... Worst of all I have used the belief in such secret pre-eminence as a compensation for things that wearied or humiliated me in real life.... The cure of this disease is not easy to find.... I was free from it at times when writing Dymer. Then I was interested in the object, not in my own privileged position as seer of the object. But whenever I stopped writing or thought of publication or showed the MS to friends I contemplated not that of which I had been writing, but my writing about it: I passed from looking at the macrocosm to looking at a little historical event inside the "Me." The only healthy or happy or eternal life is to look so steadily on the World that the representation "Me" fades away. Its appearance at all in the field of consciousness is a mark of inferiority in the state where it appears. Its claiming a central position is disease. (383–84)

Lewis went on to say the only way to cure this disease was to look away from self to the greater world so that thoughts of self would fade. What is so striking here is his brutal self-assessment. He confessed that his desire for fame as a poet was nothing less than spiritual pride, a key theme he explored later in prose fiction and apologetics. Equally, he noted that poetry per se, even his poetry, had not been nearly as interesting to him in this process as *he* had been. Additionally, we see that his hopes for literary fame had been a kind of sop for other disappointments. Indeed, he was clearly embarrassed by the recognition that his desire to be a poet veiled an intense self-absorption. Although this realization was certainly a watershed in the life of Lewis the poet, it did not mark the end of his desire for fame as a poet. Instead, it provided Lewis with a point in time for occasions later in life when his thirst for fame as a poet or more broadly as a writer was tempered by the realization that such a desire was an unhealthy exaltation of self.

After 1926, references to his efforts at writing poetry drop off substantially in his letters and diary entries as a direct result of his being elected a fellow of Magdalen College. Lewis had feared his time for poetry would be limited by this election, as a diary entry from February 29, 1924 reveals: "I saw that it [a Trinity College fellowship] would mean pretty full work and that I might become submerged and poetry crushed out" (*DCSL*, 293). Still he did not abandon writing poetry. In a letter on August 18, 1930, Lewis attempted to encourage Greeves, who had just experienced rejection of a writing project.[40] Lewis, who by this time was nearing conversion to Christ, openly admitted his belief that because achieving success as a poet had become for him an idol, God had to kill it: "From the age of sixteen onwards I had one single ambition, from which I never wavered, in the prosecution of which I spent every ounce I could, on wh[ich] I really deliberately staked my whole contentment.... Suffering of the sort that you are now feeling is my special subject, my profession, my long suit, the thing I claim to be an expert in" (*TST*, 378–79). Foreshadowing his later phrase a "severe mercy," Lewis counseled Greeves that perhaps God was dealing kindly with them by denying their desires for literary fame. Such a denial saved them from the disappointment and despair attendant upon those who briefly flame up with literary fame, only to flicker quickly before fading into oblivion.

We know, of course, that he continued to write poetry, as his pieces appeared regularly in newspapers, literary magazines, and scholarly journals.[41] In letters to other friends, he recorded this continuing impulse to write poetry. At times he was very confident of his ability as a poet. Tongue in cheek, he writes to Owen Barfield: "I have written about 100 lines of a long poem in my type of Alexandrine. It is going to make the Prelude [by Wordsworth] (let alone the *Tower* [by Barfield]) look silly" (Mar. 16, 1932).[42] Yet his discouragement about poetry in general was pronounced when he wrote Barfield seven years later: "I am more and more convinced that there is no future for poetry" (Feb. 8, 1939, *OB*, 0088). Lewis's debate with E. M. W. Tillyard published in 1939 as *The Personal Heresy* (hereafter *PH*) offers additional evidence of the primacy of poetry in Lewis's life.[43] Although this debate did not explicitly reveal Lewis's passion to be known as a poet, it clearly demonstrated how seriously he considered the necessity for right thinking about the nature of poetry and the role of the poet. Lewis rejected modern poetry's emphasis on the poet's personality or character; he came to call this emphasis the "personal heresy." Instead, he argues "that when we read poetry as poetry should be read, we have before us no representation which claims to be the poet, and frequently no representation of a *man*, a *character*, or a *personality* at all" (Lewis's emphasis).[44] Citing his as an "objective or impersonal theory of poetry," he admits that this notion "finds its easiest application in the drama and epic" (*PH*, 8). Given Lewis's consistent early efforts at narrative poetry, his point of view is not surprising. Furthermore, it is not difficult to posit that Lewis's personal heresy argument germinated in part from the diary entry of March 6, 1926, quoted above; Lewis's self-indictment provided the basis for his critical distaste for poetry focusing upon the author's personality.

Yet he did not totally dismiss the significance of the poet's personality. Instead, he articulated effectively how a poet's personality may affect the reading of a poem: "[However, when reading a poem], let it be granted that I do approach the poet; at least I do it by sharing his consciousness, not by studying it. I look with his eyes, not at him.... The poet is not a man who asks me to look at him; he is a man who says 'look at that' and points; the more I follow the pointing of his finger the less I can possibly see of *him*" (11, Lewis's emphasis). Later, he adds that while looking to where the poet points, "I must make of him not a spectacle but a pair of spectacles.... I must *enjoy* him and not *contemplate* him" (12, Lewis's emphasis).[45] Throughout, Lewis argued that poetry was not a private matter, but instead a public one: "[In a poem] it is absolutely essential that each word should suggest not what is private and personal to the poet but what is public, common, impersonal, objective" (19).[46]

Lewis's view of the role of the poet has been under attack since the great Romantic poets; Wordsworth claimed that poets wrote about "both what they half create, / And what they perceive." Lewis believed the elevation of the poet's personality led to "Poetolatry" and "the cult of poetry" displaying "religious characteristics" (65). When Lewis turns to a theory of poetry in *The Personal Heresy*, he sounds very much like he did in his early letters: "[Poetry is] a skill or trained habit of using all the extra-logical elements of language—rhythm, vowel-music, onomatopoeia, associations, and what not—to convey the concrete reality of experiences.... [A poem is] a composition which communicates more of the concrete and qualitative than our usual utterances do. A poet is a man who produces such compositions more often and more successfully than the rest of us" (108–9). Lewis's view suggests that a poet is primarily a workman using the tools of language to reflect on the universal concerns of all men and women. Because the poet is more gifted in the use of language, he can speak poignantly to universal human concerns. However, the poet as a person is no more worthy of our interest than a plumber; the poet simply articulates more effectively the same basic concerns he shares with the plumber. Near the end of *The Personal Heresy*, Lewis says there are only two questions to ask about a poem: "Firstly, whether it is interesting, enjoyable, attractive, and secondly, whether this enjoyment wears well and helps or hinders you towards all the other things you would like to enjoy, or do, or be" (119–20). It was this pragmatic view of poetry that Lewis consistently supported, and, at the same time, this view may have kept him from achieving acclaim as a poet. That is, it may be that

Lewis's workmanlike efforts to write poetry, to make himself into a poet, inevitably thwarted his poetic sensibilities.

Even so, Lewis's public discussion with Tillyard complemented his continued private correspondence. For instance, he carried on a lengthy correspondence with Ruth Pitter, an accomplished poet. In response to her critiques of several of his poems, he writes: "In most of these poems [that he has sent her] I am enamoured of metrical subtleties—not as a game: the truth is I often lust after a metre as a man might lust after a woman" (*RP*, Aug. 10, 1946).[47] He writes to Rhona Bodle commenting on the way poetry makes language concrete: "Indeed, in a sense, one can hardly put anything into words: only the simplest colours have names, and hardly any of the smells. The simple physical pains and (still more) the pleasures can't be expressed in language. I labour the point lest the devil shd. hereafter try to make you believe that what was wordless was therefore vague and nebulous. But in reality it is just the clearest, the most concrete, and most indubitable realities which escape language: not because *they* [Lewis's emphasis] are vague but because language is.... Poetry I take to be the continual effort to bring language back to the actual" (June 24, 1949).[48] In writing to Martyn Skinner about his *Two Colloquies*, Lewis says, "I didn't want to write until I had given them a sympathetic reading and somehow I never was in quite the mood for them till tonight. (Reading collection papers, like marking School Cert., I have always found a great whetter of appetite for poetry. Fact! I don't know why). The right mood for a new poem doesn't come so often now as it used to. There is so little leisure, and when one comes to that leisure untired— well, you know *Ink* is a deadly drug. One wants to write. I cannot shake off the addiction" (Oct. 11, 1950).[49] In a letter to Dom Bede Griffiths, Lewis expresses his well-known distaste for modern British poetry and a surprisingly positive evaluation of some modern American poetry: "I feel as you do about modern English poetry. American is better. [Robert] Frost and Robinson Jeffers all really have something to say and some real art" (Apr. 22, 1954, Lewis's emphasis).[50] During a dry period, he writes Pitter: "It is a long time since I turned a verse. One aches a little, doesn't one? I should like to be 'with poem' again" (Mar. 19, 1955, *RP*, 0073).

LEWIS THE CRAFTSMAN

Lewis's penchant to be "enamoured of metrical subtleties," his lusting "after a metre as a man might lust after a woman," his ache to turn a verse and "be 'with poem' again," was lifelong, so before we consider the content of his poetry, it is appropriate we consider his focus upon crafting his poetry, including both his tendency to revise his poems and his fascination with prosody. While he certainly dashed off quick initial drafts of poems, he labored to make the final draft as polished as possible. Hooper has noted that while Lewis the prose writer worked quickly and wrote few drafts, Lewis the poet was painstaking, often writing several versions of the same poem: "Most of Lewis's prose came from his head almost exactly as it appears on the printed page, with only an occasional word being changed. It was not like this with his poetry. They went through endless revisions."[51] We know, for example, that Lewis sent friends drafts of poems and asked for criticism. In the mid-twenties, he writes Leo Baker: "I am sending you the revised version of the Wild Hunt and await your criticism.... I have not time today to discuss your theory of poetry; we seem to be agreed on fundamentals, tho' there are still points of difference—real ones, not 'misunderstanding'" (*LKB*, 090). About an autobiographical poem concerning, in part, his spiritual pilgrimage, Lewis writes Barfield: "It really takes a load off my mind to hear that you like the poem ["I Will Write Down"]. Couplets, however dangerous, are needed if one is to try to give to the subjective poem some of the swing and narrative zest of the old epic.... I send ... the opening of the poem.... I am not satisfied with any part I have yet written and the design is ludicrously ambitious. But I feel it will be several years anyway before I give up" (May 6, 1932, *OB*, 0063, 0064).[52]

Lewis's extensive correspondence with Ruth Pitter also shows him seeking criticism about drafts of poems. Given Lewis's deep affection for Pitter's poetry, it is not surprising that he seeks her advice about his own poetry.[53] In her he found one who shared similar poetic sensibilities, so he felt comfortable asking her to critique his verse. In fact, he asked her to be straightforward in her criticisms: "Now remember ... you won't wound a sick man by unfavourable comment.... I know (or think) that some of these contain important thoughts and v. great metrical ingenuity. That isn't what I'm worrying about. But are they real poems or do the content and the form remain separable—fitted together only by force?" (July 24, 1946, *RP*, 005). At one point he asks her to judge between two versions of his poem "Two Kinds of Memory": "I want some advice. I have written two different versions of a poem and all my friends disagree, some violently championing A and some B, and some neither. Will you give a vote? Firstly, is either any good? Secondly, if so, which is the good one? Don't be in the least afraid of answering NO to the first question: kindness wd. only be an encouragement to waste more time.... I could almost make myself hope for your sake—and lest you spend more time and attention on them than is reasonable for me to exact—that both are bad!" (Feb. 2, 1947, 017, 019). In her recollection of this letter, Pitter writes, "Both versions are very fine, of course: the skill in form alone is enough to drive a small poet to despair: and then the melody, so strong and so unforced, and the solemn images and the contrasting moods. Strange how memory is here *polarised*, as though he could not have encompassed the paradisal without retaining a hellish pain in recollection, an ever-fresh wound. (NB. These poems should be read aloud, but only by a strong male voice.) And see how he deprecates giving trouble, when one was of course only too eager: I have sometimes thought he would devise little jobs because he knew very well what pleasure it would give."[54] In another instance, she recalls being flattered that Lewis would think her view on his poems important: "'Donkey's Delight,' 'Young King Cole,' 'Vitraea Circe,' [are] magnificent poems to my mind, the technique staggering, vocabulary so wide, learned, & choice, discrimination (moral or spiritual) so lofty. As well might a lion request a mouse to criticise his roaring: and yet I can imagine a lion doing so."[55]

On the basis of such criticisms as well as his own desire to write the best poetry possible, Lewis frequently reworked poems.[56] While any number of poems could be cited to show Lewis working as a craftsman, we will consider one here as representative. In *Poems*, Hooper published the poignant sonnet "As the Ruin Falls," an agonizing recollection about a beloved one's suffering.[57] Three holograph versions of the poem survive, but all are undated.[58] However, based on the internal evidence of the three versions, I surmise the following order of the drafts:

Draft A (written on very thin typing paper)
This is all flashy rhetoric about loving you;
I never had a selfless thought since I was born.
I am mercenary and self-seeking through and through,
I want God, Man, and you, only to serve my turn.

Pleasure, ease, reassurance are the goals I seek,
I cannot crawl one inch outside my proper skin.
I talk of "love" (a scholar's parrot might talk Greek)
But, self-imprisoned, end always where I begin.

But this at least: you have shown me, dearest, what I lack,
Revealed the gulf, and me on the wrong side of it,
Shown me the impossibility of turning back,
And pointed me the one way from[?] the noisome pit.

For this I bless you for my broken heart. The pains
You cause me are more precious than all other gains.

Draft B (written on a scrap of paper)
All this is flashy rhetoric, about loving you.
I never had a selfless thought since I was born.
I am mercenary and self-seeking through and through:
I want friends, you, and God only to serve my turn.

Pleasure, peace, re-assurance are the goals I seek;
I cannot crawl one inch outside my proper skin.
I talk of love—a scholar's parrot may talk Greek—
But, self-imprisoned, always end where I begin.

Only that now you have shown me (oh how late) my lack:
I see the chasm; and everything you are was making
Each moment a long bridge by which I might get back
From exile and grow man. And now the bridge is breaking.

Yet so, I bless you for my hammered heart: the pains
You give me are more precious than all other gains.

Draft C (written on lined, greenish paper)
All this is flashy rhetoric about loving you.
I never had a selfless thought since I was born.
I am mercenary and self-seeking through and through:
I want God, you, all friends, merely to serve my turn.

Peace, re-assurance, pleasure, are the goals I seek,
I cannot crawl one inch outside my proper skin:
I talk of love—a scholar's parrot may talk Greek—
But, self-imprisoned, always end where I begin.

Only that now you have taught me (but how late) my lack.
I see the chasm. And everything you are was making
My heart into a bridge by which I might get back
From exile, and grow man. And now the bridge is breaking.

For this I bless you as the ruin falls. The pains
You give me are more precious than all other gains.[59]

Each draft is written in alexandrines and uses the rhyme scheme of an English sonnet. In the first quatrain, there are few differences between the drafts. "B" and "C" change the opening from "This is all flashy rhetoric" to "All this is flashy rhetoric," and in line four "only" becomes "merely" in "C." In the second quatrain, the "ease" of line five becomes "peace" in "B" and "C"; the alliteration of "pleasure, peace, reassurance" in "B" is weakened in "peace, re-assurance, pleasure" in "C." The only other significant difference is that "(a scholar's parrot might talk Greek)" becomes "—a scholar's parrot may talk Greek—" in "B" and "C."

However, the minor tweaking Lewis did in the drafts of the first two quatrains contrasts to major changes in the third quatrain and final couplet. In the initial draft, the third quatrain is weak. In line nine "but this at least" is jarring, and "dearest" edges the poem to the brink of sentimentality. "Revealed the gulf" in line ten could work, but "me on the wrong side of it" is forced. Line eleven suggests the beloved has shown the speaker "the impossibility of turning back" from his love for her, and this works well with the sentiment expressed in line twelve: that their relationship has saved him from hell on earth ("pointed me the one way from[?] the noisome pit"). Also, the *it:pit* rhyme is odd. The third quatrains of "B" and "C" are considerable improvements. Both drafts remake lines nine and ten-A into the more poetically powerful "Only that now you have taught me (but how late) my lack. / I see the chasm." The next clear sign the poem evolves from weak to stronger occurs when lines ten-B and eleven of "B," "and everything you are was making / Each moment a long bridge by which I might get back" becomes "and everything you are was making / My heart into a bridge by which I might get back" of "C." The shift from the impersonal "each moment a long bridge" to "my heart into a bridge" suddenly transforms the poem from an objective, clinical analysis to a subjective, personal confession. The power of both "B" and "C" is highlighted by the shared conclusion: "And now the bridge is breaking." Lewis deftly describes the pain of heartbreak yet avoids being maudlin.

The final couplet in the three drafts undergoes the most change, particularly line thirteen. In "A," Lewis again verges on the sentimental when he writes, "For this I bless you for my broken heart." "B" is a qualitative improvement as we read, "Yet so, I bless you for my hammered heart." Indeed, the notion his heart has been hammered by a smith shaping molten iron ameliorates the hackneyed use of "bless." However, Lewis nears perfection in "C" when the line evolves to its most powerful expression: "For this I bless you as the ruin falls." Now it all comes out: As he watches her suffering—her physical ruin—he faces squarely his own ruin: his broken life as he anticipates losing her. Yet in the midst of this knowledge, the poem's final line shares the secret of one of life's greatest ironies—the pain of losing one's beloved reinforces the inestimable worth of human love: "The pains / You give me are more precious than all other gains." In reviewing the three drafts of this poem, it is clear a craftsman was at work—shaping, honing, and molding words into the best combination of sounds and meanings he could. This same dedication to making the best poetry he could informed all of Lewis's serious efforts at verse.

LEWIS'S PROSODY

As a crafter of verse, Lewis was extremely conscious of prosody, especially meter, rhyme (exact and slant as well internal and final), and stanza form.[60] As early as March 7, 1916, he writes Greeves and critiques the prosody of several of George MacDonald's poems appearing in *Phantastes*: "There are ... poems in the tale ... which with one or two exceptions are shockingly bad, so don't TRY [Lewis's emphasis] to appreciate them: it is just a sign, isn't it, of how some geniuses can't work in metrical forms" (*TST*, 93). Three months later he tells Greeves, "My verse, both in quality and quantity for the last three weeks is deplorable!" (June 6, 1916, 107). On October 12, 1916, Lewis's praise to Greeves of Shelley's *Prometheus Unbound* is tempered by his criticism of the prosody: "Shelley had a great genius, but his carelessness about rhymes, metre, choice of words etc., just prevents him being as good as he might be. To me, when you're in the middle of a fine passage and come to a 'cockney' rhyme like 'ruin' & pursuing [Lewis's emphasis], it spoils the whole thing" (136).

While Lewis's youthful criticism of Shelley may be querulous, it nonetheless demonstrates how important prosody was to him. Lewis's interest in the making of verse, especially prosody, was lifelong and is reflected in many of his scholarly writings. In "The Alliterative Metre," Lewis took it upon himself to expound "the principles of this metre to a larger public than those Anglo-Saxon and Old Norse specialists who know it already."[61] Throughout this essay he tries to make the technical aspects of alliterative meter understandable, and he gives a detailed explanation of how the half-line meter works. In addition, he explains lifts and dips, providing multiple examples (A–E plus variations of each) of how lifts and dips may be arranged in the half-line. In something of a tour de force, he ends the essays with his own model alliterative poem, "The Planets." Throughout this essay we follow the serious passion of a poet intent upon demonstrating how important a knowledge of prosody is for those who want to understand alliterative verse. In "The Fifteenth-Century Heroic Line," he offers another thoughtful discussion of prosody: "I shall give the arbitrary name 'Fifteenth-Century Heroic' to the line we find in *The Temple of Glas*, *The Pastime of Pleasure*, Barclay's *Ecologues*, Wyatt's *Complaint upon Love to Reason*, and, in general, all those poems which appear at first sight to attempt the decasyllabic line without success. The question I propose is whether the Fifteenth-Century Heroic is, in fact, an attempt at our decasyllabic; and, if it is not, what else it may be."[62] Lewis offers at one point in the essay to demonstrate what he means by an "experiment" in which he offers two contrasting four-line stanzas; while the content of each is roughly the same, the differing meters of each illustrate the point he wishes to make.

In his massive *English Literature in the Sixteenth Century* (1944), Lewis moves easily between literary history, evaluation of various poets (he dismisses some rather abruptly), and commentary on prosody. For example, about the poulter's measure (alternating lines of hexameter and heptameter), he writes, "The vices of that metre are two. The medial break in the alexandrine, though it may do well enough in French, quickly becomes intolerable in a language with such a tyrannous stress-accent as ours: the line struts. The fourteener has a much pleasanter movement, but a totally different one; the line dances a jig. Hence in a couplet made of two such yoke-fellows we seem to be labouring up a steep hill in bottom gear for the first line, and then running down the other side of the hill, out of control, for the second" (232–33). In "Metre," published near the end of his life, Lewis is still focusing upon prosody.[63] The essay attempts to consider the somewhat thorny question of how to scan lines of poetry. After admitting that scansion depends upon phonetic facts and individual differences of pronunciation, he posits, "I am going to suggest that metrical questions are profitable only if we regard them, not as questions about fact, but as purely practical. That is, when we ask 'What is the metre of this poem?,' we are not, or should not be, asking which analysis of the paradigm is 'true' but which is most useful" (281).

Lewis's earliest poems illustrate this lifelong fascination with prosody. For example, he enjoyed experimenting with meter from the heroic couplets of "Descend to Earth, Descend, Celestial Nine" to the eight-stressed catalectic trochees of "'Carpe Diem' after Horace" to the rhyme royal of "In Winter When the Frosty Nights Are Long" to the blank verse of *Loki Bound*.[64] Other examples of Lewis's earliest verse, the ten poems that survive from "Metrical Meditations of a Cod"[65] and the lyrics of *Spirits in Bondage*, offer additional insights into Lewis's youthful concerns with prosody. Of these fifty-one poems, thirty-five are tetrameter or pentameter, most often iambs, with trochees less frequent. The other sixteen poems include trimeter, hexameter, heptameter, and several cases where the meter is mixed.

TETRAMETER AND PENTAMETER POEMS

Several of Lewis's iambic tetrameter and pentameter poems employ rhyming couplets. For instance, the tetrameter couplets of "Satan Speaks" (I) and the heroic couplets of "Satan Speaks" (XIII) indicate that the two poems share more than a common title (*SB*, 3, 22). Both open similarly, including the use of a medial caesura. The "I am Nature, the Mighty Mother / I am the law: ye have none other" of the former sets the stage for "I am the Lord your God: even he that made / Material things, and all these signs arrayed" of the latter. In "The Hills of Down," Lewis disguises his heroic couplets by printing the poem as though lines of iambic dimeter alternate with iambic trimeter:

> I will abide
> > And make my dwelling here
> Whatso betide,
> > Since there is more to fear
> Out yonder. Though
> > This world is drear and wan,
> I dare not go
> > To dreaming Avalon. (*CP*, 229)

What we actually have are heroic couplets with internal rhyme. Lewis weaves the fabric of this poem even tighter when we note the assonance of *abide, my,* and *betide* in the first three lines as well as the final *–er* sound of *here, there, fear, yonder,* and *drear* in lines two through six. This assonance and sound repetition occurs throughout the other sections of the poem.

Lewis used tercets less often but to powerful effect, as in "Spooks": "Last night I dreamed that I was come again / Unto the house where my beloved dwells / After years of wandering and pain" (*SB*, 11). While the rhyme scheme here is *aba* and not the typical *aaa* of the true tercet, Lewis may have been experimenting with a kind of terza rima, since the rest of the poem rhymes *acc, dde, ffe, acca*. However, "De Profundis" utilizes the true tercet rhyme, with several sounds repeated in the twelve stanzas: *abcdefgdhige*. In addition, one stanza uses the unusual perfect rhyme: "Yet I will not bow down to thee nor love thee, / For looking in my own heart I can prove thee, / And know this frail, bruised being is above thee" (20). Another example of the true tercet is found in "Hymn (for Boys' Voices)" where Lewis uses trochaic catalectic tetrameter: "Every man a God would be / Laughing through eternity / If as God's his eye could see" (58). We also see tercets in the longest poem of *Spirits in Bondage*, "Song of the Pilgrims."

Oddly, although Lewis admired Tennyson's poetry, in these early poems we never see him attempt the *In Memoriam* stanza: iambic tetrameter with the *abba* rhyme scheme. At the same time, most of Lewis's pentameter poems, such as "Of Ships," "French Nocturne," "Victory," "Apology," and "Milton Read Again," use the *abba* rhyme. Also, among his early poems Lewis wrote two Italian sonnets, "Sonnet—To Philip Sydney" and "Sonnet" ("The stars come out; the fragrant shadows fall"), both employing the *abbaabba cdcdee* rhyme (*CP*, 237; *SB*, 33). In the sonnet to Sydney, Lewis appears to be working strictly to form, so much so that the poem is only two sentences: The octave is the first sentence and the sestet is the second. In the sonnet "The stars come out," he more freely uses the caesura, producing a poem with five sentences and medial caesuras in lines one, eight, and eleven. A final connection between the two sonnets is his use of the feminine rhyme *hour:bower* in both. While Lewis wrote other sonnets later, it was not a form he particularly favored, so these two early specimens suggest poetic "finger exercise" where he imitated and experimented with the form.

We also see Lewis experimenting with a medieval poetic form—the ballade—in his "Ballade of a Winter's Morning" and "Ballade Mystique" (*CP*, 234–35; *SB*, 53–54). The ballade, which Lewis may have encountered in imperfect form in Chaucer and almost certainly knew from Swinburne's "Ballad of Dreamland," Henley's "Ballade of Dead Actors," and Lang's "Ballades of Blue China," is highly structured. Most commonly, the ballade consists of three stanzas and a final envoy. Each stanza is eight to ten lines, and the envoy contains half as many lines as the stanzas. The rhyme in all the stanzas must be identical in the corresponding lines, although the rhyming words may vary from stanza to stanza; the most common rhyme scheme for the stanza is *ababbcbc* and for the envoy *bcbc*. However, the one element that marks the ballade is the refrain, which forms the last line of each stanza and the envoy. The envoy "is not only a dedication, but should be the peroration of the subject, and richer in its wording and more stately in its imagery than the preceding verses, to convey the climax of the whole matter, and avoid the suspicion that it is a mere postscript."[66]

Both "Ballade of a Winter's Morning" and "Ballade Mystique" are iambic tetrameter stanzas of eight lines with the *ababbcbc* rhyme scheme, and both four-line envoys use the *bcbc* rhyme scheme. The refrain in "Ballade of a Winter's Morning" undergoes progressive mutations from "A merry morning we shall spend" to "And make us merry friend by friend" to "To make us merry friend by friend" to "Of him who sang Patroklos' friend" to "Than thine or mine, oh friend, my friend" to the final line of the envoy, "We'll tread them bravely, friend by friend." In a poem almost certainly celebrating Lewis's friendship with Greeves, the refrain is most appropriate. In "Ballade Mystique," Lewis experiments with the refrain as it moves from a question to a declarative to a final combined declarative and question: "What do they know? What do they know?" (repeated in the second stanza) to "They do not know, they do not know" to the envoy's "They do not know: how should they know?" This poem, ostensibly also about friendship, uses the refrain to contrast the distance between the speaker and his friends.

Similarly, the envoy of the former is upbeat ("So while the wind-foot seasons wear / Be glad, and when towards the end / Adown the dusky ways we fare, / We'll tread them bravely, friend by friend!"), while that of the latter is dark ("The friends I have without a peer / Beyond the western ocean's glow, / Whither the faerie galleys steer, / They do not know: how should they know?"). Yet both poems link friendship with love for literature. "Ballade of a Winter's Morning," obviously set in winter when all is cold and dead outside, fairly exalts in the anticipation of rich sessions inside where the friends will "take fit books" and "old tomes full oft reread with care," those perhaps of Spenser, Horace, Malory, and Virgil, as a remedy for the outer cold. Ironically, however, in "Ballade Mystique," the speaker, whose friends think he needs to leave his house in order to enjoy Spring and "the wakening of the year," does not feel the need for their fellowship. He is not, as they believe, "piteously alone / Without the speech of comrades dear." Instead, literature is his comfort:

> That I have seen the Dagda's throne
> In sunny lands without a tear
> And found a forest all my own
> To ward with magic shield and spear,
> Where, through the stately towers I rear
> For my desire, around me go
> Immortal shapes of beauty clear.

As a result, both ballades, highly structured literary forms, center upon the value of literature. While "Ballade Mystique" underscores the speaker's isolation and alienation from his friends, "Ballade of a Winter's Morning" highlights the fellowship and camaraderie the speaker enjoys with one friend.

POEMS WITH OTHER METERS

Although Lewis favored iambic tetrameter and pentameter, he enjoyed writing poems in other meters. "Exercise," for example, utilizes iambic trimeter: "Where are the magic swords / That elves of long ago / Smithied beneath the snow / For heroes' rich rewards?" (*CP*, 242). The trimeter six-line stanzas of "Hesperus" employ a unique *ababcb* rhyme scheme (*SB*, 65–66). Three poems, "To Sleep," "Our Daily Bread," and "How He Saw Angus the God" (18, 60–62), use a kind of English form of the Sapphic stanza with rhyme: four-line stanzas of alternate rhyme, with the first three lines in pentameter and the fourth line a trimeter. Lewis plays with an even shorter form in the couplet lines of "The Autumn Morning," where we find quatrains with the first three lines in trimeter and the fourth line in dimeter: "See! The pale autumn dawn / Is faint, upon the lawn / That lies in powdered white / Of hoar-frost dight" (34–35).

Lewis's only example of hexameter in these early poems is the appropriately entitled "Alexandrines" (41). In addition to experimenting with iambic hexameter in this poem, Lewis also plays with the sonnet form by modifying both the rhyme scheme and the length of the poem. His *ababbccddeeff* is a loose adaptation of the typical English sonnet rhyme scheme, and his thirteen-line format is one short of the sonnet. The alexandrine is typically characterized by a regular and strongly marked medial caesura, and Lewis's poem includes medial caesuras in lines three, seven, nine, ten, eleven, and twelve. The effectiveness of the medial caesura is best seen in the last four lines: "For in that house I know a little, silent room / Where Someone's always waiting, waiting in the gloom / To draw me with an evil eye, and hold me fast— / Yet thither doom will drive me and He will win at last."

More frequent in these early poems is Lewis's exploration of the heptameter (or septenary). Like the hexameter, the heptameter is marked by a regular and strong medial caesura evident in "Ode for New Year's Day":

> Woe unto you, ye sons of pain that are this day in earth,
> Now cry for all your torment: now curse your hour of birth
> And the fathers who begat you to a portion nothing worth.
> And Thou, my own beloved, for as brave as ere thou art,
> Bow down thine head, Despoina, clasp thy pale arms over it. (13)

"World's Desire" is written primarily in septenarian couplets, with occasional octameters as well: "And the cold ravine / Echoes to the crushing roar and thunder of a mighty river / Raging down a cataract. Very tower and forest quiver / And the grey wolves are afraid and the call of birds is drowned, / And the thought and speech of man in the boiling water's sound" (72). Lewis uses heptameter tercets throughout "The Roads": "I stand on the windy uplands among the hills of Down / With all the world spread out beneath, meadow and sea and town, / And ploughlands on the far-off hills that glow with friendly brown" (63). In "Prologue" he employs an irregular heptameter:

> As of old Phoenician men, to the Tin Isles sailing
> Straight against the sunset and the edges of the earth,
> Chaunted loud above the storm and the strange sea's wailing,
> Legends of their people and the land that gave them birth—
> Sang aloud to Baal-Peor, sang unto the horned maiden,
> Sang how they should come again with the Brethon treasure laden. (xli)

To this oddity Lewis adds lines of octameter as in "Toiling at the stroke and feather through the wet and weary weather."

"One of the most interesting heptameter specimens is "The Satyr," where Lewis, as he does with the heroic couplets in "The Hills of Down," disguises the meter by printing the poem so it appears we are reading tetrameter quatrains rhyming *aaba*: "When the flowery hands of spring / Forth their woodland riches fling, / Through the meadows, through the valleys / Goes the satyr carolling" (5). In fact, the meter is heptameter couplets with internal rhyme occurring in the first line of each couplet as in *spring:fling*. Furthermore, Lewis emphasizes particular sounds in each couplet as in flowery, forth, fling, and valleys and carolling. He extends the connection of sounds by creating internal rhyme between pairs of couplets. For instance, the couplet following the one cited above is: "From the mountain and the moor, / Forest green and ocean shore / All the faerie kin he rallies / Making music evermore." In addition to the internal rhyme of *moor:shore*, the alliteration of *m*ountain, *m*oor, *m*aking, and *m*usic, and the emphasis on the sound—*or* as in *m*oor, *f*orest, *sh*ore, and ever*more*, Lewis links the couplets by rhyming *valleys* in the second line of the first heptameter couplet with *rallies* in the second line of the second heptameter couplet. This use of internal rhyme to connect the septenarian couplets continues in the rest of the poem as in *cloven:woven* in lines six and eight and *asunder:wonder* in lines ten and twelve. As this review of Lewis's earliest poetry illustrates, he enjoyed experimenting with meter, rhyme, and lyric forms, and this interest extended throughout his poetic career.

Nevill Coghill in "The Approach to English" commented upon Lewis's poetry, recalling as young men in the 1920s that both he and Lewis "hoped to be poets.... It was not until six or seven years later that Lewis said sadly to me 'When I at last realized that I was not, after all, going to be a great man....' I think he meant 'a great poet.'"[67] He also recalled Lewis's "'gusto' for poetry" (62). Coghill's comments are a helpful gloss to Lewis's poetic aspirations, influences, craftsmanship, and prosody. In combination they illustrate the degree to which writing poetry and being a poet were fundamental to the way Lewis saw himself. While the tepid critical reception of *Dymer* in 1926 forced him to suppress his desire to be known as a poet publicly, privately he longed to be a good one as his sustained efforts at verse demonstrate. He wanted to be a great poet in the tradition of the ancients he so admired. Consequently, he drew from the cistern of poetic impulse by frequently reading Virgil, Dante, Milton, Wordsworth, Yeats, and others. At the same time, he worked consciously as a crafter of verse, especially at prosody, in order to shape poems worthy of the same well.[68] It is now time to turn to his initial efforts in verse, poetry written and in some cases published before *Spirits in Bondage*, in order to see the earliest outpourings of his poetic impulse.

NOTES

1. Don King, "Glints of Light: The Unpublished Short Poetry of C.S. Lewis," SEVEN: *An Anglo-American Literary Review* 15 (1998): 73–96. These poems also appear in appendix 2. In addition, there are another eleven unpublished short poems that appear in appendix 3.

2. Thomas Howard, "*Poems*: A Review," *Christianity Today* 9 (June 18, 1965): 30.

3. Chad Walsh, *The Literary Legacy of C.S. Lewis* (New York: Harcourt Brace Jovanovich, 1979), 35.

4. Dabney Hart, "Editor's Comment," *Studies in Literary Imagination* 22 (Fall 1989): 128.

5. Charles Huttar, "A Lifelong Love Affair with Language: C.S. Lewis' Poetry," in *Word and Story in C.S. Lewis*, ed. Peter Schakel and Charles Huttar (Columbia: U of Missouri P, 1991), 86.

6. George Sayer, "C.S. Lewis's *Dymer*," SEVEN: *An Anglo-American Literary Review* 1 (1980): 113.

7. W. W. Robson, "The Poetry of C.S. Lewis," *The Chesterton Review* 17 (3–4) (Aug.–Nov 1991): 437.

8. Luci Shaw, "Looking Back to Eden: The Poetry of C.S. Lewis," *Bulletin of the New York C.S. Lewis Society* 23 (Feb. 1992): 3.

9. Owen Barfield, address given at Wheaton College, Wheaton, Ill., Oct. 16, 1964, Marion E. Wade Center, Wheaton College, Wheaton, Ill.

10. Lewis's shorthand allusion to Bergen-Belsen, German Nazi concentration camp near the villages of Bergen and Belsen, about ten miles northwest of Celle, then in Prussian Hanover, Germany. Anne Frank died at Bergen-Belsen in March 1945

11. *Surprised by Joy: The Shape of My Early Life* (New York: Harcourt, Brace and World, 1955), 25 (hereafter cited as *SJ*). Lewis has a poem fragment in which he provides further information about his recollection of Capron. This is discussed in detail in chapter 4.

12. See Warren Lewis's "C.S. Lewis: A Biography," unpublished manuscript, Marion E. Wade Center, 21.

13. Before Lewis enters Cherbourg House, he spends a short time at home which he thoroughly enjoys: "Curiously enough it is at this time, not in earlier childhood, that I chiefly remember delighting in fairy tales. I fell deeply under the spells of Dwarfs—the old bright-hooded, snowy-bearded dwarves.... I visualized them so intensely that I came to the very frontiers of hallucination; once, walking in the garden, I was for a second not quite sure that a little man had not run past me into the shrubbery. I was faintly alarmed, but it was not like my night fears. A fear that guarded Faerie was one I could face" (*SJ*, 54–55). This intense love for faery is a key theme in many poems in *Spirits in Bondage* and the narrative poem "The Queen of Drum."

14. Lewis goes on in this passage to connect the experience with his rediscovery of the role of joy in his life.

15. Copies of the magazine, *The Soundbox*, from this time period (1911–12) appear not to have survived. In checking the significant holdings of libraries in both Ireland and England, I have been unable to find surviving copies.

16. This 794-line fragment I have entitled "Descend to Earth, Descend, Celestial Nine" has survived, is discussed in detail in chapter 2, and the complete text is published in appendix 1.

17. The idea that he tried to write poetry rather than allowing it to flow from his pen is one that recurs many times; it may explain why he never achieved the poetic acclaim he desired.

18. Lewis has a poem fragment in which he provides further information about his recollection of Smith. This is discussed in detail in chapter 4.

19. Lewis has a poem fragment in which he provides further information about his recollection of Kirkpatrick. This is discussed in detail in chapter 4.

20. Fewer than 120 lines in four fragments of *Loki Bound* have survived. They are discussed in detail in chapter 2, and the complete text is published in appendix 1.

21. A complete scheme for an opera version of the poem is found in C.S. Lewis, *They Stand Together: The Letters of C.S. Lewis to Arthur Greeves (1914–1963)*, edited by Walter Hooper (New York: Macmillan, 1979), 50–53.

22. Hearing and reading poetry aloud was always an important principle, indicated as he writes to his brother eighteen years later: "By the way, I most fully agree with you about 'the lips being invited to share the banquet' in poetry, and always 'mouth' it while I read.... I look upon this 'mouthing' as an infallible mark of those who really like poetry" (Apr. 8, 1932, *LL*, 303).

23. Lewis includes "Milton Read Again" in *Spirits in Bondage*, a tribute to his deep affection for the blind poet. His lifelong admiration for Milton is later reflected in his *A Preface to Paradise Lost* (London: Oxford UP, 1942).

24. Later, in a telling letter to his brother on August 2, 1928, he does admit that the thrill of discovering a great new poem in English is over: "There is no longer any chance of discovering a new long poem in English which will turn out to be just what I want and which can be added to the *Faerie Queen*, *The Prelude*, *Paradise Lost*, *The Ring and the Book*, the *Earthly Paradise*, and a few others—because there aren't anymore.... In that sense I have come to the end of English poetry—as you may be said to have come to the end of a wood, not where you have actually walked every inch of it, but when you have walked about in it enough to know where all the boundaries are and to feel the end near even when you can't

see it; when there is no longer any hope (as there was in the first few days) that the next turn of the path might bring you to an unsuspected lake or cave or clearing on the edge of a new valley" (*LL*, 259). Clearly there is in this letter sadness a longing for the old thrill of discovering a new poem; Lewis's tone here recalls Wordsworth's "Tintern Abbey": "That time is past, / And all its aching joys are now no more, / And all its dizzy raptures.

25. While "The Quest of Bleheris" is a prose romance and not a poem (see the Bodleian Library, Oxford, MS. Eng. left. c. 220/5. fols. 5–43, dated 1916), it is not far from poetry. It is a fascinating piece of writing, very much in the school of Arthurian romance/allegory. One interesting point is that the old, ugly hag who thwarts Bleheris may be the prototype for the hag who similarly thwarts Dymer. A very long and involved effort, it was never finished. For recent scholarship on "Bleheris," see David C. Downing, "'The Dungeon of his Soul': Lewis's Unfinished 'Quest of Bleheris,'" *SEVEN: An Anglo-American Literary Review* 15 (1998): 37–54 and my "C.S. Lewis's 'The Quest of Bleheris' as Prose Poetry," The *Lamp-Post of the Southern California C.S. Lewis Society* 23, no. 1 (Spring 1999): 3–15.

26. The quote means "to be praised by a man who is [himself] praised."

27. *LKB*, 0087.

28. Such critical self-assessment foreshadows an even more penetrating episode several years later (discussed below); this weakness also may be related to Lewis's lifelong search for joy and his repeated realization that when he actively sought joy he never found it.

29. While this focus linked him with the ancient poets he so admired (for example, he placed great emphasis upon meter, even writing several poems expressly to experiment with various meters that fascinated him), in another way it cut him off from them. For Homer and Virgil, poetry was their natural form of expression. Yet Odysseus and Aeneas live on, less because of verse per se, and more because of their characters and the narratives about them. Lewis, lacking an Odysseus or Aeneas (although later he almost adopted Wotan/Odin), focused too much on the *form* of poetry rather than on the *creation* of a story, whether original or borrowed. Happily, Lewis's prose is not encumbered by a similar focus.

30. Lewis writes Greeves on December 2, 1918, about this prose version: "I have just finished a short narrative, which is a verse version of our old friend 'Dymer,' greatly reduced & altered to my new ideas. The main idea is that of development by self-destruction, both of individuals & species…. The background proceeds on the old assumption of good *outside & opposed to* [Lewis's emphasis] the cosmic order. It is written in the metre of [Shakespeare's] Venus and Adonis: 'Dymer' is changed to 'Ask' (you remember Ask and Embla in the Norse myths) & it is in the 3rd person under the title of 'The Redemption of Ask'" (*TST*, 239).

31. Lewis offers his own chronology for the development of *Dymer* in "The Lewis Papers: Memoirs of the Lewis Family, 1850–1930," 11 vols., Wade Center, 9:129–30.

32. *All My Road Before Me: The Diary of C.S. Lewis 1922–1927*, edited by Walter Hooper (New York: Harcourt Brace Jovanovich, 1991), 20–21.

33. See *The Beacon* 3, no. 31 (May 1924): 444–45. This poem is discussed in chapter 4.

34. Unfortunately, only the opening eight-line stanza has survived. It is discussed briefly in chapter 2.

35. Though a poem by this title has not survived, I believe "The Carpet Rises in the Draught" is in fact the fragment referred to here. This fragment is discussed in detail in chapter 4.

36. "Foster" has not survived.

37. In a footnote on this same page, Walter Hooper says: "The first version of this sonnet sequence survives in the same notebook as the last portion of the Diary. A revised version of it, entitled 'Infatuation,' is found in Lewis's *Poems* (1964)."

38. "Wild Hunt" has not survived, though its relationship to "The King of Drum" will be discussed in chapter 4. "Sigrid" has not survived. A fragment of a poem on Cupid and Psyche has survived, will be discussed in detail in chapter 4, and the complete text is in appendix i. Of course, Lewis's fullest realization of this theme appears in *Till We Have Faces: A Myth Retold* (London: Geoffrey Bles, 1956).

39. These included the fact that Heinemann had already published *Spirits in Bondage* and that Lewis had hoped to make a profit, desired personal fame, desired that the poem itself achieve a place in literary history, and desired that his poem validate his poetic ability.

40. This letter contains the diary entry for March 6, 1926, cited above.

41. Hooper collects both the published poems and others he discovers after Lewis's death in *Poems* (New York: Harcourt Brace Jovanovich, 1964) and later *The Collected Poems of C.S. Lewis* (London: Fount, 1994). As noted earlier, my "Glints of Light: The Unpublished Short Poetry of C.S. Lewis" includes ten more poems previously unpublished; they are reprinted in appendix 2.

42. *OB*, March 16, 1932, 0054.

43. Lewis addressed this topic as early as March 30, 1930, in a paper he read to the literary group, the Marlets. Entitled "The Personal Heresy in Poetics," the paper introduced themes Lewis expanded upon in his debate with Tillyard in *The Personal Heresy* (London: Oxford UP, 1939) (hereafter *PH*). In *C.S. Lewis: A Biography* (New York: Harcourt Brace Jovanovich, 1974), Roger L. Green and Walter Hooper note that the paper "attacked the notion that poetry is the 'expression of personality' and is useful for putting us into contact with the 'poet's soul': in short, that a poet's 'Life' and 'Works' are two diverse expressions of a single quiddity" (125).

44. *The Personal Heresy*, 4.

45. Later, in *An Experiment in Criticism* (Cambridge: Cambridge UP, 1961), Lewis makes a similar point: "[Literature is valuable] not only nor chiefly in order to see what [the authors] are like but [because] ... we see what they see [and] occupy, for a while, their seat in the great theatre, [and] use their spectacles and [are] made free of whatever insights, joys, terrors, wonders or merriment those spectacles reveal" (139).

46. Interestingly, Lewis appears here to be endorsing something similar to T. S. Eliot's "objective correlative," in spite of the fact that elsewhere he disagrees with Eliot's literary perspective. Joe R. Christopher says, "I'm not certain that Lewis really meant what he was saying [here]" (e-mail to author, Nov. 18, 1997). At the same time, Lewis's claim here is tied to his frequent celebration of the core values of civilized life, what he terms "stock responses." Tracing these back to the Greek and Roman writers he so admired—Homer, Virgil, and Ovid—as well as the towering figures of Western literature—Dante, Chaucer, Shakespeare, Milton, Wordsworth, Shelley, Keats, and Yeats—Lewis infuses his work with passages promoting honor, courage, bravery, honesty, charity, respect, and related values.

47. *RP*, 0008.

48. Lewis to Rhona Bodle, Miscellaneous Letters, June 24, 1949, 0192–0193, Wade Center. Jerry Daniel in his "The Taste of the Pineapple: A Basis for Literary Criticism" (in *The Taste of the Pineapple: Essays on C.S. Lewis as Reader, Critic, and Imaginative Writer*, ed. Bruce L. Edwards [Bowling Green, Oh.: Bowling Green State U Popular P, 1988])

emphasizes how wonderfully effective Lewis is in describing the "essence of things." Calling this focus an "emphasis on the quiddity of things" (10), Daniel offers thoughtful commentary and numerous examples from Lewis's work to sustain his argument. As a reader, Lewis, according to Daniel, "immersed himself in the quality of a story or a poem he was reading," and "whether prose or verse, all works were 'poetry' to him in the sense that the 'feel' or 'taste' was primary" (10–11). Indeed, Daniel uses throughout the image of the "taste" of a poem as a way of describing Lewis's acquisition of poetry. In addition, Daniel applies this same rubric to Lewis as literary critic and imaginative writer. He finds Lewis's love of stock responses in poetry a connection to his desire for the essence of things: "Lewis felt ... that literature *ought* to produce stock responses: if a story presents a scene of cruelty, we ought to respond with horror; if a poem describes a mother's love for her child we ought to respond with warm satisfaction. Since he, as an artist, was attempting to impart a vision, he was attempting to elicit a response to that vision; and, believing in absolute values, he preferred to elicit a stock response.... [Lewis forces] us to attend to the great reality of the poetry, the vision, inherent in so many works written by so many different persons in different ages of our history" (25). Daniel's essay is must reading for anyone interested in Lewis's use of poetic language.

49. Lewis to Martyn Skinner, Miscellaneous Letters, Oct. u, 1950, 942, Wade Center.

50. Lewis to Dom Bede Griffiths, Letters of CSL to Dom Bede Griffiths, Vol 2, Apr. 22, 1954, 0070, Wade Center.

51. Introduction to *Collected Poems*, xv–xvi.

52. This poetic fragment is discussed in chapter 5.

53. Lewis's correspondence with Pitter and their shared interest in poetry is discussed more fully in chapter 9.

54. Feb. 2, 1947; MS. Eng. lett. c. 220/3, fol. 38, Bodleian Library.

55. July 6, 1947; MS. Eng. lett. c. 220/3, fol. 52, Bodleian Library.

56. According to Hooper, Lewis even revised poems after they had been published. Until recently it has been difficult to verify this contention. This task is somewhat easier now because, in the fall of 1997, Hooper deposited in the Bodleian Library the typescript of *Young King Cole and Other Pieces* as well as holographs of many other Lewis poems. Still problematic, however, is verifying whether the changes to or various versions of a poem occurred *before* or *after* the published version, since in most cases neither the typescript of *Young King Cole and Other Pieces* nor the holographs are dated. In appendix 4, I provide a complete list of the contents of this deposit as well the publication history of each poem.

57. This poem (and its possible connections to Lewis's wife, Joy) is discussed in detail in chapter 7.

58. The holographs are available in Hooper's 1997 deposit to the Bodleian Library. See the bibliography for a complete listing of holographs.

59. This is the version Hooper published in *Poems*.

60. Charles Huttar's, "A Lifelong Love Affair with Language: C.S. Lewis's Poetry," is the best piece of criticism available on Lewis's prosody. Huttar focuses upon both Lewis's love of language and his technical expertise as poet. While relegating Lewis to the role of minor poet, Huttar finds Lewis's "attitudes toward language [include] a respect for its illusive and elusive nature and at the same time an overflowing enjoyment of it" (87). Among the chief characteristics of Lewis's poetry is his "sheer love of the sounds of words ... [often revealed] in his virtuoso deployment in poem after poem of intricate patterns of exact or slant rhyme, both final and internal" (87). Another notable characteristic of his

poetry "is semantic change, specifically the alteration of meaning which may disrupt communication between members of a speech community" (92). Huttar then cites poems revealing Lewis's use of semantics as a tool for critiquing contemporary culture, and he comments upon the way that "Lewis examines language as a fundamental human attribute, one that reveals, both our greatness and our limitations" (103). Huttar reviews several poems that celebrate the birth of language, human reason and dominion, and freedom of the will. In addition, he cites letters showing Lewis's admission of the inadequacy of language to communicate anything effectively. Huttar believes Lewis's poems on God best demonstrate the shortcoming of language, and he offers from "Footnote to All Prayers" the following as an example: "To 'attempt the ineffable Name' ... is to risk worshipping an 'idol' shaped by one's 'own unquiet thought'; the language of prayer references only 'frail images' in the speaker's mind, 'which cannot be the thing Thou art' ... 'Take not, oh Lord, our literal sense. Lord, in Thy great, / Unbroken speech our limping metaphor translate'" (106). Huttar's work in this essay is thorough and keen; his critical focus upon Lewis's use of language in his poetry is essential reading.

61. *Selected Literary Essays* (Cambridge: Cambridge UP, 1969), 15. Originally published as "A Metrical Suggestion," *Lysistrata* 2 (May 1935): 13–24.

62. *Selected Literary Essays*, 46. Originally published in *Essays and Studies by Members of the English Association* 26 (1939): 28–41.

63. *Selected Literary Essays*, 280–85. Originally published in *A Review of English Literature* 1 (Jan. 1960): 45–50.

64. These poems are discussed at length in chapter 2.

65. These ten poems appear in the "Miscellany" from *Collected Poems*. The poems are "The Hills of Down," "Against Potpourri," "A Prelude," "Ballade of a Winter's Morning," "Laus Mortis," "Sonnet—To Philip Sydney," "Of Ships," "Couplets," "Circe—A Fragment," and "Exercise." All date from 1915–17.

66. Gleeson White from his *Ballades and Rondeaus* (1893) cited in Raymond MacDonald Alden, ed., *English Verse: Specimens Illustrating Its Principles and History* (1929; reprint, New York, AMS, 1970), 360.

67. "The Approach to English," *Light on C.S. Lewis*, ed. Jocelyn Gibb (New York: Harcourt Brace Jovanovich, 1965), 53.

68. Joe R. Christopher offers this insight: "I'd say that Lewis wanted to be a Romantic poet and he actually was (most often) a classical epigrammist—he wanted to be John Keats and he was actually Ben Jonson" (e-mail to author, Nov. 18, 1997).

Chronology

1898	Clive Staples Lewis is born November 29 in Belfast, Northern Ireland, to Albert James Lewis and Flora Augusta Hamilton Lewis. His brother, Warren Hamilton Lewis, was born on June 16, 1895.
1905	The Lewis family moves to their new home, "Little Lea," on the outskirts of Belfast.
1908	Mother, Flora, dies of cancer; C.S. Lewis and brother are sent to Wynard School in England.
1910	Attends Campbell College boarding school in Belfast.
1911–1913	Lewis studies at Cherbourg School, Malvern, England.
1914	Under the private tutoring of William Kirkpatrick, Lewis begins extensive literary and philosophical studies (Latin, Greek, French, German, and Italian).
1916	Wins scholarship to University College, Oxford.
1917	Lewis attends University College, Oxford, but enlists in the British army during World War I.
1919	Returns to his studies at Oxford. Publishes *Spirits in Bondage*, his first book.
1921	Lewis's mentor, William Kirkpatrick, dies.
1924	Serves as philosophy tutor at University College.
1925	Elected a Fellow of Magdalen College, Oxford, where he will serve as tutor in English Language and Literature for 29 years.

1926	Publishes *Dymer.*
1929	Father, Albert, dies on September 24.
1930	The Inklings, a sort of literary society, first meets in Oxford. Members, who will continue to meet for the next sixteen years, include J.R.R. Tolkien, Hugo Dyson, Charles Williams, Dr. Robert Harvard, Owen Barfield, Neville Coghill, and others.
1931	Lewis returns to belief in Christianity.
1933	*The Pilgrim's Regress* is published.
1936	*The Allegory of Love: A Study in Medieval Tradition* is published.
1938	*Out of the Silent Planet*, the first novel in the Ransom Trilogy, is published.
1940	*The Problem of Pain* is published.
1941	Gives radio addresses on "Right and Wrong: A Clue to the Meaning of the Universe?" From May 2 until November 28, *The Guardian* publishes 31 *Screwtape Letters* in weekly installments.
1942	The first meeting of the Socratic Club is held in Oxford. *The Screwtape Letters* is published.
1943	*Perelandra*, the second novel in the Ransom Trilogy, is published.
1944	*The Abolition of Man* is published.
1945	*That Hideous Strength*, the final novel in the Ransom Trilogy, is published. *The Great Divorce* is published.
1947	Lewis appears on the cover of *Time* magazine.
1950	*The Lion, the Witch and the Wardrobe*, the first of seven books in *The Chronicles of Narnia*, is published.
1951	*Prince Caspian* is published.
1952	*Mere Christianity* is published. *The Voyage of the Dawn Treader* is published.
1953	*The Silver Chair* is published.
1954	*The Horse and His Boy* is published. In June, Lewis accepts the Chair of Medieval and Renaissance Literature at Cambridge.
1955	*The Magician's Nephew*, the sixth of the seven Chronicles of Narnia, is published; *Surprised by Joy* is published.

1956	*The Last Battle*, the seventh and final book in *The Chronicles of Narnia*, is published; Lewis receives the Carnegie Medal in recognition of it. *Till We Have Faces* is published. Lewis and Joy Gresham are married in a civil ceremony in Oxford. Joy is diagnosed with cancer.
1957	Lewis and Joy have a religious wedding ceremony at her hospital bed.
1958–59	Joy's cancer goes into remission. Lewis is elected an Honorary Fellow of University College, Oxford. *Reflections on the Psalms* is published.
1960	Joy dies on July 13 at the age of 45. *Studies in Words* and *The Four Loves* are published.
1961	*A Grief Observed* is published under the pseudonym of N.W. Clerk. *An Experiment in Criticism* is published.
1963	Lewis dies one week before his 65th birthday on Friday, November 22, after a variety of illnesses, including a heart attack and kidney problems.

Contributors

HAROLD BLOOM is Sterling Professor of the Humanities at Yale University. He is the author of 30 books, including *Shelley's Mythmaking* (1959), *The Visionary Company* (1961), *Blake's Apocalypse* (1963), *Yeats* (1970), *A Map of Misreading* (1975), *Kabbalah and Criticism* (1975), *Agon: Toward a Theory of Revisionism* (1982), *The American Religion* (1992), *The Western Canon* (1994), and *Omens of Millennium: The Gnosis of Angels, Dreams, and Resurrection* (1996). *The Anxiety of Influence* (1973) sets forth Professor Bloom's provocative theory of the literary relationships between the great writers and their predecessors. His most recent books include *Shakespeare: The Invention of the Human* (1998), a 1998 National Book Award finalist, *How to Read and Why* (2000), *Genius: A Mosaic of One Hundred Exemplary Creative Minds* (2002), *Hamlet: Poem Unlimited* (2003), *Where Shall Wisdom Be Found?* (2004), and *Jesus and Yahweh: The Names Divine* (2005). In 1999, Professor Bloom received the prestigious American Academy of Arts and Letters Gold Medal for Criticism. He has also received the International Prize of Catalonia, the Alfonso Reyes Prize of Mexico, and the Hans Christian Andersen Bicentennial Prize of Denmark.

CHAD WALSH is the author of several books, including *C.S. Lewis: Apostle to the Skeptics* and *The Literary Legacy of C.S. Lewis*. One of the original founders of the *Beloit Poetry Journal*, a national literary quarterly, Walsh was also a professor at Beloit College.

MARGARET BLOUNT is the author of *Animal Land: The Creatures of Children's Fiction*.

MARGARET PATTERSON HANNAY is the author of *C.S. Lewis* and the editor of *Silent but for the Word: Tudor Women as Patrons, Translators, and Writers of Religious Works* and *As Her Whimsey Took Her: Critical Essays on the Work of Dorothy L. Sayers*.

DABNEY ADAMS HART is a scholar and frequent lecturer on C.S. Lewis. A 1948 Agnes Scott graduate, Hart earned her doctorate in English from the University of Wisconsin and taught at Florida State University, the University of Wisconsin, and Georgia State University as associate professor of English until she retired in 1993.

LEE D. ROSSI is the author of *The Politics of Fantasy: C.S. Lewis and J.R.R. Tolkien*.

C.N. MANLOVE taught English literature at the University of Edinburgh until 1993. He is the author of *Modern Fantasy: Five Studies; Literature and Reality, 1600–1800; The Gap in Shakespeare: The Motif of Division from "Richard II" to "The Tempest"; The Impulse of Fantasy Literature; Science Fiction: Ten Explorations; C.S. Lewis: His Literary Achievement; Critical Thinking: A Guide to Interpreting Literary Texts; Christian Fantasy: From 1200 to the Present;* and *From Alice to Harry Potter: Children's Fantasy in England*.

JOE R. CHRISTOPHER is the author of *C.S. Lewis: An Annotated Checklist of Writings About Him and His Work* and *C.S. Lewis*. He teaches at Tarleton State University.

DAVID C. DOWNING is the R.W. Schlosser Professor of English at Elizabethtown College in Lancaster County, Pennsylvania. He is the author of *Planets in Peril: A Critical Study of C.S. Lewis's Ransom Trilogy* and *The Most Reluctant Convert: C.S. Lewis's Journey to Faith*.

KATH FILMER is a Celtic researcher and twice winner of the Mythopoeic Society's Scholarship Award in Myth and Fantasy Studies. She is the author of *The Fiction of C.S. Lewis: Mask and Mirror; Skepticism and Hope in Twentieth Century Fantasy Literature;* and *Fantasy Fiction and Welsh Myth: Tales of Belonging*.

LIONEL ADEY is a Professor Emeritus for the Department of English at the University of Victoria. He is the author of *C.S. Lewis' "Great War" with Owen Barfield*; *Hymns and the Christian "Myth"*; *Class and Idol in the English Hymn*; and *C.S. Lewis: Writer, Dreamer, and Mentor.*

DON W. KING is professor of English at Montreat College in Montreat, North Carolina. He is the author of *C.S. Lewis, Poet: The Legacy of his Poetic Impulse.*

Bibliography

Adey, Lionel. *C.S. Lewis's 'Great War' with Owen Barfield.* Univ. of Victoria, B.C.: ELS Monographs, 1978.

———. *C.S. Lewis: Writer, Dreamer and Mentor.* Grand Rapids, MI: Eerdmans, 1998.

Blount, Margaret. *Animal Land: The Creatures of Children's Fiction.* London: Hutchinson, 1974.

Bowman, Mary R. "'A Darker Ignorance': C.S. Lewis and the Nature of the Fall." *Mythlore: A Journal of J.R.R. Tolkien, C.S. Lewis, Charles Williams, and Mythopoeic Literature* 24:1.91 (Summer 2003): 62–78.

Carpenter, Humphrey. *The Inklings: C.S. Lewis, J.R.R. Tolkien, Charles Williams, and Their Friends.* London: Allen & Unwin, 1978.

Christopher, Joe R., and Joan K. Ostling. *C.S. Lewis: An Annotated Checklist of Writings about Him and His Works.* Kent, OH: Kent State University Press, 1973.

DuPlessis, Nicole M. "EcoLewis: Conservationism and Anticolonialism in *The Chronicles of Narnia.*" *Wild Things: Children's Culture and Ecocriticism.* Eds: Sidney I. Dobrin and Kenneth B. Kidd. Detroit, MI: Wayne State UP, 2004.

Duriez, Colin. *The C.S. Lewis Encyclopedia: A Complete Guide to His Life, Thought, and Writings.* Wheaton, IL: Crossway Books, 2000.

Edwards, Bruce L. *Taste of the Pineapple: Essays on C.S. Lewis as Reader, Critic, and Imaginative Writer.* Bowling Green, OH: Bowling Green State University Popular Press, 1988.

Filmer, Kath. *The Fiction of C.S. Lewis: Mask and Mirror*. New York: Macmillan, 1993.

Ford, Paul F. *A Companion to Narnia*. San Francisco: HarperCollins Publishing Company, 1994.

Fredrick, Candice, and Sam McBride. *Women Among the Inklings: Gender, C.S. Lewis, J.R.R. Tolkien, and Charles Williams*. Westport, CT: Greenwood Press, 2001.

Gibson, Evan K. *C.S. Lewis, Spinner of Tales: A Guide to His Fiction*. Grand Rapids, MI: Eerdmans, 1980.

Glover, Donald. *C.S. Lewis: The Art of Enchantment*. Athens, OH: Ohio University Press, 1981.

Graham, Jean E. "Women, Sex, and Power: Circe and Lilith in Narnia" *Children's Literature Association Quarterly* 29 1–2 (Spring–Summer 2004): 32–44.

Green, Roger L., and Walter Hooper. *C.S. Lewis: A Biography*. New York: Harcourt Brace Jovanovich, 1974.

Griffin, William. *Clive Staples Lewis: A Dramatic Life*. New York: Harper and Row, 1986.

Hannay, Margaret Patterson. *C.S. Lewis*. New York: Ungar, 1981.

Hart, Dabney Adams. *Through the Open Door: A New Look at C.S. Lewis*. Montgomery, AL: University of Alabama Press, 1984.

Holbrook, D. *The Skeleton in the Wardrobe: C.S. Lewis' Fantasies, a Phenomenological Study*. Lewisburg, PA: Bucknell University Press, 1991.

Holmer, Paul L. *C.S. Lewis: The Shape of His Faith and Thought*. New York: Harper, 1976.

Hooper, Walter. *C.S. Lewis: A Companion and Guide*. San Francisco: Harper, 1996.

————. *Past Watchful Dragons: The Narnian Chronicles of C.S. Lewis*. New York: Collier Books, 1979.

Howard, Thomas. *The Achievement of C.S. Lewis: A Reading of His Fiction*. Wheaton, IL: Harold Shaw Publishers, 1980.

Keefe, Carolyn, ed. *C.S. Lewis: Speaker and Teacher*. Grand Rapids, MI: Zondervan, 1971.

King, Don. *C.S. Lewis, Poet: The Legacy of His Poetic Impulse*. Kent, OH: Kent State University Press, 2001.

Kreeft, Peter. *C.S. Lewis: A Critical Essay*. Grand Rapids, MI: Eerdmans, 1969.

Lindskoog, Kathryn A. *The Lion of Judah in Never-Never Land: The Theology of C.S. Lewis Expressed in His Fantasies for Children.* Grand Rapids, MI: Eerdmans, 1973.

Manlove, Colin. *The Chronicles of Narnia: The Patterning of a Fantastic World.* New York: Twayne, 1993.

———. *C.S. Lewis: His Literary Achievement.* Basingstoke, Hampshire: Macmillan Press, 1987.

Mills, David, ed. *The Pilgrim's Guide: C.S. Lewis and the Art of Witness.* Grand Rapids, MI: Eerdmans, 1998.

Myers, Doris T. *C.S. Lewis in Context.* Kent, OH: Kent State University Press, 1994.

Patterson, Nancy-Lou. "The Visionary Woman in C.S. Lewis' *Chronicles of Narnia* and *That Hideous Strength.*" *Mythlore: A Journal of J.R.R. Tolkien, C.S. Lewis, Charles Williams, and the Genres of Myth and Fantasy Studies* 6 (Summer 1979): 6–10.

Reilly, R. J. *Romantic Religion: A Study of Barfield, Lewis, Williams, and Tolkien.* Athens, GA: University of Georgia Press, 1971.

Rossi, L.D. *The Politics of Fantasy: C.S. Lewis and J.R.R. Tolkien.* Ann Arbor: University of Michigan Press, 1984.

Schakel, Peter J., ed. *The Longing for a Form: Essays on the Fiction of C.S. Lewis.* Kent, OH: Kent State University Press, 1977.

——— and C.A. Huttar, eds. *Word and Story in C.S. Lewis.* Columbia, MO: University of Missouri Press, 1991.

Sibley, Brian. *Shadowlands.* London: Hodder, 1985.

Walsh, Chad. *C.S. Lewis: Apostle to the Skeptics.* New York: Macmillan, 1949.

———. *The Literary Legacy of C.S. Lewis.* New York: Harcourt, 1979.

Ward, Michael. "Through the Wardrobe: A Famous Image Explored." *Seven: An Anglo-American Literary Review* 15 (1998): 55–71.

Wilson, A.N. *C.S. Lewis: A Biography.* London: Collins, 1990.

Acknowledgments

Reprinted with the permission of Scribner, an imprint of Simon & Schuster Adult Publishing Group, from *Apostle to the Skeptics* by Chad Walsh. Copyright © 1949 by Chad Walsch; copyright renewed © 1976 by Chad Walsh.

"Fallen and Redeemed: Animals in the Novels of C.S. Lewis" by Margaret Blount. © 1974 by Margaret Ingle-Finch. Reprinted by permission.

"The Inconsolable Secret: Biography" by Margaret Patterson Hannay. *C.S. Lewis*. © 1981 by Frederick Ungar Publishing Co., Inc. Reprinted by permission of Continuum Publishing.

"The Power of Language" by Dabney Adams Hart. *Through the Open Door: A New Look at C.S. Lewis*. © 1984 by The University of Alabama Press. Reprinted by permission.

"Logic" and "Romance": The Divided Self of C.S. Lewis" by Lee D. Rossi. *The Politics of Fantasy: C.S. Lewis and J.R.R. Tolkien*. © 1984 by Lee D. Rossi. Reprinted by permission.

"The "Narnia" Books" by C.N. Manlove. *C.S. Lewis: His Literary Achievement*. © 1987 by C.N. Manlove. Reprinted by permission.

"The Apologist" by Joe R. Christopher. *C.S. Lewis:* Twaynes English Authors Series. © 1987 by G.K. Hall & Co. Reprinted by permission of the Gale Group.

"The Recovered Image: Elements of Classicism and Medievalism." by David Downing. *Planets in Peril.* © 1993 by the University of Massachusetts Press. Reprinted by permission.

"Masking the Misogynist in Narnia and Glome" by Kath Filmer. *The Fiction of C.S. Lewis: Mask and Mirror.* © 1993 by Kath Filmer. Reprinted by permission.

"Children's Storyteller" by Lionel Adey. *C.S. Lewis: Writer, Dreamer and Mentor.* © 1998 by William B. Eerdmans Publishing. Reprinted by permission.

"C.S. Lewis, Poet" by Don W. King. *C.S. Lewis, Poet.* © 2001 by The Kent State University Press. Reprinted by permission.

Every effort has been made to contact the owners of copyrighted material and secure copyright permission. Articles appearing in this volume generally appear much as they did in their original publication with few or no editorial changes. Those interested in locating the original source will find bibliographic information in the bibliography and acknowledgments sections of this volume.

Index

Characters in literary works are indexed by first name (if any), followed by the name of the work in parentheses